The Delamere Saga
(The Untold Story of Vale Royal Abbey)

Written and researched by Geoffrey Hebdon

Glass House Books
Brisbane

Glass House Books
an imprint of IP (Interactive Publications Pty Ltd)
Treetop Studio • 9 Kuhler Court
Carindale, Queensland, Australia 4152
ipoz.biz/glass-house-books/
ipoz.biz/ipstore

First published by IP in 2020

© 2018 Geoffrey Hebdon, the MTC International Foundation, and IP

All rights reserved. Without limiting the rights under copyright reserved above, no part of this publication may be reproduced, stored in or introduced into a retrieval system, or transmitted, in any form or by any means (electronic, mechanical, photocopying, recording or otherwise), without the prior written permission of the copyright owner and the publisher of this book.

Printed in 12 pt Baskerville on 14 pt Avenir Book

ISBN 9781922332110 (PB); ISBN 9781922332127 (eBook)

Library of Congress (LOC) #TXu 002-109-237

 A catalogue record for this book is available from the National Library of Australia

Contents

Author's Note & Introduction	v
Preface	ix
Acknowledgments	xx

Part One: The Life & Chronicles of Thomas Cholmondeley, 1st Lord Delamere, 1767-1855

Chapter One: The Forebears of 1st Lord Delamere of Vale Royal Abbey	3
Chapter Two: Thomas Cholmondeley (1627-1702)	21
Chapter Three: Charles Cholmondeley (1684-1756)	44
Chapter Four: Thomas Cholmondeley (1726-1779)	85
Chapter Five: Thomas Cholmondeley, 1st Lord Delamere of Vale Royal Abbey (1767- 1855)	93

Part Two: Life & Chronicles of Hugh Cholmondeley, 2nd Lord Delamere (1811-1887)

Chapter Six: Hugh Cholmondeley, 2nd Lord Delamere (1811-1887)	143

Part Three: Life & Chronicles of Hugh Cholmondeley, 3rd Lord Delamere (1870-1931)

Chapter Seven: Hugh Cholmondeley, 3rd Lord Delamere	179
Chapter Eight: Hugh Cholmondeley, 3rd Lord Delamere, Moves to Africa	183
Chapter Nine: Sybil Burnaby (1871-1911)	255
Chapter Ten: The Vicissitudes of Vale Royal Abbey from 1907 to the Present	267
Postscript	279
Appendix 1: English Civil Wars	281
Appendix 2: King Henry II	282
Appendix 3: South Sea Bubble	284
Appendix 4: Osborn Collection	286
Appendix 5: Newstead Abbey	288
Appendix 6: Rochdale & Rochdale Town Hall	290
Appendix 7: Royton Hall	295
Appendix 8: Peterloo Massacre	297
Appendix 9: Cowlishaw Village or Hamlet in Crompton, Lancashire	301
Appendix 10: Carnegie Library in Royton, Lancashire	303
Appendix 11: Mau Mau Uprising in Kenya (1952-1960)	306
Selected Bibliography	313

Author's Note & Introduction

For many centuries the outstanding landmark that dominates the skyline in the beautiful, peaceful countryside around the small village of Whitegate, in the ceremonial county of Cheshire, has been the impressive Vale Royal Abbey, which for most visitors to the area proved to be an enigma. When I was asked to write a comprehensive report on the history of Vale Royal Abbey and its occupants over the years, this presented an enormous personal challenge.

This book is about the intriguing history of Vale Royal Abbey, England, and is written from the vantage point of my first visit in the year 1946, up to the latest visits that I made during the years 1999 and 2000, at the invitation of the management of the current new owners of the estate. Being able to dig deep into the archives of some of England's most famous institutions, museums and libraries, which revealed and uncovered such fascinating information and details about the County of Cheshire and more particularly the elegant, inspiring estate of Vale Royal Abbey, proved to be one of the most exciting endeavors I have ever undertaken.

With the assistance of a dedicated team of researchers and genealogists, I also cover in this 'saga', over eight generations of the well-known Cholmondeley family line associated with the Vale Royal Abbey in Cheshire, from 1615, when Lady Mary Cholmondeley bought the estate from the Holford family, which later was to become the home of the Lords' Delamere; and up to the 1940s when the bankrupt estate, controlled by the mortgagees and subject to the rules and restrictions of the British Crown, was sold and disposed of to the present owners.

To the more informed reader; while I acknowledge that some of the events and incidents related to our main characters in this account cannot always be accurately confirmed or irrefutably authenticated from available and reliable sources and may appear to some readers like 'fiction' or in fact may question whether these incidents actually happened and are based simply on rumors, innuendoes and hearsay. I have never the less thought it expedient and appropriate to include most of these details in this book, based on my sincere effort to expand and embellish for our readers benefit, the life style and conduct of the aristocracy and nobility in England over the past few centuries, being contemporaries of our main characters during their lifetime. I like to describe myself as a writer, author, researcher and a reporter of truth. All references, quotations, opinions and views expressed in this narrative based on our research, are not necessarily those of the author or members of our research team.

However, much of the material, especially in Chapter Five and Six, which is related to Hugh, 2nd Lord Delamere is also based on information and material contained in our private family Bibles, plus personal letters and copious hand written notes and other details orally passed down from my various family ancestors.

Especially important to me was the writing of Chapters Seven and Eight of the book related to the country of Kenya, and based on the fact that I spent many years living in Africa as a freelance missionary related to the educational field, I undertook this task as a pleasure and personal privilege. Also being able to research and write about this beautiful country and to be able to undertake the extensive reading of many books and articles related to the checkered history, background and development of this awe inspiring country of Kenya, was a delight in itself and I hope our readers will enjoy ruminating; being captivated and enlightened about this country, as much as I did in my personal experience of researching and the writing of this informative material. Africa is such a highly diverse continent full of fascinating cultures, beautiful scenery and of course the incredible array of its majestic wildlife.

In Chapter Eight we also draw a parallel between eastern and southern Africa in the 20th century, and especially include a short overview of the Apartheid system in South Africa during the years 1948-1994, which legally introduced racial laws and regulations that were part of one of the most obscene systems known to man, as it reduced the status of the South African blacks to nothing more than animals; in fact many animals owned by white citizens of South Africa were treated to a higher standard.

I hope you also get as much satisfaction from reading about some of the fascinating, albeit, short extracts of the past history of Cheshire and Wales, and experience as much pleasure as I did undertaking this research and the uncovering and recording of this descriptive, detailed material. Much of the information in the Preface, plus Chapters One and Two was gleaned from the archives of the sources acknowledged, some of which is available to the general public; other sources are only available by special permission. Material related to the politics of the characters involved, especially in Chapter Three, connected to Charles Cholmondeley, Member of Parliament for Cheshire, is also available in the public domain, but in all cases we have acknowledged the sources. Charles Cholmondeley provides a magnificent example of how to handle a major setback in life and still retain your dignity in any given situation, but especially how to deal with a serious defeat if you are contemplating or planning to run for political office or taking up a career in politics.

This book is not so much a 'history' book but rather an intimate view and insight of the 'dramatic chronicles' of the lives of our main characters that lived at Vale Royal Abbey. This narrative also forms part of a trilogy. The second book, titled "Zero Hour of the Apartheid Regime of Suid Afrika", covers the 30 years that the author spent living in Southern Africa as a witness and contributor to the end of Apartheid and the beginning of a new democracy. This book is also in celebration of 25 years of the end of Apartheid in 1994. Book three, titled "The Birth, Life and Death of King Cotton", covers the establishment of the slave trade, especially from Africa to the Americas, the development of the cotton plantations of the southern States of America and includes the history of Lancashire families and ancestors of the author plus their experiences related to the cotton trade and the 'dark and satanic' cotton mills of Lancashire.

When asked under which category this book, *The Delamere Saga*, is to be published I was presented with a conundrum! Is it a historical narrative; a genealogical report and also partly autobiographical, or is it a political summary and observation of British politics of the past or maybe just another fictional, romantic, historical novel? I ruminated that it's probably a mix or 'witches' brew' of all of these categories? However I will let you, our revered readers decide.

The publication of this book and all rights to the original manuscript and proceeds thereof is now the property of the "MTC International Foundation" (Reg. No.16650 in California, USA), to be incorporated as a non-profit corporation and recognized as a Section 501(c) (3) organization by the Internal Revenue Department of the US Government as a non-profit company based in the USA and therefore all donations are tax deductible. A percentage of the proceeds from this book will be donated to nominated wildlife sanctuaries in Kenya, which are registered members of the "Kenya Wildlife Conservation Association" as decided by the management committee of the MTC International Foundation.

Preface

My first visit to Vale Royal Abbey in the county of Cheshire, was as a young boy in 1946. I had been invited to visit the town of Northwich by a friend of our family, a Mr. Norris Jopson, who was the chauffeur for Mr. Dunkerley, a local wealthy businessman, who owned and lived in the large mansion house known as 'Higher House', located at the top of our local street where I was born; Rochdale Lane in Royton, Lancashire. Plus this well-known family; the Dunkerley's, who along with the Cheetham and Gartside families, owned numerous cotton factories and businesses in the local area of Royton, Crompton and Shaw. Higher House, one time home of the Dunkerley family, was what many Royton residents will remember, later became the 'Tramtracks' Pub (public house) and after that a nightclub named 'Scandals'. It was later demolished and the site is now where the new houses exist at the corner of Rochdale Road and Rochdale Lane, opposite Dogford Road and the Junction Inn.

Mr. Jopson, a phlegmatic sort of person, was assigned by his employer, Mr. Dunkerley, to drive down to Cheshire and collect some Polish refugees who were being housed on the Vale Royal Abbey Estate after the Second World War (1939-1945), and who were to be transported back to our local town of Royton in Lancashire for much needed employment.

Royton, in the North West of England was an industrial centre with many cotton mills providing essential employment for most of the towns' residents. In as late as the 1950s, 80% of Royton's population was employed in the over 40 textile mills. As imports of cheaper foreign goods increased during the mid-20th century, Royton's textile sector declined gradually to a halt; cotton spinning being reduced in the 1960s and 1970s. To quote from the local history society of Royton:

> After the Great War the Cotton industry went into decline due to competition mainly, from India, which had imported Lancashire machinery and had the advantage of

cheap labour and accessible cotton fields. Production and population growth ceased for the first time in a hundred years of steady growth, but it took a long time for Roytonians to grasp the fact that the Lancashire cotton trade was in long-term decline.

In Chapter Eight, we provide a little more background and an overview of the textile industry in Lancashire, England.

Mr. Norris Jopson, also known to me personally as 'Uncle Norri', besides being a chauffeur was also an amateur but very knowledgeable historian, so on our visit to Vale Royal Abbey in 1946, he recounted many intriguing details about the Cholmondeley (pronounced *Chumley*), Vale Royal branch of the well-known Cheshire family, plus some fascinating aspects about Vale Royal Abbey itself and its checkered history. For me to be driven in a brand new Bentley limousine, a 1946 Mark VI was an exciting event in itself, but to visit and behold Vale Royal Abbey that year was an experience that would profoundly affect my future life. Do you remember everything that happened to you when you were seven years? Most of us can't. Well, science has proved that your subconscious mind does. It's remarkable and so is our story!

The Cholmondeley family name goes back to William Le Belward in the 11th century, but the most accurate records are taken up from Sir Hugh Cholmondeley (1552-1601) whose descendants became also Marquess of Cholmondeley, and was responsible for the building and completion of the original Cholmondeley Castle near Malpas, Cheshire. The Marquess also held many other titles including, Earl Rocksavage, Earl Cholmondeley, Viscount Malpas, Baron Newsburgh, Viscount Cholmondeley, Baron Newborough (Ireland). This line of the family goes right through to today, with the present (7th) Marquess of Cholmondeley who is also the current Lord Great Chamberlain being appointed in the 1990s. William Le Belward was the father of the surname Cholmondeley; William Le Belward was the Lord of the Barony of Malpas. He married Tanglust, natural daughter of Hugh Kevelioc, palatine Earl of Chester. The surname of Le Belward was changed to Cholmondeley after the Norman invasion of William the Conqueror in 1066. William Le Belward had a son named Robert De Cholmondeley, who was a second son. They lived in the Cheshire area of England.

Preface

According to an article in the *Country Life* magazine,

> The name Cholmondeley (pronounced chum-lee) is also recorded in various registers, church records, etc. under various spellings (or misspellings) for example Cholmonderley, Cholmonderly, Cholmonly, Chelmundlegh, Chumleye, plus about 6 others renditions. Cholmondeley village in Cheshire has always been the family's principal seat, though, giving its name to the family and having descended through the male line of the family since before Domesday. The founder of this distinguished lineage was the younger son of a Norman Marcher baron, Robert de Chelmundeleigh, whose name eventually evolved to the present spelling, the pronunciation of which is, of course, "chumley".

The lands around the village of Malpas, Cheshire, were given to the Cholmondeley family, who were originally Norman barons and knights who came to Cheshire with the Norman Conquest of 1066 AD and were descended from the half-sister of William the Conqueror. The Cholmondeley Castle in Cheshire today [Note this is not an original castle but a comparatively new mock, somewhat incongruous (re-built) Gothic castle] was constructed in the 1800s and is now home to Lavinia, Marchioness of Cholomondeley mother of the current 7th Marquess, and is not open to the public, only the impressive gardens are open for public viewing. Originally the family was given the lands in return for defensive services on the Welsh border, and since then the family has always played a prominent role in the military affairs of the County of Cheshire. Hugh Cholmondeley was rewarded with a peerage as Baron of Nantwich in 1689 and was given the Earldom of Cholmondeley in 1706. Today, Cholmondeley Village is a civil parish in Cheshire, north-east of Malpas and west of Nantwich. It includes the small settlements of Croxton Green and Dowse Green, with a population of a little over a hundred, increasing to 157 at the 2011 Census.

Most of the records and journals of the Cholmondeley family of Cholmondeley Castle, Cheshire, plus also some important records of the Vale Royal Abbey branch of the family, have been given to the University of Cambridge in 1951 and they are still in the process of sorting and cataloging them. To quote from the University archive section:

The Delamere Saga

> The Marquess of Cholmondeley deposited the bulk of these papers in 1951, the collection subsequently being purchased by the Library. Formerly held at Houghton, the papers include working records of the estate office, papers of the Pell family, and collections relating to various generations of the Walpole family, including a large collection of political papers collected by Sir Robert Walpole, first Prime Minister of Great Britain, in the course of his long political career.

The following report was also received from the Rylands Library in Manchester, England, regarding Mary Cholmondeley (nee Holford) and the village of Holford:

> Holford village adjoins the ancient manors of Lostock and Plumley. About 1119 AD this manor was given by Roger de Mainwaring to the Abbey of Chester under which it was held by Mesne lords until the dissolution. About 1227, half the manor passed in marriage with Joan, daughter of Richard de Lostock, who was heir to her two brothers, who had died without issue. Joan married William de Toft, younger brother of Roger de Toft, whose posterity settled at Holford and assumed the name Holford. Joan had a son, Roger de Holford. The Holfords possessed the manor until the death of Christopher Holford, Esq., about 1581 to 1600, when it passed by marriage with his heiress to the Cholmondeley family.

> The heiress was Mary Holford who had married Sir Hugh Cholmondeley, the younger, of Cholmondeley in Cheshire, and had five sons and three daughters among whom were: Robert Lord Cholmondeley; Hatton Cholmondeley (died in 1605); Thomas Cholmondeley, from whom the Cholmondeleys' of Vale Royal Abbey descend; and Hugh Cholmondeley. "In Peover Church, Cheshire there is a monument to Thomas Cholmondeley late of Holford, Esq., only son of Robert Lord Cholmondeley, Earl of Leinster, son and heir of Mary, daughter and heir of Christopher Holford of Holford, Esq., which said Thomas died 6 January 1667.

> Mary Cholmondeley was involved in a forty years lawsuit with her father's brother George Holford of Narborough over the estate. Lady Mary Cholmondeley meantime had recently bought Vale Royal Abbey in 1615 AD for £9000.

Later King James the 1st visited, holding court at Vale Royal Abbey for three days, dubbing Mary the 'bolde lady of Cheshire.'

Eventually there was a division of land; Mary Cholmondley had the manor of Holford and George Holford the manor of Iscoit bordering Flintshire, Wales. Further division took place later with one part of Plumley divided between the Mainwarings and the Leicesters. The manors of Plumley and Holford were purchased in 1791 by Thomas Langford Brooke, Esq., of Mere from Thomas Asherton Smith, Esq., to whose grandfather Thomas Asherton they were given.

Regarding more detailed information about the history and background of the Old Cistercian Abbey that later became the Great House of Vale Royal Abbey, this will be fully revealed and covered in Chapter Three of our story, as it was Charles Cholmondeley (1684-1756) who was a devout student of English history and he accurately recorded many details in his journals based on his intricate knowledge and research into the history of this old Cistercian Abbey and its eventual, partial demolition in 1539. Most of these journals are now found in the archives of Rylands Library in Manchester, England. Charles Cholmondeley was also the individual who expanded the massive library at Vale Royal Abbey that contained books, manuscripts and records, covering a vast area of knowledge and history, and it very soon became one of the largest private libraries throughout the whole of England and was the envy of many, even including the Vatican in Rome.

However, in the meantime and to whet your appetite the following is a brief extract from a book called *Summer Rambles in Cheshire, Derbyshire, Lancashire & Yorkshire* written by Leo Hartley Grindon[1] in 1866 and provides a delightful description of Vale Royal.

---

[1] This 289-page book *Summer Rambles in Cheshire...* written and published in 1866 by Leopold Hartley Grindon (1818-1904) especially the short section on Vale Royal Abbey, pps 146-149, was written while the Vale Royal estate was still occupied by Hugh Cholmondeley, 2nd Lord Delamere (1811-1877). From copious handwritten notes and diaries written by Botanist Leo Grindon, who was Lecturer on Botany at the Royal School of Medicine, Manchester, and most of his records, diaries and manuscripts were donated and are now archived in the Manchester Museum (located in the University of Manchester), plus some in the Manchester Central Library. It appears from Leo's diaries that he was privately introduced to Hugh, 2nd Lord Delamere, plus he was personally escorted and given a tour of the Great House and Great Hall by his Lordship himself.

The Delamere Saga

The immense stretch of country spread at our feet when standing on Beeston castle rock is that famous part of Cheshire designated 'Vale Royal', which name was given by King Edward I to the Abbey founded by him on the River Weaver.

Vale Royal Abbey was later adapted to the purposes of a modern mansion during the reign of King James I and is the seat of the Cholmondeleys, the head of which family was in 1821 created Lord Delamere. Vale Royal Abbey lies about two and one half miles west by south from Northwich, occupying the crown of a gentle elevation near the banks of the River Weaver of which provides a commanding, delightful view of the Cheshire countryside. The approach is through a spacious park that in many parts is singularly picturesque; while in the interior of the manor are the most striking decorations with which a residence can be enriched, including ancient implements of war and of the chase with antlers in profusion."

Adding still further to the interior beauty are the stained glass windows that are entirely covered with heraldic devices. In the time of King Henry VIII the original Abbey, like all other abbeys in the land, it suffered dismemberment and all that remains of the original building is that part of it which now forms the basement of the present mansion.

On my first visit in 1946, being accompanied by Mr. Norris Jopson (Uncle Norri), to Vale Royal Abbey, the one time home and residence of the Cholmondeley family and the Lords' Delamere, it was a sorry sight indeed to behold as it was being used as a storage and warehouse facility, with unkempt rooms, which were foul smelling with a sulphuric stench. Plus this ancient historic building was also being used as local offices for the Cheshire salt mining industry. In later years it was supposedly in the process of gradually and slowly being improved and converted into a stark, rather severe institute to eventually care for mentally handicapped children and to be operated under a registered British Charity, the Michaelmas Trust. This project was eventually abandoned in 1981. From existing records it also appears that Vale Royal Abbey was even being considered to be converted into a H. M. Government Prison, plus also at one stage an asylum for the mentally and criminally insane, both of these considerations brought major objections from the local residents and adjoining property owners in Cheshire and quite rightly were ultimately discarded.

Of great interest to our readers who are fascinated with English and Cheshire history, especially the once lucrative salt mining industry is that during the 19th century it became uneconomical to physically mine for the salt for which Cheshire was famous. Instead, hot water was pumped through the mines, which dissolved the salt. The resultant brine was then pumped out and the salt extracted from the brine. This technique unfortunately weakened the mine shafts and tunnels, which led to serious land subsidence as they collapsed. Subsidence definitely affected the town centre of Northwich, the surrounding areas and landscape, the evidence of which can clearly be seen today, this subsidence also included in days gone bye; fortunately to a much smaller degree, even the Vale Royal Abbey. The four mines identified for this experimental work were Baron's Quay, Witton Bank, Neumann's and Penny's Lane. These mines were chosen and later closed because their subsidence was causing major problems for the town centre of Northwich in Cheshire.

Salt was a valuable commodity in days gone bye and is the basis for our modern English word 'salary'. The Latin word *salarium* originally was (Lat. *sal*, salt) salt money, i.e. the sum paid to soldiers for their 'work-for-hire' and gave rise to such expressions as 'being worth one's salt'.

Typical buildings in Northwich Town Centre, courtesy of *Cheshire Life Magazine*

The Delamere Saga

This extract from the book *History of Cheshire (Its Traditions & History)* by Alfred Ingham (1920), held in the archives of Rylands Library, reveals a very graphic and accurate report of the terrifying, frightening experience of the subsidence and resultant explosion of a Cheshire salt mine in 1880:

> A most remarkable, if not the most remarkable subsidence on record, took place at Northwich on Monday, 6th December 1880. About six o'clock on the morning of that day, a rumbling noise was heard in a district on the outskirts of Northwich, known by the name of Dunkirk, which is completely honeycombed with abandoned salt mines.
>
> Immediately, the ground seemed to be heaving as if from an earthquake and the small lakes in the neighbourhood varying from nearly half an acre to nearly two acres in area, and thirty to forty feet in depth, commenced to boil and bubble all over, the water being forced up violently some feet above the surface. The whole area of these lakes was in a furious state of commotion, and the noise of the bubbling water could be heard three hundred yards away. All around, for a space of two thousand feet in diameter, at every weak point in the ground, air and foul gas were being expelled; and where in its course the gas met with water, it forced it up in jets, usually accompanied with mud and sand.
>
> For a space of at least one-fourth of the circumference of the largest lake, called Ashton's Old Rock Pit Hole, which covered nearly two acres, there were at intervals regular mud geysers, spouting intermittently to a height of about twelve feet. In one space of about thirty yards in extent, there were at least twenty of these playing at one time. The more violent ebullitions subsided after three or four hours; though in some cases the bubbling and gurgling mud craters continued in action for two days and the ablution in the various pits continued on a smaller scale for three days. The whole of this bubbling and boiling was evidently caused by the air that filled the old mines being violently driven out by the inrush of descending water and earth. The whole surface of the River Weaver and the top of the Brook was lowered fully a foot, over one hundred and sixty acres, in about four hours, and if we add to this the whole of the water of the Wincham Brook for twelve hours, we shall find

that not less than six hundred thousand tons of water rushed below. Many hundreds of tons of rock salt that had been brought to the surface, as well as the tramways, wagons, tubs, tools, and all materials were totally lost, and the mine as a mine, totally destroyed.

For some years the future of Vale Royal Abbey was in doubt, like many other ancient historic houses and manors throughout the country of England, mainly through neglect and ignorance, and the main dwelling possibly faced eventual demolition until it was fortunately purchased and taken over by the Vale Royal Abbey Golf Club in 1998, and has now been extravagantly upgraded, restored and expertly resembles its previous golden days of glory, as when the Cholmondeley family and the Lords' Delamere resided there.

This book is divided into three sections:

Part One. The life of Thomas Cholmondeley, 1st Lord Delamere (1767-1855)
Part Two. The life of Hugh Cholmondeley, 2nd Lord Delamere (1811-1887)
Part Three. The life of Hugh Cholmondeley, 3rd Lord Delamere (1870-1931)

This third section is somewhat abbreviated as a biography has already been written by Elsbeth Huxley (1935): *White Man's Country: Lord Delamere and the Making of Kenya.*

We will however reveal in our narrative—plus clarify many incidents in the life of Hugh, 3rd Lord Delamere and also the country of Kenya—events and facts based on our extensive research that are not included in his biography; a project that the 3rd Lord Delamere knew nothing about, as it was personally authorized and instructed by his second wife and young widow, Gwladys, Lady Delamere, a task that was undertaken by her personal friend the English writer, the late Elsbeth Huxley (1907-1997). But there are some established details, independently and factually recorded regarding his history, life style and that also relate to his questionable personal conduct both in England and also Kenya—somewhat private matters, many of them relating to Vale Royal Abbey and his immediate family, information that his widow (second wife, Gwladys, Lady Delamere) had no knowledge or if she did then simply would not permit the writer Elsbeth Huxley to include in her official biography that was published in 1935, four years after the death of Hugh Cholmondeley, 3rd Lord Delamere.

These three main characters form the basis of our story, and we will cover the period of time from 1538-1931, but many other interesting and fascinating individuals will be woven into this saga as they played important influential roles in the lives of our three main characters. For example, Sybil Burnaby (nee Cholmondeley, 1871-1911) the poor, unhappy, miserable, victimized, disillusioned daughter of Hugh, the 2nd Lord Delamere, who was driven to commit suicide at the young age of 39 years. We will reveal previously undisclosed facts related to the official inquest into her tragic death in 1911. We also expose her ex-husband, Algernon Edwyn Burnaby of Baggrave Hall, Leicestershire, also known as the "Leicestershire Scoundrel" whom she divorced in 1902. Plus we reveal the endearing and touching character of Lady Sophie Scott, the pretty, indulged youngest daughter of one of the richest men in the land, George, the 5th Earl Cadogan. Lady Sophie was seduced and humiliated by Algernon Burnaby while he was still married to Sybil Burnaby (nee Cholmondeley). Also we include details of the first wife of Hugh, 3rd Lord Delamere; the Lady Florence Anne Cole of Enniskillen, Ulster, Northern Ireland and the pathetic, degrading circumstances she endured and eventually that killed her whilst living in East Africa, later to become Kenya, during her short life of 36 years.

We also highlight in our account, Henrietta Charlotte Cholmondeley (1823-1874), who was the unfortunate victim of an arranged marriage by her overbearing, manipulative father, Thomas Cholmondeley, 1st Lord Delamere. Plus we learn of the loyal and faithful housekeeper of Hugh, 2nd Lord Delamere, Margaret Green (1835-1908) and Mildred Duffy (1845-1902), the very attractive, head cook in the Vale Royal Abbey household and her fascinating, complex involvement with the head butler, William Clarke of Tatton Park, Cheshire, the home of Lord William Tatton Egerton (1806-1883) a relationship that was both complex; sad but inspiring, despite all of William's idiosyncrasies. Both of these two intriguing characters, Margaret Green and Mildred Duffy, being part of the downstairs staff at Vale Royal Abbey during the lifetime of Hugh, 2nd Lord Delamere (1811-1887), had both personally

Preface

witnessed the decline and deterioration of the Great House at Vale Royal Abbey and parlous state of the once elegant Cheshire estate. Plus they saw firsthand the negative and weakening effect that these aggravating circumstances had on Hugh, 2nd Lord Delamere, his degenerating health and the very serious personal family problems he had to cope with during his lifetime, up until his eventual death in 1887.

On my latest visit to Vale Royal Abbey, England, approximately 53 years after my first visit in 1946, I was totally awe struck and indeed very pleasantly surprised by the beautiful and skillful restoration that had taken place by the current owners, the Vale Royal Abbey Golf Club, and this experience brought back many vivid memories and reflections of how Thomas, 1st Lord Delamere must have truly enjoyed the opulence and pleasure of residing in one of the most pulchritudinous historic residences in the whole of England. So let's take up the story of the Cholmondeley family of Vale Royal Abbey and relive their fascinating lives, exploits, disappointments, intrigues, disasters and conquests.

Vale Royal Abbey today, courtesy of Steve Leech, Vale Royal Abbey Golf Club and the *Creative Commons*

Acknowledgments

Many of these historic events and descriptions contained in this book have been reproduced, confirmed and acknowledged using information freely provided from *Wikipedia*, plus other numerous external sources. Our team of researchers has independently checked and verified as far as humanly possible all these details for accuracy and authenticity.

We gratefully acknowledge the access we have been provided by the University of London, University of Cambridge, University of York, Historic England Research Project, The Royal Collection Trust & Georgian Papers, English Heritage, the archives of the British History, the National Archives, the Rylands Library of Manchester, Grosvenor Museum in Cheshire, History Department of Hull University and the Historic Manuscripts Commission, plus resources of the Institute of Historical Research the Cheshire Records Office in Chester and the National Portrait Gallery in London.

We are also grateful to The Corpus Vitrearum Medii Aevi (CVMA) of Great Britain, plus the Kings College of London and the British Academy. The JANET Network and JISC, plus the National Education & Research Network (NREN). We also profusely thank "The Peerage" web site; created and maintained by the truly amazing, talented Darryl Lundy of New Zealand for the use of all the research material freely provided by him and his excellent web service. Also, we especially thank our friends, associates and students of the History Department of the University of Utah in Salt Lake City, who wish to remain nameless but who volunteered and provided much of their time, plus the valuable material related to the background history of our narrative and the characters involved. We gratefully acknowledge also the assistance we received from the Family History Library and Genealogy Department of the LDS Church in Temple Square, Salt Lake City. We also wish to thank the research information regarding the serious structural issues at Vale Royal Abbey, provided by Allan Challoner, Managing Trustee of the Michaelmas Trust, a British

Acknowledgements

Charity that owned Vale Royal Abbey for a number of years and also to the management of the current owners, the Vale Royal Abbey Golf Club for their cooperation in our research.

Most of the images and diagrams used in this narrative are in the public domain. Many of the photos used were taken by the author himself or members of his family and associates and these also are now in the public domain, a few other photos have been used after a request was made for permission from the copyright owners and these have been acknowledged accordingly.

Some images were sourced from the 'non-profit' organization *Wikipedia*, the online encyclopedia, especially their ShareAlike 4.0 International and Creative Commons (CC By-SA 4.0) service, referenced in the captions as *Creative Commons*, as well as other external sources. Our researchers have checked and verified as far as humanly possible these details for accuracy and authenticity.

All the names of the additional characters mentioned in this narrative are unrelated and unconnected to any living person who may have a similar name.

This is primarily a work of non-fiction as more fully explained in the Author's Note, although we expect some criticism from a section of our readers, but it is also loosely based on real places, events and actual people who lived in the annals of human history from 1538 to 1931. We have also included known and established facts regarding the history and development of Africa, especially Eastern and Southern Africa, which we hope will edify our readers regarding this important but often ignored, developing area of the world.

This narrative is dedicated to my dear wife Pauline and our three living children, Bradley, Kimberley and Garrick, who all taught me the qualities of patience, forbearance and perseverance involved with this 25-year project, and also to my two precious grandchildren, Natalie Claire Hebdon and Myles Peel Hebdon Hunter. In addition, also in memory of the many happy years our family spent living on the beautiful, exquisite continent of Africa and the close, dear friendships we made and all still enjoy even to this day. I also want to thank the input, information and recollections that my immediate family peers provided, especially my four dear sisters, Patricia Joyce, Judith Ann, Delia and Janice Margaret and also my beloved brother, Leslie.

Part One: The Life & Chronicles of Thomas Cholmondeley, 1ˢᵗ Lord Delamere, 1767-1855

Chapter One: The Forebears of 1st Lord Delamere of Vale Royal Abbey

Travelling through the beautiful, luxurious, green countryside of Cheshire, Thomas Cholmondeley (1594-1652), the great-great-grandfather of Thomas the 1st Lord Delamere; sitting comfortably in his horse drawn 'coach and four', was on his way from Holford Manor Hall in Newborough-in-Dutton to Vale Royal Abbey, on the outskirts of Delamere Forest. He was of course totally oblivious and unaware of his future destiny and what lay ahead. Thomas was however in a reflective, pensive mood this day as he was about to undertake his first official visit as the new owner of Vale Royal Abbey, the auspicious and elegant estate that he had just recently inherited from his mother, Lady Mary Cholmondeley, earlier in this year of 1625.

Lady Mary Cholmondeley had already undertaken extensive reconstruction and improvements to the Vale Royal Abbey manor, and was still purchasing furniture and expensive household items for the estate, right up until the day of her death on 15 August 1625. Her will, dated 20 January 1623, carefully enumerated her beneficiaries and her bequests. She designated her eldest son, Robert and his children as the lawful heirs to the Holford Manor Hall near the village of Plumley, Cheshire, plus the estate in addition to all the surrounding vast Cholmondeley lands. Her fourth son, Thomas, was bequeathed Vale Royal, the site of an ancient abbey, along with all the oxen, cattle, ploughs and other 'implements of husbandry' found at the estate, plus all the surrounding forests and lands.

Holford Manor Hall, inherited by Robert Cholmondeley, is a country house standing to the west of the village of Plumley, Cheshire. It consists of a fragment of a much larger timber-framed house, built in 1601 for Mary Cholmondeley on a moated site. The house is recorded in the National Heritage List for England as a designated Grade II listed building.

Cheshire Country Houses, by Peter de Figueiredo and Julian Treuhertz Phillimore, Chichester (1988), shows a photograph of the hall as it was in 1880 and states:

A very pretty fragment of a much larger moated timber house rebuilt for Mary Cholmondeley nee Holford, after the death of her husband, Sir Hugh Cholmondeley in 1601. There is a fine double arched stone bridge over the moat. Mary Cholmondeley lived at Holford until 1616 when she moved to Vale Royal.

Sir Hugh Cholmondeley, of Cholmondeley in Cheshire, the younger, married Mary daughter and sole heir of Christopher Holford of Holford, aforesaid, and had issue, Robert Lord Cholmondeley; Hatton Cholmondeley, second son, who died in London, 1605; Hugh Cholmondeley, third son who died before his eldest brother, whose issue afterwards became heirs of Cholmondeley lands; Thomas Cholmondeley, fourth son, from whom the Cholmondeleys of Vale Royal in Cheshire descend. And young Francis, died in infancy; Mary, eldest daughter, married Sir George Caveley of Leanigh Eaton-Boat; Lettice married Sir Richard Grosvenor, of Eaton-Boat, afterwards baronet; and Frances, youngest daughter, was second wife of Peter Venables of Kinderton, Esq. commonly called baron of Kinderton.

Holford Manor Hall near Plumley, Cheshire, today

Chapter One: The Forebears of 1st Lord Delamere of Vale Royal Abbey

Thomas Cholmondeley, the younger and only surviving brother of Robert had meantime inherited Vale Royal Abbey, which was a medieval Cistercian abbey, and later became a country house, located in Whitegate, between Northwich and Winsford in Cheshire.

Artist's impression of the Abbey as originally planned and envisioned, courtesy of Rylands Library

According to the *Dictionary of National Biography* (1885-1900), Lady Mary Cholmondeley was born as Mary Holford in late 1562 or January 1563 to Christopher Holford and Elizabeth Mainwaring in Holford, Great Budworth, Cheshire and christened (baptised) on 20 January 1563. She married Sir Randall Brereton of Malpas but he soon died. Around 1581, she married Sir Hugh Cholmondeley. They had eight children—Robert, Hatton, Hugh, Thomas, Francis, Mary, Lettice, and Frances—before Sir Hugh's death in 1601. Mary Cholmondeley died on 15 August 1625 at the age of sixty-three in Vale Royal Abbey, Whitegate, Cheshire.

Lady Mary Cholmondeley (1562-1625), unknown artist, courtesy of Winsford History Society

The Delamere Saga: Part 1

Vale Royal Abbey was founded in 1270 by King Edward I, for monks of the austere Cistercian Order. The King intended the abbey to be on the grandest scale, even larger than Westminster Abbey in London; however, financial difficulties meant that these ambitions could not be fulfilled and the final building was considerably smaller than planned. The project ran into problems in other ways too; the abbey was frequently grossly mismanaged, relations with the local population were so poor as to result in large scale violence on a number of occasions and internal discipline was frequently bad.

The Abbey was closed in 1538 by King Henry VIII as part of the Dissolution of the Monasteries. Much of the Abbey, including the church, was demolished but some of the cloister buildings were later incorporated into a mansion by Thomas Holcroft, an important government official, during the 1540s. Over subsequent centuries this house was considerably altered and extended by successive generations. The building remained habitable and contained surviving rooms from the original medieval abbey, including the refectory and kitchen. The foundations of the church and cloister have also been excavated. Today it is a scheduled ancient monument, and recorded in the National Heritage List for England as a designated Grade II listed building.

The *Imperial Gazetteer of England & Wales* by John Wilson (1870) describes Vale Royal Abbey as follows:

> Vale Royal, the seat of Lord Delamere, in Whitegate parish, Cheshire; on the river Weaver, near the Northwestern railway, 3 miles SW of Northwich. A Cistertian abbey was founded here in 1266, by Prince Edward, afterwards Edward I.; and was given, at the dissolution, to the Holcrofts. The mansion occupies the site of the abbey; was built in the time of Elizabeth by the Holcrofts; has been greatly altered by modern renovations and extensions; includes a portion of the old abbey in its basement; comprises a centre and two wings; is adorned in front with several towers; includes a great hall 70 feet long, hung round with interesting portraits, some of them by Rubens; was visited, in 1617, by James I.; and was plundered, in the civil wars of Charles I., by the soldiers of Cromwell.

Chapter One: The Forebears of 1st Lord Delamere of Vale Royal Abbey

The widowed Lady Mary Cholmondeley (1562-1625), a powerful woman in her own right with extensive properties in the area, had bought the Abbey as a home for herself when her eldest son inherited the primary family estates of Cholmondeley. In August 1617 she had entertained King James the 1st to a stag hunting party at the Vale Royal estate. The king enjoyed himself so much that he gave knighthoods to two members of the family. Shortly afterwards, in a letter he offered to advance the political careers of Lady Mary's sons if they would come to court. This offer was so firmly refused that the King named her "the Bolde Lady of Cheshire". Upon her death in 1625, Lady Mary passed the Abbey and estate on to her fourth son, Thomas, who founded the Vale Royal branch of the Cholmondeley family.

Artist's impression of the completed Abbey of St. Mary the Virgin, and St. Nicholas, Vale Royal, Cheshire, courtesy of Rylands Library

The church of the tenants of Vale Royal Abbey was made parochial at the Dissolution and the associated parish was called New Church or Whitegate. The township of Over was divided between Over Parish and Whitegate Parish, both of which are in Eddisbury Hundred and Middlewich Deanery. Wharton on the east of the Weaver was in Davenham Parish in Northwich

Hundred and Deanery (Dunn, 1987, 20, 38). Today, Winsford, which includes both Over and Wharton, is an Urban District and a Civil Parish in the District of Vale Royal.

Meanwhile, in 1625, the year that his mother Lady Mary died, Thomas Cholmondeley, was now on his way to visit Vale Royal Abbey, but this time as the proud and exalted new owner, and whose heart was now beating heavily with excitement as Vale Royal Abbey came into view. This day in the autumn of 1625 had come with sharpness in the air and the view across the Cheshire countryside was exhilarating. Thomas after leaning over to lightly kiss his wife on the cheek, he then fully turned unabashed to his much younger, demure and pretty wife Elizabeth, sole daughter and heir of John Minshull of Minshull, and enthusiastically he tightly grasped her shoulders, and said to her in a conspiratorial whisper, "What a great life we will now enjoy, especially now that I own and I am the "lord and master" of Vale Royal Abbey," and then gesturing with his hand sweeping across the expansive view of the graceful, undulating Cheshire countryside, plus the dense Delamere Forest beyond, he continued ruminatively, "and it's all mine!" He was of course, being the new owner and grand master of Vale Royal Abbey and the large estate, also holding the prestigious position of inheriting plus now owning one of the largest private estates in the whole of England, now experiencing for the first time the real taste of absolute power. His young, innocent wife Elizabeth meantime was somewhat bemused by his gesture and his headstrong remarks; she gently nodded and smiled, but she kept her tumultuous private feelings to herself.

Elizabeth, the recently married wife of Thomas, very quietly and with her usual wifely subjection, as she had been carefully taught by her mother, but with private reservations, said to Thomas, "I am so proud of you my dear husband". Thomas reacted with a disdainful glance toward Elizabeth and in a laconic, sarcastic tone stated, "Are you, my dear wife; thank you so very much." Little did Thomas and Elizabeth realize that day as they approached Vale Royal Abbey, the trauma and heart aches that faced them and their future family in the coming years; events, tragedies and serious issues that would ultimately tear the family apart?

Chapter One: The Forebears of 1st Lord Delamere of Vale Royal Abbey

Painting of a 'coach and four' possibly on the way from Holford Manor Hall to Vale Royal Abbey in the Cheshire countryside, unknown artist, courtesy of the Grosvenor Museum, Chester

Their coach, after driving up the attractive curved gravel driveway, eventually arrived at the grandiose front entrance of the Great House at Vale Royal Abbey, the entourage of household servants, all of whom were orderly and neatly arranged in advance, stood waiting to welcome their new 'lord and master' plus their new mistress of the household, Elizabeth, the recently married wife of Thomas Cholmondeley.

What the pre-occupied Thomas did not notice, as he was completely obsessed and blinded with the whole new experience of now being a celebrity for the first time, was the furtive glance the outstandingly handsome and physically powerful head groom, but also an audacious character, Hubert Broxup gave Elizabeth, the young and still very inexperienced wife of Thomas. Plus Thomas Cholmondeley never even noticed the blush that Elizabeth displayed and of course the flutter she had felt in her heart upon seeing Hubert for the first time. But someone else amongst the gathered downstairs staff, who were all neatly lined up on the front steps of the Great House at Vale Royal Abbey, had indeed shrewdly noticed this brief interchange between Hubert Broxup and the new 'mistress of the household' Elizabeth Cholmondeley.

The chambermaid Ethel was seething with anger as she observed this intimate reaction between Hubert Broxup and Elizabeth Cholmondeley, her new mistress of the household, and turned to her friend Agnes, the kitchen maid, her closest friend and confidant, and whispered to Agnes, while displaying a pout and facial grimace, "Hubert is mine, and over my dead body, I will not allow anyone else to take him away from me." Little did she know of the eventual truth and outcome of this statement to her close friend Agnes, and thus started the great animosity between the two rivals for the attention of Hubert Broxup the head stable groom; a feud that caused havoc for many years to come in the downstairs and upstairs household of Thomas Cholmondeley, now being the new owner of Vale Royal Abbey.

After Thomas and his new wife Elizabeth had been introduced to all the downstairs staff, they made their way to their private chambers, and intimately sharing a glass of the finest sherry, provided by their butler and which came from the well stocked wine cellar at Vale Royal Abbey that had been established by the late Lady Mary Cholmondeley, and reminiscing on the recent past events that had led up to this most important and significant day in their lives, now being the proud, exalted owners; master and mistress of this exquisite, expansive, and elegant estate of Vale Royal Abbey. But their idyllic private time being enjoyed in their secluded chambers was soon disturbed and broken with an urgent call from the head butler, Harold Fawcett, as he vigorously and repeatedly knocked on their bedroom door, but with no reply. So Harold insistently continued knocking and when Thomas after adjusting his clothes and putting on his britches again, eventually called out "Enter". The self-disciplined butler Harold humbly entered the bedroom with his eyes cast downwards, conveyed in a serious, solemn voice the urgent message to his master Thomas, "a violent fight had broken out in the downstairs tackle room of the stables, and the master must come immediately".

Dragging himself away from the comfort of his private chambers, his excellent glass of sherry and also from the enjoyment

Chapter One: The Forebears of 1st Lord Delamere of Vale Royal Abbey

of the company of his amorous new wife, Thomas braced himself, adorned his new smoking jacket, a gift from his new wife and following Harold his butler down to the basement room that held the tackle for all the numerous horses and stables he had inherited and that he now owned on the elegant Vale Royal Estate.

Thomas Cholmondeley was not prepared for, or even forewarned of, the shocking site and morbid scene that met him when he stepped into the annex room of the stables, plus the dank, musty smell of the place that made him retch. There lying face down upon the floor was the frail body of James the stable hand with a pitch fork embedded in his back with a large pool of blood now running and freely flowing over the stone cobbled floor. Plus Thomas also noted and was repulsed by the sight of the slop stone sink in the stables, as there was a disgusting pile of blood soaked clothes and sacking.

The stable boys, all cowering in the shadows, were silent and in a state of fear as they had just witnessed a murder that would eventually be judged as a mere "accident". The head groom Hubert Broxup stepped forward with his head bowed, and, with an artificially forced humility, admitted to his new master Thomas Cholmondeley that a fight and scuffle had ensued, and that James the stable boy had stumbled backwards and fallen onto the pitch fork, which unfortunately was unseen and hidden in the pile of straw against the rear wall of the stables.

Harold Fawcett the butler boldly stepped forward but in his usual lethargic manner and politely suggested to Thomas Cholmondeley that he send for the Sheriff of Chester, who lived in Chester Castle, Bridge Street, and resided in the nearby City of Chester. Thomas raising his shoulders and holding his head high with pride and with his usual arrogance stared directly with a glaring look and screaming at his butler, he shouted and said, "Harold you fool, *I am* now the Sheriff of Chester." So this traumatic evening concluded with instructions from Thomas Cholmondeley that the now befuddled Harold his butler send for the local Reverend Alan Higgs and that he would instruct him to take care of the body of the young James Greenwood, and the next day an inquest would be held by Thomas in his role as the new Sheriff of Chester, plus now being the official owner of Vale Royal Abbey, which was to be convened in his private study and he would personally interview the stable boys who had witnessed this horrifying incident

The Delamere Saga: Part 1

This October evening in 1625, on his first day spent at Vale Royal Abbey as lord and master was nevertheless definitely not concluded for Thomas, as he vigorously and quickly with bounding steps returned to his private chambers where his attractive new wife Elizabeth was still waiting patiently, and that evening plus many more evenings in the coming months of impregnating his young vulnerable delicate wife, and, after many miscarriages by Elizabeth, eventually the son he had always wanted and dreamed of was conceived in the January of 1627 and nine months later was born on 15 September 1627, when Thomas celebrated the birth of his new first born son and heir, also with personal pride and adulated self-image, to be also named Thomas.

This first day was thus marred by the death of an innocent young stable boy from Oldham, Lancashire who had done no harm to anyone, but it was also to eventually lead to the start of the new life in the Cholmondeley family line at Vale Royal Abbey. These events would seriously mark and feature in his newly inherited role of being owner and master of Vale Royal Abbey, plus it would also effectively influence and dominate him for the rest of his life, right up until his eventual death on 3 January 1652.

The following day, Thomas, now invigorated with his manly performance of the previous evening, came strutting down the stairs like a cock in his new red hunting jacket and buckskin breeches. Whistling his favourite tune "Greensleeves", he presented a fine handsome figure indeed. Thomas had just been recently appointed Master of the Hunt by the local gentry, a group of local wealthy land owners in Cheshire, who eventually formed the Tarporley Hunt Club in 1762, a tradition that continued with the Cholmondeley males for many years to come.

Thomas now called into his study the Reverend Higgs, plus three selected deacons from the local church of St. Chad's in the village of Over, Cheshire. This hurriedly arranged inquest now began that was to decide on the verdict of the "accidental" death of James Greenwood the young stable hand that had occurred the previous evening. It soon became clear after interviewing the stable boys that the fight that had ensued in the basement tackle room was primarily between James the young stable hand who lived in the local village of Weaver with his pregnant girl friend Brenda, James also happened to be the half-brother of the chamber maid

Chapter One: The Forebears of 1st Lord Delamere of Vale Royal Abbey

Ethel, and with the head groom, Hubert Broxup from the City of Chester. Poor Ethel had for some years laid claim on Hubert as belonging to her, but getting nowhere with her ambitions, except for the regular private intimate meetings and mutual sex they shared during the secret, private occasions they had together in the stables, primarily in order to satisfy Hubert's male lustful desires.

"What was the fight about?" Thomas Cholmondeley asked the bedraggled stable boys, most of whom had come from poor Lancashire families and were sarcastically known by the 'nickname' as "roughyeds"[2] and added, using his very limited knowledge of the Lancashire dialect, "Naythen now" (now see here), I want the truth "abaht" (about) this incident, does thee hear me lads?" They reluctantly replied as best as they could, "awlreet" (*all right*) the leader of the stable boys replied and explained that it was related to the insulting names that Hubert, acting like a "barmpot" (silly fool) used to describe Ethel the chamber maid that "neet" (night), and who with frenzied swearing language calling her a "slut" (sleaze) and even more denigrating terms; words the stable boys could not even pronounce correctly, and added that Hubert was "addled" (*not thinking straight*) and they all had too much "booze" (*ale*) that evening. Hubert "mun" (must) have pushed James "backarts" (backwards) and not "worriting" (bothering or worrying) to check the pile of straw."[2]

Unknown to Thomas Cholmondeley and the others sitting in on this quickly arranged 'local board of enquiry' being held in the study at Vale Royal Abbey that morning, Hubert Broxup the head groom already had his sights set on greater things than a poor lowly chamber maid called Ethel, his sight was ambitiously set on conquering and seducing Elizabeth the attractive young wife of Thomas and who was now the new mistress of the household at Vale Royal Abbey, but this private knowledge and evidence was not

---

[2] *Roughyed* is a nickname for a person from Oldham, derived from the rough felt used in the hatting and textile industry in the past, which once employed many local people. Since the mid-20th century, Oldham has seen the demise of its textile industry, and the troubled integration of new cultural traditions and religions. With respect to the ensuing depression that followed Oldham's slump in textile manufacture, one author remarked that "when the fall finally came, it was the town that crashed the hardest". An enlightening comment in the archives of the *Morning Chronicle*, a London Newspaper of 1849, offers this description of Oldham: "The visitor to Oldham will find it essentially a mean-looking straggling town, built upon both sides and crowning the ridge of one of the outlying spurs which branch from Manchester, the neighbouring "backbone of England". The whole place has a shabby underdone look. The general appearance of the operatives' houses is filthy and smouldering."

revealed or exposed at this time or at this morbid, macabre inquest. Most of the young, innocent, inexperienced stable boys appeared to be totally flummoxed over the whole unfortunate incident. The eventual decision and ruling by Thomas Cholmondeley, now acting in his new role as the official Sheriff of Chester, and after carefully studying Hubert's expressions while he was being questioned, was that this dreadful incident was an unfortunate and tragic accident caused by heavy drinking of ale by his staff, so with a sharp, critical reprimand of the ones involved, the matter was quietly and discreetly dropped. This was a decision that Thomas Cholmondeley would regret for the rest of his life.

From this cold dank autumn day in 1625, events and household concerns settled into a fairly regular boring routine for many months. The amorous ambitions of Hubert Broxup the head groom were put on hold and could not be personally pursued, as his sexual desires for the mistress of the household, namely Elizabeth Cholmondeley, who was having great difficulty settling down and adapting to her new life at Vale Royal Abbey, also after suffering several miscarriages was now having difficulties carrying her unborn son. Her poor state of health and debilitating pregnancy severely restricted her activities and she seldom left her private chambers for weeks or even months at a time.

It was springtime, 1626, when next Thomas welcomed his older brother Robert from Holford Hall, now known as Viscount Cholmondeley of Kells, and his attractive wife Catherine, daughter of John, Lord Stanhope of Harrington, this being their first official visit to Vale Royal Abbey, and what an event that proved to be. The siblings of Thomas and Robert Cholmondeley, namely their three brothers and three sisters had either died, joined the clergy or gone insane, so now to be the most successful surviving offspring of the Cholmondeley family of Holford Hall, these two sons of the now famous; the late Lady Mary Cholmondeley, deserved to celebrated, and this they indeed did for a whole month, with drinking, debauchery and conduct that was so extreme and lascivious that it cannot be included in this narrative. Putting it more succinctly, the local wenches from the villages of Over and Weaver in Cheshire had the time of their lives!

Upon his departure from Vale Royal Abbey, Robert Cholmondeley, in June, 1626, was to return initially to his home at

Chapter One: The Forebears of 1ˢᵗ Lord Delamere of Vale Royal Abbey

Holford Hall near Plumley, Cheshire, and then travel on to the City of London to attend to business related to the complicated estate of his late mother, Lady Mary Cholmondeley. His wife Catherine was to remain behind, as usual, at Holford Hall, as Robert, like most of the Cholmondeley males, he had arranged to meet his secret lover at his rented house in Wilton Place, Belgravia, in London. He invited his brother Thomas to join him, but as Elizabeth the wife of Thomas Cholmondeley, now again being heavy with child, having recently and unfortunately experiencing another miscarriage, but as she was now hopefully bearing his first son and heir, his vested interest was primarily at Vale Royal Abbey and his heir to be, and certainly not at this pending important eventful time in his life was he interested in the whore houses and brothels of London; that indeed would come later.

September, 1627, soon came around and ultimately the day that the child of Elizabeth and Thomas Cholmondeley was due, and indeed on the date due, the boy child was born, but not without great trauma for Elizabeth during the birth, which Thomas completely ignored and was only keen on hearing the first loud, squalling cry demonstrating and announcing his first born sons entry into the world of the esteemed Cholmondeley family of Vale Royal Abbey and of seeing his new heir; the son he had always dreamed of, now to also be proudly named Thomas Cholmondeley (1627-1702). This new era of bringing up a son and heir, introducing and exposing his son to all the grandeur and benefits of being a future "lord of the manor" kept the new father Thomas close to home and also preoccupied with the serious, grave responsibilities of running the now prosperous, opulent estate of Vale Royal Abbey and also completing the new renovations that his late mother, Lady Mary Cholmondeley, had already started before she died, an obligation that he personally felt must still be administered and completed.

Thomas's new, first born son, Thomas junior, born in 1627, was completely under the guidance and influence of his mother Elizabeth and the new recently appointed governess, Mary Parsons, whom she had employed from the nearby City of Chester. Thomas the father was so preoccupied with his duties as new "lord of the manor" he hardly ever took notice of his wife and any personal time they spent together was only to discuss and boast of his accomplishments and ambitions, plus his goals to increase the prestige and reputation of Vale Royal Abbey and create it to become the most desirable and ostentatious private estate in the whole of England.

What Elizabeth, the wife of Thomas, did not realize at the time she employed the new governess was that Mary Parsons was a distant cousin of Hubert Broxup, the Head Groom, and very soon Hubert wormed his charming way into the intimate private life of Elizabeth Cholmondeley. Using the pretext of helping the young boy Thomas to learn to ride his new pony, a gift from his now disinterested father, a pony that Thomas had bought for his son's fourth birthday, Hubert Broxup was soon spending more and more time each day with Elizabeth and the young Thomas, taking riding lessons and enjoying trotting through the intoxicating, lush countryside of the county of Cheshire. To experience the scents of the summer months in Cheshire is a delight in itself to all the fortunate people who live there, but also being privileged to own and to ride a well groomed, healthy stallion through the graceful Cheshire countryside enhances that delight. So passed 1631, a year that Elizabeth, the sadly neglected wife of Thomas Cholmondeley experienced her growing loneliness and emptiness in her life, now a seemingly interminable and tedious existence, little wonder that she fell into the snare laid by her insistent suitor, the extremely handsome, manipulative and virile Hubert Broxup, and she soon found she was pregnant once again.

Thomas Cholmondeley, the husband of Elizabeth, who meantime was completely preoccupied with expanding and improving his grand residence in Cheshire, the Great House and Great Hall, plus the now well established estate at Vale Royal Abbey, determined to make it the most admired and palatial manor house in the whole of England. Each evening when he finished his daily duties, he soon started drinking heavily and after dinner he relaxed, enjoyed his brandy and then soon quickly fell asleep, slumped in his favorite over-stuffed chair, much to the anguish of his young neglected wife Elizabeth. She was meantime seriously contemplating how to break the news to her husband that she was again three months pregnant and knowing that Thomas did not have the energy in the evenings to even make love anymore to his emotionally starved wife, and also knowing that they had not been

Chapter One: The Forebears of 1st Lord Delamere of Vale Royal Abbey

intimate now for over six months, her secret would soon have to be revealed and uncovered, plus the morbid curiosity of Thomas her husband would have to be appeased somehow.

The ambition of Thomas, that by this time had become his main obsession in life, was to acquire works of art and a library of classical literature and books to the ever expanding, growing library started by his late mother Lady Mary at Vale Royal Abbey. He spent much of his spare time in visiting local auction houses and deceased estates, acquiring and accumulating a library that ultimately would become one of the largest private libraries in the whole of England, containing many priceless books of great value. Plus his interest in acquiring works of art to proudly display in his property, eventually took him to Amsterdam in Holland, and there he visited the showrooms of art dealers and local artists. It was during one of his annual trips in 1645 that he acquired several paintings from the local Dutch artist, Pieter Brueghel the Younger, and one of the paintings he acquired costing him 200 florins at the time [two shillings or 10 new pence today], and was titled *Census at Bethlehem*. This same painting was recently sold by one of the descendants of Thomas Cholmondeley (1594-1652) for the amazing price of almost $10 million.

To quote from a recent article in the *London Times* regarding this work of art:

> A painting found in Africa, which falls under the category of an ancient masterpiece, sold in London for 9.6 million dollars on 16 October 2013. The work, entitled *Census at Bethlehem* by Pieter Brueghel the Younger, was discovered in a house in Kenya by art dealer Johnny van Haeften, who specialises in the field of ancient masters. The oil painting, dating from 1556, was sold by van Haeften at the Frieze in London. The work comes from a descendant of Lord Delamere, whose family owned the painting for more than a century. According to the Bloomberg website, a dead gecko lizard fell from the top of the painting when Mr. van Haeften took it off the wall. It was bought by and is now owned by the Royal Museum of Fine Arts of Belgium.

The Delamere Saga: Part 1

Census at Bethlehem by Pieter Brueghel the Younger, courtesy of the Royal Museum of Fine Arts, Belgium

The pride and joy of Thomas Cholmondeley was to stroll through the main west gallery and library at Vale Royal Abbey, to salivate and gloat over his worldly possessions, unfortunately his wife and his two sons; yes he had reluctantly accepted the son of Elizabeth his wife and Hubert Broxup as his own and named him Robert after his only living older brother, but they did not receive the same attention as his collection of valuable books, armory, collectibles and works of art. Elizabeth meantime in the following years, apart from several more miscarriages was to bear seven more sons and four daughters, six of these children died through illness early in infancy as they did not have the physical stamina of Thomas, but had inherited the frail, weak physical characteristics of their mother. Hubert Broxup the head groom had of course been dismissed by his master Thomas Cholmondeley with vilifying terms on the feeble excuse and pretext that he had been accused of stealing some of his property, namely bridles and saddles from the stables, also they had now become very antagonistic towards each other. So Hubert Broxup, smiling whimsically gladly moved on to even greater pastures and conquests, so he took up the role of farm manager of Haggate Farm in Royton, Lancashire, which was the

Chapter One: The Forebears of 1st Lord Delamere of Vale Royal Abbey

location of one of the largest Friesian cattle herds in the north of England, and ironically Hubert met and married a local girl called Ethel who worked on the farm.

Hubert and Ethel Broxup remained childless up until their eventual death at Haggate Farm in Royton and the only son that Hubert ever had was his illegitimate son, born back in Cheshire from the illicit affair he had experienced with Elizabeth (1600-1661), the wife of Thomas Cholmondeley (1594-1652) while Hubert was still working there as the Head Groom at Vale Royal Abbey. Thomas had meantime reluctantly accepted this illegitimate child as his own and had named him Robert after his older brother Robert, Viscount Cholmondeley of Kells, Ireland, who lived in the nearby Holford Manor Hall.

Robert Cholmondeley, the adopted son of Thomas, never knew who his real biological father was, but the stunning appearance of Robert, being tall, dark and handsome, he proved to be the 'spitting image' of his biological father Hubert Broxup, and he also had the same identical swaggering walk and way of attracting and charming the young beautiful women of Cheshire. Robert never married and made his life vocation in the military as a high ranking member of the Royalist Cavaliers (known as the Royalists) army fighting the Parliamentarian army (known as the Roundheads) during the English Civil Wars (1642-1659) and he presented a most stunning figure of a man when dressed in his official uniform.

A typical Cavalier (Royalist) Soldier, by unknown artist, courtesy of the British Museum

The *Encyclopædia Britannica* quotes a contemporary authority's description of the members of the Parliamentary army:

> They had the hair of their heads, very few of them longer than their ears, whereupon it came to pass that those who usually with their cries attended at Westminster were by a nickname called 'Roundheads'. The demonstrators included London apprentices and Roundhead was a term of derision for them because the regulations to which they had agreed included a provision for closely cropped hair.

Thomas Cholmondeley was reminded every single day and every time he looked at his adopted son Robert as he grew into a physically powerful young man, and how much he looked like and resembled his biological father Hubert Broxup, which made Thomas extremely bitter and irritated, plus he was also reminded with repulsion and hatred in his heart of the act of unfaithfulness and the adultery of his wife Elizabeth with his now dismissed "head groom" Hubert Broxup. Thomas did not think for one minute that possibly he could have been the prime cause of this unfaithful action by his wife, because of his own neglect and remiss, spending far too much time pursuing his ambitious goals of trying to make Vale Royal Abbey the most prosperous and envied private estate in the whole of England. Thomas Cholmondeley spent the rest of his life harboring this hatred of his wife and her brief relationship with Hubert Broxup, which permeated Vale Royal Abbey for many years and he had no remorse for his attitude toward his wife, right up until his eventual death in 1652.

Robert Cholmondeley (1630-1658), the illegitimate son of Hubert Broxup and Elizabeth Cholmondeley, was a devout Royalist as was his adoptive father Thomas Cholmondeley and young Robert died aged only 28 years. He eventually died in the arms of his loving mother Elizabeth at Vale Royal Abbey in 1658, as a result of his severe wounds received during the English Civil Wars of 1650-1659 (see Appendix 1), while he was fighting Cromwell and his Parliamentary army and today he is buried at Church Minshull in Cheshire.

Chapter Two: Thomas Cholmondeley (1627-1702)

After the death of Thomas Cholmondeley in 1652 and his wife Elizabeth, who died in 1661, both were buried in the village of Church Minshull in Cheshire. Their son, born on 15 September 1627, also named Thomas, took over the reigns at Vale Royal Abbey.

By this time, the main house had been extensively improved and renovated and now had the reputation of being one of the grandest places of great prestige in the whole of England. To be invited to visit Vale Royal Abbey at this time was the dream of most of the wealthy inhabitants of the land, including nobility and even members of the Royal Family. These were to be the glory days of Vale Royal Abbey.

The new master, Thomas, had recently married Jane, daughter of Sir Lionel Tollemache, 2nd Baronette of Helmingham, Suffolk, in 1644, who was 17 years old at the time. Thomas was as prolific as his father, as Jane gave birth to five sons and seven daughters, but she died, understandably, at 39 years in 1666. Thomas was also very keen to marry again after her death and very soon took up a serious relationship with Ann St. John from Wiltshire, described as a "gentlewoman", whom he had known intimately in any case now for several years when he had visited London on a regular basis as Member of Parliament for Cheshire.

Ann was the daughter of Sir Walter St. John (1622-1708) of Battersea, London. Sir Walter was Member of Parliament for Wiltshire (1656-1658 and 1659); for Wootton Bassett (1660-1679); and again for Wiltshire (1679-81 and 1690-95). He was famed for his "piety and moral virtues". In 1700, Sir Walter signed a trust deed that led to the formation of a local school in London, which later became the world-famous Sir Walter St John's School of Battersea.

The Delamere Saga: Part 1

Sir Walter St. John (1622-1708) courtesy of the National Archives

To quote from Enitan Bereola's *The Good Gentlewoman* (2013):

> Anne St. John was baptised at St Mary's Church, Battersea on December 8, 1650 the first of Sir Walter and Lady Johanna St. John's thirteen children. She grew up at the manor house in Battersea, spending summer holidays at the family's country seat in Lydiard Tregoze, Wiltshire. On May 20, 1684 Anne married Thomas Cholmondeley at the Charterhouse Chapel in London and left for her new home at Vale Royal, a former abbey founded by Edward I on the River Weaver in Delamere Forest, Cheshire.
>
> Anne, Thomas's second wife, was described as being 'a lady not esteemed very young,' who was a bit of a problem for the Cholmondeley family, as Thomas was in dire need of a male heir. Ann was almost 35 years by the time she married Thomas Cholmondeley in 1684. His first wife, Jane, daughter of Sir Lionel Tollemache had produced 12 children, but all five sons had died during their father's lifetime.

Ann St. John was born in 1650, and married Thomas Cholmondeley in 1684 and was 34 years younger than Thomas. She died 1 December 1742, aged 92 years at Vale Royal Abbey, and is buried at Minshull, Cheshire. Ann, the second wife of Thomas, also had four sons and one daughter during her lifetime.

Thomas became the first Cholmondeley male of Vale Royal Abbey to achieve the position of becoming the Member of Parliament (MP) for Cheshire in 1669, a position that his descendants continued to hold for many years to come, and this new appointment required that he spend much of his time in London to attend to his duties at the House of Commons, but unfortunately his reputation closely followed him and he was soon noted as being a 'rake' and he also mixed freely with the royal household of King William III, who reigned as King of England from 1688 to 1702.

To quote from a record of the time regarding King William:

> The King's position was not a happy one. He never loved England and they never loved their 'Dutch William'. The leading men around him were a sorry crowd; quarrelsome, spiteful, self-seeking and faithless. Queen Mary, wife of William, with her bright smile and warm heart, helped greatly to smooth his path; but when she died in 1694 and William was left alone, he became even more unpopular than before. Unfortunately he was not a man to command affection. He was surly and unsociable and his wretched health often made him peevish. Moreover, he was only interested in English affairs for a particular purpose and that was to save Holland, from the grasping ambition and cruel Catholic bigotry of Louis XIV, King of France.

London in 1699 was noted for its immoral, depraved conduct amongst the rich and wealthy, plus in direct contrast the extreme poverty and traumatic conditions in the slums of London, especially with the poor Jewish immigrants fleeing from the radical, fanatical persecution in Eastern Europe and most of whom were now settling in the ghettos of the east end of London.

Special mention must be made regarding the appalling conditions of these Jewish immigrants in London as the grandparents of one my special friends were amongst this group. In later years, especially from 1850s to the beginning of the 20th century, Jewish communities received particular interest from the now world famous Charles Booth and his survey team. During the late nineteenth century, London was home to a new and large scale migrant Jewish population, which had arrived from Eastern Europe, fleeing persecution and seeking new lives. As a point of comparison, Jewish migrants in London were second only to Irish settlers in number.

Charles Booth (1840-1916) was a British businessman and social reformer born in Liverpool, Lancashire in 1840 and remembered today mostly for his efforts to document poverty in nineteenth-century London. In 1866, Booth and his brother Alfred began a shipping service between Europe and Brazil. The business was reorganized as Booth Steamship Company, Ltd., in 1901. He documented these efforts in his multivolume work (17 volumes) of over 450 notebooks, *Inquiry into Life and Labour in London*, which was published between 1889 and 1903.

Bored with running his successful business, Booth had decided to investigate the incidence of pauperism in the East End of the city of London; he also recruited a team of researchers to assist him in his campaign. These notebooks that are now stored in the archives of the London School of Economics comprise over 450 volumes of interviews, questionnaires, observations and statistical information. They document the social and economic life of London, highlighting all of its contrasts, complexities and contradictions. These notes are now available in the public domain and are open for inspection by genuine historians.

Members of Parliament and the British Government at that time had very little interest or concern in the pathetic, wretched conditions of the poor in London or for that matter throughout the whole of England, their primary concern was for power and advancement of their lucrative careers, and Thomas Cholmondeley was no exception, he continued to display his acerbic character more and more. Thomas after arriving in London soon befriended Ned Ward (1667-1731) an ebullient fellow from Oxford, also known as Edward Ward, who was a satirical writer and publican in the late seventeenth and early eighteenth century while he was based in London. His most famous work is *The London Spy*, published in 18 monthly installments from November 1698. It was described by the author as a "complete survey" of the London scene.

What attracted Thomas Cholmondeley of Vale Royal Abbey to the tempestuous Ned Ward is an enigma, plus a very perplexing, bewildering question. Ned Ward was born in the year 1667 in Oxfordshire, and, historian Theophilus Cibber in his book, *Lives of the Poets of Great Britain & Ireland*, wrote that Ward was

Chapter Two: Thomas Cholmondeley (1627-1702)

"a man of low extraction, [...] who never received any regular education", and he was likely to have been educated at one of the local grammar schools of Oxfordshire or possibly Coventry in Warwickshire, England. When Thomas Cholmondeley first met Edward Ward, Edward was an impecunious, budding writer and he was trying to get a foothold in the City of London but he had very few meaningful connections.

By 1691 Ned Ward had made his way to London. Edward Ward was also involved in political controversy from as early as 1698. Being a "High-Church Tory", he launched several scurrilous attacks on low-church moderation and conformity, the first of them being the 'Ecclesia et factio' (1698). He also had a propensity for violence and aggression, which displayed itself in his life style and reputation, but Ned Ward also quickly learned how to conciliate the conflicting moods of the Church and the State. However it was an issue of endurance to hear Ned Ward bloviate about his accomplishments.

Portrait of Edward (Ned) Ward, approximately 1731, by Michael Vandergucht, courtesy of the National Gallery, London

Ward's best-known political publication, *Hudibras Redivivus*, issued in twenty-four monthly parts between 1705 and 1707, drew upon topical material from the political struggle of the day. Ned Ward also wrote *The London Spy*, which was published in eighteen monthly parts from November, 1698. Written in the authorial voice of a philosopher who abandons his scholarly pursuits in favour of actual experience, *The London Spy* established Ward's name and style within the literary world, and was so successful that for over a decade Ward's writings were sold and advertised under the caption of "by the Author of *The London Spy*".

In *The London Spy*, Ward presented the seamier side of life by using graphic description, racy anecdotes and character sketches. Some of these satires were expanded into periodicals, allowing for an extended commentary on specific human and individual vices that Ward experienced personally, particularly within London and also what he saw in his own taverns. He also further elucidated the various practices of corruption by the clergy and politicians in London. *The London Spy* was followed by over one hundred satires of prose and verse, of which typical targets included alehouse keepers, dissenting ministers, lawyers and booksellers; he extended some of these works into periodicals, such as *The Weekly Comedy*. He was taken into custody by the local police authorities both in February and June of 1706 and Ned Ward was charged with seditious libel for accusing the Queen of failing to support the Tories in parliament and was condemned to stand in the pillory.[3]

The loquacious Ned Ward was also a publican at the King's Head Tavern, next door to Gray's Inn, in London, and from the habits and reputation of Thomas Cholmondeley, this is the likely place they first met and their clandestine bi-sexual relationship began. It is also rumoured, based on related archived documents, in which Thomas Cholmondeley had helped, privately and anonymously, to finance Ned Ward in many of his literary projects, which Thomas later grudgingly admitted was a mistake.

In 1699 Thomas Cholmondeley was introduced to the very attractive, provocative Emily Williams from Merthyr Tydfil, Wales by his mutual friend Ned Ward, probably while Thomas was on his usual evening visit to the beer hall at the King's Head Tavern, an introduction for which Thomas gave Ned his fervid thanks. Emily was celebrated as a young woman of great beauty and charm, who later established a questionable reputation as an actress but she was extremely equable. In May 1699, even the famous Robert Dyer, painter and poet, from Llanfynydd, Carmarthenshire, invited her to "an evening at home", attended by some of the famous artists of the day. Emily's looks and personality attracted interest, commentary, and invitations from artists and society hostesses; she was also a very capricious girl who would do anything to get her

---

[3] A *pillory* was a wooden framework with holes for the head and hands, in which an offender was shackled, imprisoned and being exposed to public abuse. They were often placed on platforms to increase public visibility of the person and often a placard detailing the crime was placed nearby.

Chapter Two: Thomas Cholmondeley (1627-1702)

own way and she really knew how to tantalise her admirers. Plus of course she now had in tow; like a drooling puppy, the disreputable Thomas Cholmondeley of Vale Royal Abbey, the very wealthy and prosperous Member of Parliament and Sheriff of Chester.

What was England like in the 1700s? Apart from the life style of the rich and famous, such as Thomas Cholmondeley, and the royal family, nobility and their friends who enjoyed the opulence and the excessive life style of the wealthy, life was a miserable experience day in and day out for the great majority of the inhabitants of the land. To quote from a reliable historical record of the time:

> Britain suffered such great poverty during this time. A foundling hospital is opened in London for the unwanted children of the poor and many have to beg and are simply dying in the streets, as for others, a study shows of the 2339 children admitted into London work houses, only 168 remain alive after five years. To combat the rampant alcoholism, a gin tax is also levied.

An additional historical record, *Looking at History* by R. J. Unstead (1963), reflects the trends of the changing times in England in the 1700s:

> It was a time of great change in England. The population was expanding rapidly, and new methods of agriculture were developed to cope with the increasing population. Many people who had lived in the country lost their jobs due to enclosure of land, as small farms were amalgamated into large farms to make farming more efficient. At the same time, new methods of manufacture were devised, and towns expanded. The population began to shift from the country to the towns.
>
> Although the Church of England was still very much the official religion of England, Methodism was spreading, especially in the West Country; it was hugely popular in Cornwall for instance. Over three hundred and fifty Methodist chapels were built in the 1700s. There was still strong anti-Catholic feeling in England, in 1780, after a mild measure in Parliament to ease restrictions on Catholics, Lord George Gordon led a mob on the rampage in London. They pillaged Catholic chapels, broke open prisons, and set fire to a distillery. The orgy of destruction lasted for a week, and almost five hundred people were killed or wounded.

Travel was on foot or on horseback or in horse-drawn vehicles. Wealthy people kept their own carriages; poorer people might travel on public stagecoaches. Those who could not afford stage-coaches might travel on stage-wagons, which were pulled by eight or ten horses, and might carry as many as 30 or 40 passengers. The mid-1700s was also the great era of canal building in England, and a network of canals was built for transporting goods all across England, including Cheshire. Besides the respectable tradesmen, workers and street sellers, there were hordes of poor and destitute who seldom had regular work, but lived as best they could. Thieving, robbery, and murder were common crimes and punishments were savage. A man could be hanged for any one of two hundred crimes, such as sheep-stealing, pocket-picking, or, indeed, for the theft of any amount above five shillings.

Regarding the punishment that was meted out to convicted criminals from 1780-1825, during our research we uncovered a brilliant project that was launched in 2017. The Digital Panopticon is the "collaboration between the Universities of Liverpool, Sheffield, Tasmania, Oxford, and Sussex," with Barry Godfrey, professor of Social Justice at the University of Liverpool, as its principal investigator. The project explores the impact of various punishments on approximately 90,000 people who were sentenced at London's Old Bailey between 1780 and 1825. This project brings together "millions of records from around fifty datasets" into a searchable database, including trial records, transportation records of convicts who were sent to Australia, and many more. Of particular interest are the "convict lives" pages, which feature brief biographies of individual convicts whose life histories were "reconstructed using the Digital Panopticon website," while the historical background section offers helpful contextual information about the British criminal justice system at that time.

A sample of the records in this project is of one James McDonald, a married man with three children to feed and illustrated a typical victim of the time. He was brought before the judge at Old Bailey, London in 1744. Accused of grand larceny while working at the Fox and Hounds in Shoreditch of "stealing a shirt, value 3s. three silver buckles, value 6s. a pair of stockings, value 2s." and he was found guilty. He was sentenced to transportation to the convict

Chapter Two: Thomas Cholmondeley (1627-1702)

colony in Australia and probably died there.

Of course none of these very serious national or social issues experienced by the poor and victimized in England, affected or even touched the 'thick skinned' and callous Thomas Cholmondeley, as he was living a life of luxury, mixing with the royal family of the day and also now being in the City of London, was also enjoying the decadence that was the normal life style of those who belonged to his class. Thomas was however foolishly, naively and completely unaware of what intrigues, quirks and vagaries that were taking place and being experienced by the family household back at his estate, Vale Royal Abbey.

Meantime back at Vale Royal Abbey, Ann (1650-1742) the second wife of Thomas Cholmondeley, in 1699, with her husband being away in London most of the time, supposedly at the House of Commons, eventually grudgingly admitted to herself that she was hardly able or even capable of managing the large estate, now bordering on going 'haywire'[4] even with the sincere, devoted help of the recently appointed but unfortunately incompetent, so-called estate manager, James Barry Jones of Runcorn, Cheshire. At least she had the support of her indefatigable dedicated downstairs staff and her very competent and qualified governess, Miss Delia Davies from Denbigh, Wales, assigned to take care of her three surviving children—two sons and one daughter.

Speaking in confidence to Harold Fawcett the Butler one day, Ann poured out her troubles and concerns of not being able to fully understand or comprehend the figures of the estate accounts, and could no longer manage or control the overwhelming task of the bookkeeping and also paying the local Cheshire merchants and suppliers of the household goods on time. Plus she was also very worried that possibly she was being swindled and exploited on many occasions by many of these very shrewd local merchants because of her ineptness, ignorance and lack of experience. Harold Fawcett, always being the helpful supportive butler quickly came to her rescue and he already previously had also privately observed the erratic behavior of his 'mistress of the household' Ann Cholmondeley in recent months. So Harold suggested that he introduce her to a young man whom he had recently met in the taproom of the Old Star public house in Swanslow Lane in the

---

[4] This term was originally referred to the tendency of wire spooled under tension and used in the baling of hay to spring into an unmanageable tangle and out of control.

village of Winsford. This new resident of Cheshire, Horace Farrell had just recently moved from Warrington, with his young wife Charlotte, and they were now living comfortably in Kersal Lodge, in the village of Delamere, in a small cottage they had rented from Lord Egerton of Tatton Hall.

According to the butler Harold Fawcett's knowledge and recollection; as he informed his mistress, Ann Cholmondeley that drab, rainy morning in 1699, Horace Farrell had previously managed a large military food store in Warrington and while he was enlisted in the Royal Cheshire Militia had gained a great deal of experience in managing and controlling the quarter master's store and was very capable in handling the tasks of book keeping, plus he could very easily take care of the Vale Royal Estate records. Harold the butler also pointed out that Horace had only recently moved to the Cheshire countryside because of the poor health of his new wife, who had suffered a dreadful accident that had left her paralyzed from the waist down. The butler also quickly added that Horace Farrell was also a very friendly, likable and affable fellow and was currently available to be employed.

The following week, Horace Farrell thus entered into the heady and intoxicating atmosphere of Vale Royal Abbey, to be introduced to the mistress of the household, Ann Cholmondeley. Horace was completely taken aback when he saw Ann for the first time, as he was under the clear impression that Ann was an elderly woman of 51 years of age, and he being only 29 years of age was still in his manly, youthful masculine pride. Unknown to him of course was that Ann had made an especially great effort to make sure she looked her best, dressed in her finest attire and represented herself as belonging to one of the wealthiest and most prosperous families in Cheshire, if indeed not the whole country of England and Wales, whose husband just happened to be the Member of Parliament for Cheshire and also the Sheriff of Chester. Horace had also of course put on his most impressive attire consisting of his black riding britches, his highly polished black riding boots and his Harris Tweed jacket, and being over six feet tall, eyes that were a penetrating deep blue and with a mass of wavy blonde hair; he also made a very marked impression on Ann. When their eyes locked, they both knew immediately that this relationship would be more than just an employee and employer, and so began a secret, tempestuous but very private memorable love affair that would lead to a major catastrophe in the course of time.

Ann Cholmondeley soon learned that the young wife of Horace was now bedridden because of a dreadful horse riding accident a few years ago when they lived in Warrington and as they had only recently been married they had no children and now because of the unfortunate infirmity of his wife Charlotte due to the accident, she was unable to have relations with her husband, and therefore would remain childless and barren for the rest of their lives together.

After spending the rest of the afternoon in consultation together, also discussing some of their respective and personal particular problems, plus in addition their mutual unfortunate circumstances in life, the bond between them soon progressed to a more comfortable, relaxed, understanding of each other, and a solace that would soon progress and develop into a relationship that neither of them could or even wanted to control. Horace had assured Ann that he would accept his appointment and would begin his duties the following day and, if there was anything she needed to be explained about the estate records, he would be only too happy to assist. Ann's furtive mind quickly grasped on these words of Horace, "anything she needed" and in her sub-conscious she visualized the young man standing before her, who now appeared like a Greek God in her fertile mind—tall, craggy and unbelievably handsome—and she knew there and then that he surely would be able to supply "all her needs".

Horace however took the initiative and informed Ann that he must now return to his home at Kersal Lodge to attend to his severely handicapped wife, Charlotte, and Ann snapping back to reality, quickly retorted that she agreed, so after their first day in each others company they parted, both knowing that when Horace returned the next day to commence his duties as bookkeeper of the Vale Royal Estate, but the atmosphere and aura between them would now be completely different from when they first met a few hours earlier.

The following day, Horace Farrell arrived at Vale Royal Abbey promptly at noon, and began his specific task of trying to sort out the mess and muddle that the estate records had fallen into. He was instructed by Harold Fawcett that he was to undertake his duties in the family study, which was now rarely used because the master,

Thomas Cholmondeley, being always absent in London in his town house in Craven Terrace.

Southern View of Vale Royal Abbey by Peter Varley, courtesy of *The Gentlewoman*

Although Horace Farrell was not greeted personally by the mistress of the household, Ann Cholmondeley, he was fully aware of her presence in the adjoining sitting room, where she was trying to distract her mind by reading one her favourite books, but her mind kept flitting back to the recent meeting with Horace on the previous day and the strange emotional feelings she was now experiencing. So despite the thick stone walls of the Great House of Vale Royal Abbey separating them, the powerful vibrations and palpitating trauma that they were both experiencing, and was being felt by both of them respectively, and no matter how thick the walls were, the atmosphere of romance was overpowering that day at Vale Royal Abbey.

As the time of 6pm was approaching, the time that Horace was to end his duties for the day, Ann now determinedly decided to enter the study and looking her most stunning and ravishing, dressed in her beautiful green gown and accompanying jewelry, poor beguiled Horace was absolutely smitten with the sight he was

Chapter Two: Thomas Cholmondeley (1627-1702)

beholding, and he quickly jumped to his feet and then slowly walked across the room and now knowing what the true feelings of Ann were toward him, hesitatingly he gently took Ann into his arms, and although at first Ann slightly resisted, she soon succumbed to this bold action of Horace, and the emotions that they were both experiencing and now both deeply felt, they kissed passionately.

At the insistent request of Ann Cholmondeley, Horace was to stay for dinner that evening so that they could both further discuss the findings and observations of Horace, as he had just completed his first day of checking, scrutinising and the handling of the estate affairs. At first Horace declined, as he guiltily explained that his infirmed wife back at Kersal Lodge would be requiring his attention, but Ann was not going to give in so easily and upon her insistence that he was to stay at least for dinner, Horace's guilt was soon erased and he acquiesced as he knew that Kitty the girl from across the street from Kersal Lodge in the village of Delamere, would call in as usual that evening and she would take care of any personal needs that his poor bedridden wife Charlotte required.

So the evening began as carefully planned in advance by Ann Cholmondeley, and dinner was served and between them they talked about minor issues related to the estate plus some inconsequential suggestions on how to improve the management of the records and then they soon progressed and moved on to the more serious, intimate personal feelings they had experienced for each other. Of course dinner was also accompanied with some excellent French Chardonnay, and soon they were both flushed with the delightful company of each other and the many things they had discovered that they had in common. It was simply a matter of time before Ann after completing dinner, invited Horace to a short tour of the house and Great Hall of Vale Royal Abbey, now ghostly silent and peacefully quiet with most of the downstairs staff enjoying their evening meal and probably many of them also drinking themselves into a stupor in the staff kitchen, which by the way was also against the rules of the absent master Thomas Cholmondeley, and eventually Ann and Horace came to the door of her bed chamber, and without a second thought they both slowly entered, quietly closed the door and then shared the most erotic sex that neither of them had ever experienced or enjoyed before.

Horace soon realized that the hours had simply flown by while he was being entertained with Ann and the techniques of love-making that she surely must only have learned from her very experienced, now often absent husband Thomas Cholmondeley, and as it was now 2am the following morning, so he graciously gave Ann another goodbye kiss and descending to the stables to collect his horse and then commenced his gallop home and to his sick, helpless wife. One person though who saw Horace leave in the early morning hours was Harold Fawcett the very observant butler, and as he had heard the horse's hooves on the gravel driveway of Vale Royal Abbey fade into the distance, he displayed a benign smile and said to himself, "Today was a good day and we have successfully achieved immeasurable progress, accomplishments and great satisfaction for more than me." So raising his glass of brandy to himself, also to Vale Royal Abbey and to all citizens in the absent world beyond, he solemnly declared, "Long Live Vale Royal Abbey."

As the weeks and months passed, Horace Farrell was very soon promoted to estate manager and his salary increased accordingly for services rendered and this was obvious to all the gossiping on-lookers that this was because his duties now included much more than simply managing the accounts, bookkeeping and estate records. It was only a matter of time before Thomas Cholmondeley, who was doing very nicely living in London at his townhouse in Craven Terrace, and still enjoying the raunchy company of his now established lover, Emily Williams from Wales, would soon learn of the goings-on back at the Abbey. Friends of his in London often sniggered behind his back with a non-stop stream of sarcastic comments, which puzzled him, and then eventually one of his oldest, very close friends and fellow MP Samuel Egerton of Tatton Hall in Cheshire, courageously stepped forward one day after a long session in the House of Commons, and privately informed Thomas that he should promptly return to Vale Royal Abbey as soon as possible, as the gossip was now rampant amongst the staff and leading wealthy families and households of Cheshire and possibly the whole of the North of England, regarding the rumors of the conduct of his so-called frail and drab wife Ann.

Chapter Two: Thomas Cholmondeley (1627-1702)

Painting of the House of Commons in London, circa. 1699 by George Hayter, courtesy of the Parliamentary Art Collection

As Parliament was now just starting its summer recess, Thomas thought it expedient and opportune to make a quick surprise visit back to Vale Royal Abbey to investigate these wild rumors regarding his drab and characterless wife Ann and this newly appointed young estate manager, Horace Farrell. So after effusively thanking Lord Egerton, Thomas Cholmondeley started his return and journey back to Vale Royal Abbey that same day by means of his private "coach and four" and headed up the Roman Road of Watling Street, through St Albans and on to the City of Chester.

Upon his arrival back at Vale Royal Abbey in the late evening, which he had originally planned as a complete surprise to his wife, but which was thwarted as his wife Ann also had influential personal friends who had tipped her off about this impending "surprise visit", and Ann was not as stupid or the fool her husband thought her to be. As her unfaithful husband was on his way back from London for this 'surprise' visit, Ann said to herself, "what a fool he is for thinking that he would surprise me?" After discretely warning Horace Farrell, her now established lover, who was also performing his other less meaningful duties such as estate manager and bookkeeper of the estate, Ann was fearful of the consequences of what the erratic behavior of Thomas, her tempestuous husband would display, as he was well-known for his aggressive, violent and truculent character. Ann was also very worried and concerned that her husband would wreak his vengeance upon poor Horace and that pandemonium would break out upon his return. She was also afraid of what vituperative remarks and criticism her husband would bombard and blast upon poor Horace. Horace was known for his gentle, affable, warm and loving personality, so with trepidation Ann was dreading the first meeting of these two men now involved and intricately complicating her private and personal life.

Upon his arrival that evening, the strained, tense relationship of Thomas and his wife Ann pervaded the whole household. Thomas claimed that he was exhausted from his journey up from London, and he just simply requested that some refreshment be taken to his private bedroom. Thomas and Ann had used separate bedrooms now for some years, so this custom was no surprise to the staff, who were now scurrying around at the 'beck and call' of the unexpected return of their 'lord and master'. Poor Ann by contrast had a fretful, turbulent night and slept very little as she had to face the traumatic event and ominous meeting the next day, when Horace Farrell arrived at Vale Royal Abbey for his usual "mundane" estate duties, but Horace also now had to face the abrasive, pugnacious and hard-headed Thomas for the first time.

As expected, this ill-boding meeting did not go well at all, apart from the fact that Horace had been using Thomas's private study while undertaking his estate duties and also using his treasured oak desk that once belonged to Sir Josiah Child, major stockholder in the East India Company, and Member of Parliament for Petersfield, in Hampshire. This antique desk was now holding pride of place in his personal study. Thomas had also very quickly noticed a 'deep' scratch in the oak top of his treasured desk, (whether imaginary or not) and immediately this caused him to surge in anger and slamming his fist on the desk he immediately accused Horace that he was responsible that his most treasured property had been damaged, the final degradation is that Thomas did not consider for one moment the more serious issue of what had also been happening and what had been going on between Ann his 'so-called' drab wife and Horace the estate manager in his absence, as he still thought of his wife Ann as his 'private property', but of less value than his prized oak antique desk! If Thomas

Chapter Two: Thomas Cholmondeley (1627-1702)

were so angry over a 'small' scratch on his oak desk, how would he react when he found out the full truth of his wife's conduct and her immoral brazen behavior with the humble, gentle, estate manager Horace Farrell?

Thomas Cholmondeley though, had by now confirmed his suspicions and the local gossip of the secret love affair between his now despised and abominated unfaithful, immoral wife Ann and her secret lover Horace Farrell, but he discretely held his temper under tight control as he did not want to tarnish his reputation as a leading Member of Parliament and also especially as he was currently being considered for a cabinet post in the 4th Parliament of King William III. Being pragmatic, Thomas simply and directly informed the subjective Horace at this first private meeting, that now as he was back at Vale Royal Abbey, he would be taking over his duties again as master of the estate and that he would now personally take care of all the management of the estate matters and affairs involved, therefore the services of Horace would no longer be required and he would be immediately discharged with a handsome purse of 50 florins. Thomas Cholmondeley knew very well that this forceful decision of his would probably create permanent and lasting damage to his wife's delicate emotions and mental stability, as she had already previously displayed signs of emotional distress and was vulnerable to any traumatic event happening to her personal life. Ann was also, on a daily basis and over the past years, currently having to handle and trying to ignore the many previous affairs and illicit immoral conduct of her husband Thomas, plus all the destructive gossip related thereto in the local community. Coping with this common knowledge had previously caused Ann to be very ill indeed and in regular need by the local doctor in Chester of medication to sedate her, but Thomas was totally without any feelings or compassion to the plight of his much younger wife and simply dismissed her behavior or conduct as an inconsequential quirk and a feature of the weaker sex, and she would simply have to cope with her female emotional idiosyncrasies and instability.

As Horace Farrell was now leaving Vale Royal Abbey and the Cholmondeley household for the very last time, he was being personally escorted by Thomas as they walked toward the impressive front entrance hall. Walking down the west gallery, that was previously part of the refectory in the old Abbey, Thomas could not resist in boasting to the young vulnerable Horace of the many acquisitions that he now owned in his palatial home of Vale Royal Abbey, including the old antique weapons proudly displayed on the walls, many collected from the wars of the Crusades, some dating back to 1122 AD, plus suits of armor from the days of King Henry the Second (1133-1189).

From the archives and journals related to Thomas Cholmondeley (1627-1702) it appears that he had an extreme, macabre and morbid fascination with the English Monarch, Henry the Second (1133-1189). No doubt this was partially based on the mutual connection with their French background related to both King Henry and Thomas, both of them having their ancestral roots based in France. However it appears it went far beyond pure obsession by Thomas, but it also included his fascination with the violence and the barbaric weapons used in warfare at this time in history. According to *The History of the Life of Henry the Second* [in five volumes], by George Lyttelton (1772), these weapons included for example, Danish Axes, Pikes, Short Lances, Darts, Arrows plus other atrociously violent weapons of war. Many of these antiques were collected by Thomas Cholmondeley and displayed in the basement Armory at Vale Royal Abbey (see our comments on King Henry II in Appendix 2).

However the major prized asset of Vale Royal Abbey that exalted the egotism of Thomas Cholmondeley, as he boasted to the now trembling and very nervous poor Horace Farrell, was the spectacular stained glass window holding pride of place in the west wall, and which also displayed the Vale Royal Abbey coat of arms, a feature that his great-grandmother, Lady Mary Cholmondeley had so painstakingly and skillfully had carefully preserved while she was alive, during the supervision many years ago related to the rebuilding and renovations of the Vale Royal Abbey plus the Great House.

As they both walked down the West Gallery, Thomas Cholmondeley gently pulled Horace to one side while they were still admiring the strikingly beautiful stained glass window in the west gallery. Thomas, who by this time had mollified his anger, leaned over toward Horace and quietly spoke to him, but still in his usual arrogant, bombastic manner, whispering in subdued

Chapter Two: Thomas Cholmondeley (1627-1702)

but very clear terms, "Mark my words young man, if you ever set foot in this household again, you will leave in a pine box with a dagger plunged between your shoulder blades". This was the true, unvarnished Thomas Cholmondeley speaking, displaying his real self and his dogmatic, opinionated, unctuous view of anyone who dared cross him or touch his property without his permission. Poor Horace was so taken aback and shocked, having never in his short life, seen, heard or known of such resentment, bitterness and hatred displayed with such vehemence.

Recent photograph of the stained glass window taken in the West Gallery of Vale Royal Abbey as admired by Thomas Cholmondeley and Horace Farrell in 1699 on the very last day Horace spent at the Abbey, courtesy of Penny Hebgin-Barnes

Poor dejected Horace Farrell now had to return to his previous normal, mundane life again, a routine that was not going well at all for him and he now lived as though a dark cloud was hanging over his head. His pitiful poor young wife's health was suddenly deteriorating at an alarming rate and the doctor from the local village informed him that her breathing was now becoming a very serious issue. Horace looked down with melancholic, tristful, sad eyes upon his now very frail wife as she lay in her sickbed with no hope of recovery. Within the week Horace was struck with the additional dreadful blow of seeing his young wife, his first love, slowly dying before his very eyes and she, still being only 26 years. Poor Charlotte died the following day and was buried in the local church yard of Saint Bartholomew's Church, in Church Minshull, Cheshire. Apart from seeing his young wife die, who was once a bright healthy young woman with a brilliant discerning mind and a beautiful body, plus having ambitions of being one of the first female doctors in England, before her disastrous accident while horse riding in the rough countryside around Warrington. Horace had to now say a permanent farewell to this once beautiful young woman who had shared a small part of his life while living in Warrington, plus for a short time in the graceful Cheshire countryside, and this broke his heart.

Horace also now had to cope with the inner struggle of his guilty conscience related to his recent love affair with Ann and for almost six months being part of an adulterous relationship and being an unfaithful husband to his extremely sick young wife—thoughts which plagued him night and day. Horace also looked back on that day almost four years ago, when he and his dear Charlotte married in the church of St. Elphin's in Warrington. Had he not during his marriage ceremony vowed to his young beautiful wife, "to have and to hold from this day forward, for better for worse, for richer for poorer, in sickness and in health, to love and to cherish, till death us do part, according to God's holy ordinance; and thereto I plight thee my troth. With this ring I thee wed, with my body I thee worship, and with all my worldly goods I thee endow: In the name of the Father, and of the Son, and of the Holy Ghost. Amen". Ruminating again on these sacred words, it tore his emotions in shreds and Horace said to himself, "God Almighty, What have I done? In God's name how could I have allowed this dreadful thing happen to our marriage?" His life was now slowly disintegrating before his very eyes and poor Horace could not take much more of this self-recrimination.

All of these negative thoughts and introspective ruminations were racking the brain and inner conscience of poor Horace, so that evening of 1 July 1699; he calmly and calculatingly decided to take the dramatic steps to end his now miserable life, which he considered was not worth living. So Horace methodically walked to the tool

Chapter Two: Thomas Cholmondeley (1627-1702)

shed at the bottom of the garden at Kersal Lodge in Cheshire, took a rope that was hanging on the wall and dispassionately threw the rope over the beam in the roof of the tool shed and climbing onto the carpenters stool, he skillfully tied a noose around his neck and kicked the stool out from under his feet. He was found the following day hanging from the beam of the tool shed, still dressed in his best riding britches and Harris Tweed jacket but his britches now all soiled as a result of the last desperate struggle in life that he was to experience, this time at the end of a rope.

Thomas Cholmondeley had meantime returned to his lover in London and his life style as a notorious lothario, plus his many other so-called important duties as a Member of Parliament and he had cared very little about what had happened to the distraught, pathetic, now deceased Horace Farrell and he repudiated any accusations made by the local gossip of citizens against him; claiming that he was probably indirectly responsible for the death and suicide of Horace. When poor Ann, the wife of Thomas Cholmondeley learned of this dreadful, devastating awful incident, she immediately collapsed and the local doctor, Richard Ross from the village of Weaver, had to prescribe sedatives to keep her calm and rested. Ann never fully recovered from this period of her otherwise wretched, forlorn life, but she still had the vivid, clear memories of a brief but meaningful relationship with a young man who had treated her with compassion and pure love, an experience she had never had with any other human being.

As the years passed, the eldest son of Thomas and Ann, namely Charles, who was born on 12 January 1684, gradually took over control and the management of Vale Royal Abbey and the estate. Upon the death of his father Thomas in 1702, who was now riddled with syphilis, Charles, being the sole heir of the family estate now became the master of Vale Royal Abbey at 18 years of age.

According to the records of the *History of Parliament Trust*, Thomas Cholmondeley died on 26 February 1702 and was buried at Church Minshull, Cheshire. In contradictory terms "Had he not lived in times of difficulties and divisions", wrote his Whig neighbour Sir John Crewe, "he had been the most popular commoner at home and abroad." His son Charles sat for Cheshire as a high Tory in the last two Parliaments of Queen Anne and again from 1725 and up to his death in 1756.

Also contained in the *Records of Parliament* is this entry,

> He (Thomas Cholmondeley 1627-1702) was a moderately active Member of the Cavalier Parliament, being named to 63 committees, most of which were for private bills, and acting as teller in three divisions.

Probably the author of *A Seasonable Argument* was not far from the truth when he alleged that Cholmondeley had been "promised a great place at Court, but was not only deceived, but laughed at; the poor gentleman". Although he was inactive in the closing sessions of the Cavalier Parliament, Shaftesbury marked him as 'doubly vile' and he was included in the 'unanimous club' of court supporters; but his name does not appear on the final list drawn up by the Government.

The youngest son of Thomas and Ann, William, had decided to move to London, as his ambition was to become a barrister and to join the illustrious circle of friends he had made through his fathers influential connections. The fact that William Cholmondeley was a homosexual caused extreme grief and anguish to his mother Ann, and as he always had his friend and lover Gilbert Winslow staying at Vale Royal Abbey, both she and the servants always having to hide their embarrassment upon hearing the strange groans and weird noises coming out from the private bedroom of William. Ann was at last relieved when William her son told her he was leaving Vale Royal Abbey and Cheshire for good, and was moving to London to join his cousin Reginald Percy Cholmondeley, who already lived there, and according to a private letter from one of his friends, Reggie was a "nebbish nobody, non-descript without charm or talent". Plus William also proudly added and announced to his mother that his very best and affectionate 'special' friend Gilbert Winslow was moving to London also, to accompany him in setting up his new home in the city.

Ann was now approaching 92 years of age and her deteriorating health was compounded by severe arthritis, but she was finally at peace with herself, especially after her intensely despised husband had died, an event that did not make her at least one bit sad in any way whatsoever. She had tried, but without success, she admitted to herself, to be a loyal and faithful wife even though knowing that her late husband had been a wild philanderer. During the evening of 1

Chapter Two: Thomas Cholmondeley (1627-1702)

December 1742, Ann was lying peacefully in her comfortable bed at Vale Royal Abbey. She was now addicted to laudanum, which had been prescribed in order to relieve and alleviate the extreme pain of her arthritis. Ann reflected, contemplated and thought back over her long life at the beautiful estate of Vale Royal Abbey. Smiling to herself, she was reminded that the happiest and most fulfilling few months she had experienced in her whole life was with Horace Farrell, who had become her close friend and brief lover. With these thoughts of that valuable precious time firmly planted in her memory, our dear Ann, the true "gentlewoman" of Vale Royal Abbey slipped into a perpetual sleep.

Chapter Three: Charles Cholmondeley (1684-1756)

The household and estate at Vale Royal Abbey in 1702 was now under the diligent control of Charles Cholmondeley, after the death of his father. Charles later married Essex Pitt the daughter of the very wealthy and well-known, Thomas "Diamond" Pitt of St. Mary Blandford, Dorset in 1714 and they had three sons of whom the eldest died in infancy and five daughters. Life at Vale Royal Abbey was now also running smoothly under the skillful, adept management of Charles, who unselfishly was totally dedicated to the ongoing success and expansion of the Estate, plus he was also still involved with his additional duties as a hard working diligent MP for Cheshire, a duty he commenced in 1710, which he took very seriously, according to the parliamentary archived records.

An interesting sideline that is connected to the new wife of Charles Cholmondeley, namely Essex Pitt, which is also related to his new father-in-law, Thomas "Diamond" Pitt the father of Essex Pitt, and it makes fascinating reading.

Thomas "Diamond" Pitt (1653-1726), father of Essex, was born at Blandford Forum, Dorset, to the Reverend John Pitt, a Church of England cleric and Sarah Jay, who was an English merchant prominently involved in the expanding trade between England with India and the Far East. He served in India as part of the East India Company. Pitt also became the President of the East India Company in Madras, India on 7 July 1698 and remained in his post until 1709. His most famous quote related to the local inhabitants of India, and is somewhat racist:

> These native governors (Subedars and Nawabs) have the knack of tramping upon us and extorting what they please of our estate from us...they will never forbid doing so till we have made them sensible of our power.

Thomas Pitt placed a very high value on education and was also a great believer in expansive learning plus the acquiring of as much knowledge as humanly possible. Although back in the 1600s and 1700s the education of daughters was treated as inconsequential and in most cases totally unnecessary, he made sure his daughter Essex obtained the best education available and employed private tutors in his endeavors, which proved to be of tremendous benefit to his sons but especially so to his daughter Essex. It is also suggested, based on his writings, that Thomas Pitt was probably the original source of the quotation often used by many educationalists, "No thief, however skillful, can rob one of knowledge, and that is why knowledge is the best and safest treasure to acquire."

From correspondence and records related to Thomas Pitt, it appears that Thomas had an inordinate fascination regarding the relationship between Queen Elizabeth I and Robert Devereux, the Earl of Essex, who was 30 years younger than the Queen. From available records it also appears that Thomas Pitt had an intense piquancy with the background and history of Queen Elizabeth I and the superior education that she had received while a young girl and lived at Hatfield House in Herefordshire, England. Elizabeth was the only child

Portrait of Thomas Pitt, approximately 1709, courtesy of the National Archives, London

and daughter of Henry VIII and Anne Boleyn, his second wife, who was executed two-and-a-half years after Elizabeth's birth. Anne's marriage to Henry VIII was later annulled, and Elizabeth was declared illegitimate.

Princess Elizabeth had received her education under the supervision of Roger Ascham (1515-1568), a sympathetic teacher who believed that learning should be engaging. Roger is also well-known for his sayings of wisdom, for example: "There is no such whetstone, to sharpen a good wit and encourage a will to learning, as is praise." Roger Ascham developed a curriculum for the Princess that would allow her to play an important political role in the future. He taught her history, geography, mathematics, and the elements of architecture, astronomy and at least six languages. In a private letter to a friend he commented about Elizabeth, "Her mind has no womanly weakness, her perseverance is equal to that of a man, and her memory long keeps what it quickly picks up… the younger, the more tender; the quicker, the easier to break… and so her grace… by little and little, may be increased in learning." When Ascham died in 1568 at 55 years, Queen Elizabeth grieved and declared that "she would have rather lost ten thousand pounds than to have lost "her" Ascham." From the *Oxford Bibliographies* we read:

> Ascham's legacy will always abide in his three great works, which made important developments in English prose and travel writing as well as educational theory. Add to this his service as Royal Tutor and Secretary and his adeptness at surviving financial penury as well as religious and political change and we have a portrait of a most remarkable man.

By the time her formal education ended in 1550, young Lady Elizabeth was one of the best educated women of her generation, and it appears from private records that Thomas Pitt, who was mesmerized with the history of Lady Elizabeth, visualized his daughter Essex also becoming one of the nobility, plus in using the glamorous terms in one of his letters: "she [Essex] being recognized and classified also as 'one of the best educated women' in the country". A review of the excellent book written by Kathryn Lasky, *The Royal Diaries of Elizabeth, the Red Rose of the House of Tudor*, covering the daily life of Elizabeth between 1544 and 1547, as personally recorded by Elizabeth in her diaries and the private details of her daily routine at Hatfield House, reveals the depth, intensity and wide scope of her education and learning.

In his *History of the English Speaking Peoples*, Winston Churchill describes Queen Elizabeth I:

> She had a commanding carriage, auburn hair, eloquence of speech, and a natural dignity that declared her as King Henry's daughter…and an almost inexhaustible fund of physical energy. She could speak six languages, and was well read in Greek and Latin.

Chapter Three: Charles Cholmondeley (1684-1756)

It is little wonder that Thomas 'Diamond' Pitt, being aware of this history of Queen Elizabeth I, liked to dote on and compare his daughter Essex to this incredible woman, who became such an outstanding individual in the history of England. This is further confirmed by Churchill:

> The times demanded a politic, calculating devious spirit at the head of the state, and this Elizabeth possessed. She gave to her country the love that she never entirely reposed in any one man, and her people responded with a loyalty that almost amounted to worship. It is not for nothing that she has come down in history as Good Queen Bess.

Elizabeth I was also known as the "Virgin Queen" and "Gloriana", plus her 44 years on the throne of England provided welcome stability for the kingdom and helped forge a sense of national identity. The one major incident that cast a shadow and was a blemish on the reign of Elizabeth I was the way her cousin Mary Stewart, Queen of Scotland (1542-1587) was treated and finally executed in the year 1587.

Mary Stewart, the only surviving legitimate child of King James V, was six days old when her father died and she acceded to the throne of Scotland. She spent most of her childhood in France while Scotland was ruled by regents and in 1558 she married the Dauphin of France, Francis. He ascended the French throne as King Francis II in 1559, and Mary briefly became queen consort of France, until his death in December 1560. Widowed, Mary returned to Scotland, arriving in Leith on 19 August 1561. Four years later, she married her first cousin, Henry Stuart, Lord Darnley and in June 1566 they had a son, James, who later became James VI of Scotland and James I of England in 1603 as the son of Mary Queen of Scots, a descendent of King Henry the Seventh.

After eighteen and a half years in custody, Mary was found guilty of plotting to assassinate Elizabeth in 1586. She was beheaded the following year at Fotheringhay Castle. Mary was not beheaded with a single strike. The first blow missed her neck and struck the back of her head. The second blow severed the neck, except for a small bit of sinew, which the executioner cut through using the axe. Afterwards, he held her head aloft and declared, "God save the Queen." At that moment, the auburn tresses in his hand turned out to be a wig and the head fell to the ground, revealing that Mary had very short, grey hair. Mary's courage at her execution helped establish her popular image as the heroic victim in a dramatic tragedy. When the news of the execution reached Elizabeth, she became indignant and asserted that William Davison, head of the Privy Council of England had disobeyed her instructions not to part with the warrant and that the Privy Council had acted without her authority. Elizabeth's vacillation and deliberately vague instructions gave her plausible deniability to attempt to avoid the direct stain of Mary's blood.

Students of English history have often asked, "Why did Thomas Pitt christen his daughter with the name "Essex", a most unusual name for his special, favourite daughter?" In a private letter to a friend, Pitt commented, which gives some credence to his motive and perhaps the real underlying reason behind the selection of this odd name for his daughter, "Without the support of the brilliant Earl of Essex, Queen Elizabeth would not have been able to establish and develop England into becoming the greatest power and monarchy in the world, and also having the Greatest Navy the world has ever known."

Notes from *British History* archived records reveal:

> The Earl of Essex, Robert Devereux was born on 10 November 1566, the son of Walter Devereux, first Earl of Essex. When he was nine his father died, and Robert inherited the title of Earl. In 1596, Essex became a national hero when he shared command of the expedition that captured Cadiz from the Spanish as part of the conquest of the Spanish Armada. Essex and Elizabeth had a tempestuous relationship and there were many quarrels but his charm ensured that she continued to grant him royal appointments for some time. Elizabeth's patience eventually had been worn thin, and consequently, the Earl's fall from grace was swift and sure.
>
> In mid-February of 1601, he was tried and found guilty of treason, and then sentenced to die a traitor's death of hanging, drawing and quartering. In her mercy, Elizabeth commuted the sentence to simple beheading - most likely because of the love and kindness she had shown him previously. The death warrant was signed on 20 February

from the many deceased estates and clearance auctions being held occasionally throughout England, plus assisting in filing and cataloging them, which resulted in helping to create and expand one of the largest private and extremely informative libraries in the land. She also played a vital role in helping Charles her husband in his intensive research into the history of Vale Royal Abbey, plus other local projects that Charles was involved with, as she was very knowledgeable and also conversant with the old English language and writings.

Essex Cholmondeley had been tutored especially in "Middle English", (12th to 15th century) and also "early modern English", (1480-1650), and she was an advanced student of these important subjects. The rare books and manuscripts collected and held in the Vale Royal Abbey library, would have been the delight of any serious students of the day and many did indeed visit Vale Royal Abbey just to see and inspect these items and they must have relished the sight of this remarkable collection being undertaken and supervised by Charles and Essex Cholmondeley. From records of the day, early copies and in some cases the original text were held in this incredible library, for example, *Paradise Lost* by John Milton, *Leviathan* by Thomas Hobbes, very rare copies of early Bible translations and Bible commentaries, Nicholas Culpeper's *The English Physician*, Chaucer's *Canterbury Tales* and Malory's *Morte d'Arthur*, these items are just to name a few listed in the archives.

Charles Cholmondeley had also acquired an original manuscript of an old English tale called *Partenope of Blois*, dated 1420 AD, which he added to the impressive library at Vale Royal Abbey. This now priceless manuscript originally written in Old French but then re-written in Middle English was held in the library at Vale Royal Abbey until the clearance sale about the year 1907 by Hugh Cholmondeley, 3rd Lord Delamere and was purchased and now owned by the British Library. The existing manuscript only contains fragments of this touching love story, as over the years much of the manuscript became damaged through gradual decay.

"Partonopeus de Blois"[6] is a long poem in the chivalric romance

---

[6] In this poem, Partenopeus is represented as having lived in the days of Clovis, king of France. He is seized while hunting in the Ardennes, and carried off to a mysterious castle with invisible inhabitants. Melior, empress of Constantinople, comes to him at night, stipulating that he must not attempt to see her for two and a half years. After successfully fighting against the Saracens, led by Sornegur, king of Denmark, he returns to the castle, armed with an enchanted lantern that breaks the spell. The consequent misfortunes have a happy ending.

Chapter Three: Charles Cholmondeley (1684-1756)

genre written in Old French in the 1170s or 1180s. Its author is not accurately known but thought possibly that it was Denis Pyramus.[7]

In the 19th century the original story of Parthénopéus de Blois served as a broad basis for Alfred Blau's libretto *Esclarmonde*, later turned into an opera by Jules Massenet.

This brief extract from this now priceless manuscript includes the following:

> Partonope, the young Earl of Blois, goes hunting in the forest of Ardennes with his uncle King Clovis, who is descended from the Trojans. He becomes lost and wanders to the shore, where he boards a mysteriously empty ship. It carries him to a beautiful deserted city where he enters the palace and is served a meal by invisible hands. Afterwards, he is led to a bedchamber, but is unable to sleep until an unseen lady joins him. Although she asks him to leave, he has sex with her. She then informs him that she is Melior, Empress of Byzantium and has loved him from afar. She will fulfill all his desires, provided that he does not attempt to see her for two-and-a-half years. He reluctantly agrees and, after being reassured of her Christian faith, falls asleep.

Unfortunately this world famous private library at Vale Royal Abbey was broken up and sold off by public auction under the instructions of a later descendant of Charles Cholmondeley, namely Hugh Cholmondeley, 3rd Lord Delamere, in approximately 1907, who now lived in Kenya, Africa, but more about this destructive, irresponsible and erratic act later in Chapter 7.

Why was the nickname "Diamond" used when referring to Thomas Pitt, the father of Essex Pitt, wife of Charles Cholmondeley? The reason was that Thomas Pitt is best known for his purchase of a 410-carat (82g) uncut diamond acquired from an Indian merchant named Jamchand in Madras, India in 1701. The merchant had purchased the diamond from an English sea captain, who had, in fact, stolen the diamond from a servant of Abul Hasan Qutb Shah. According to another version, the servant found the diamond in one of the Golconda mines on the Krishna

---
[7] Denis Pyramus was a Benedictine monk of Bury St. Edmunds Abbey and an Anglo-Norman poet who was active in the second part of the 12th and the beginning of the 13th century. In 1150 AD he wrote Parthénopéus de Blois. Partonopeus de Blois is one of the most important works of twelfth-century French fiction; it shaped the development of romance as a genre, gave rise to adaptations in several other medieval languages and even an opera.

River and had concealed it inside a large wound in his leg, which he had suffered as he fled the Siege of Golconda.

Thomas Pitt bought the diamond for £20,400, and sent it back to England in 1702 concealed inside his eldest son Robert's shoe. For two years from 1704-1706, the jeweler Harris laboured in London to hew a 141-carat (28.2 g) brilliant unique gem from the rough stone. Several secondary stones were also produced from the cut that were sold to Peter the Great of Russia. After many attempts to sell it to various European royals, including Louis XIV of France, Pitt and his sons went with the diamond to Calais, France, in 1717. With John Law acting as agent, it was sold that year to the French regent, Philippe II, Duke of Orléans, for £135,000, eventually becoming one of the crown jewels of France. Today, "Le Régent", as it came to be known, remains in the French Royal Treasury at the Louvre in Paris, where it has been on public display since 1887.

England in the late 1700s was involved in many wars and rebellions. Apart from later losing the American War of Independence in 1783, it was generally successful in warfare, and was especially successful in financing its military commitments. France and Spain, by contrast, went bankrupt. Britain maintained a relatively large and expensive Royal Navy, along with a small standing army. When the need arose for additional soldiers it hired mercenaries or financed allies who fielded armies on behalf of Britain.

The rising costs of warfare and the military forced a shift in government financing from the income of the royal agricultural estates and special imposts and taxes, to the reliance on customs and excise taxes and, after 1790, an 'income tax'. Working with bankers in the City, the government raised large loans during wartime and paid them off in peacetime. The rise in taxes by the government amounted to 20% of the national income, but the private sector also benefited from the increase in economic growth. The demand for war supplies stimulated the industrial sector, particularly naval supplies, munitions and textiles, which gave Britain an advantage in international trade during the postwar years. The citizens and workers of Cheshire and Lancashire also greatly benefited from the production of these vital products.

Conflict between Great Britain and France again broke out in 1754-1756 when the British attacked disputed French positions in

Chapter Three: Charles Cholmondeley (1684-1756)

North America and seized hundreds of French merchant ships. Charles Cholmondeley, who had recently volunteered in the Royal Cheshire Militia was very soon seconded to serve in the position of a senior officer with rank of Colonel and was part of the British army being sent to Canada to protect the British interests there. The Cheshire Regiment (also known as the Young Buffs, so named after the colour of their buff facings and waistcoats) was a line infantry regiment of the British Army, part of the Prince of Wales' Division. The 22nd Regiment of Foot was raised by the Duke of Norfolk in 1689 and was able to boast an independent existence of over 300 years.

The boundary between British and French possessions in North America was largely undefined in the 1750s. France had long claimed the entire Mississippi River basin. This was disputed by Britain. In the early 1750s the French began constructing a chain of forts in the Ohio River Valley to assert their claim and shield the Native American population from increasing British influence.

The British settlers along the coast of America were very upset that French troops would now be too close to the western borders of their colonies. They felt the French would encourage their tribal allies among the North American natives to attack them. Also, the British settlers wanted access to the fertile land of the Ohio River Valley for the new settlers that were flooding into the British colonies seeking farmland.

It was a very sad day indeed when Charles Cholmondeley had to leave his wife Essex and his children at his beloved home at Vale Royal Abbey and travel to Liverpool to embark on the ship *HMS Dolphin* sailing west across the Atlantic for Canada, along with the British soldiers committed and assigned to the war against the French.

The adventures and exploits of Charles Cholmondeley, while he was in the King's service in North America and Canada during the two years, 1751 and 1752, was to orientate, familiarize and survey the position of the French troops and report back to his superiors in England. These duties led to his first meeting with Daniel Boone (1734-1820), the American pioneer, explorer, woodsman and frontiersman, whose exploits made him one of the first folk heroes of the United States. Ironically Daniel Boone was also later a militia officer during the American Revolutionary War (War of Independence, 1775-1783) and ended up actually fighting against England. Daniel Boone is also famous for his discovery in July of 1769 of the State of Kentucky that is known as the "Bluegrass State", a nickname based on the bluegrass found in many of its pastures due to the fertile soil. Plus Boone records in his journal how impressed he was when he first saw the magnificent forests and valleys. One of the major regions in Kentucky is the Bluegrass Region in central Kentucky, which houses two of its major cities, Louisville and Lexington. It is a land with diverse environments and abundant resources. In 1792 Kentucky became the 15th State to join the Union.

During his service in Canada, Charles Cholmondeley, while he was busy working alongside the American soldiers and frontiersman trying to contain the French army, Charles unfortunately was severely wounded during one of the scuffles and skirmishes with the French army just prior to the Battle of Lake George and he had the lower half of his right leg amputated as a result of gangrene.

The Battle of Lake George goes down in history as a major incident in the French and English wars in Canada and North America. In 1755, Sir William Johnson, British Indian Supervisor of the Northeast, established a military camp at the southern end of Lake George, with the objective of launching an attack on Fort St. Frédéric, a French fort at Crown Point on Lake Champlain. The French commander, Baron Dieskau, decided to launch a preemptive attack on Johnson's support base at Fort Edward on the Hudson River. Their movements precipitated the somewhat inconclusive Battle of Lake George on September 8 1755, part of which was fought on the ground of Johnson's Lake George camp. Following the battle, Johnson decided to construct a fortification near the site, while the French began construction of Fort Carillon near the northern end of the lake.

Design and construction of the new fortification was overseen by British military engineer William Eyre of the 44th Foot. Fort William Henry was an irregular square fortification with bastions on the corners, in a design that was intended to repel Indian attacks, but not necessarily withstand attack from an enemy armed with artillery. Its walls were 30 feet (9.1 m.) thick, with log facings around an earthen filling. Inside the fort were wooden barracks two

Chapter Three: Charles Cholmondeley (1684-1756)

stories high, built around the parade ground. Its magazine was in the northeast bastion, and its hospital was located in the southeast bastion. The fort was surrounded on three sides by a dry moat, with the fourth side sloping down to the lake. The only access to the fort was by a bridge across the moat. The fort could house 400 to 500 men; additional troops were quartered in an entrenched camp 750 yards (690m) southeast of the fort, near the site of the 1755 Battle of Lake George.

Charles Cholmondeley, according to his personal journals related to his days in Canada, he had also met up with Jean Baptiste Lagimodiera (1730-1811), grandfather of Louis David Riel (1844-1885) who made a major contribution to the recognition of the Métis people of Canada.

Who were these Métis people? During the height of the North American fur trade in the late 18th and 19th centuries, many French Canadian and British fur traders married First Nations and Inuit women, mainly First Nations Cree, Ojibwa, or Saulteaux located in the Great Lakes area and to the west. The majority of these fur traders were French and Scottish; the French were Catholic. These marriages are commonly referred to as marriage "à la façon du pays" or marriage according to the "custom of the country." Their children often grew up primarily in their mothers' cultures but were often also introduced to Catholic and indigenous belief systems, thus exposed to two cultures. In many cases, as the fur trappers lived with women at the location of their tribes, the children grew up in primarily First Nations societies.

But, as more Métis lived in communities with a fur trapping tradition, they created a new distinct aboriginal people in North America. First Nations women were the link between cultures; they provided companionship for the fur traders, introductions to their people and culture, and also aided in their survival. First Nations women were able to translate the native languages, sewed new clothing for their husbands, and generally were involved in resolving any cultural issues that arose. The First Peoples had survived in the west for thousands of years, so the fur traders benefited greatly from their First Nations wives' knowledge of the land and its resources. Métis people were thought of as the bond between the Europeans and First Nations and Inuit peoples of Canada. As adults, the men often worked as interpreters as well as fur trappers in their turn.

The Delamere Saga: Part 1

According to historian Jacob A. Schooley, the Métis developed over at least two generations and with different classes. In the first stage, "servant" (employee) traders of the fur trade companies, known as wintering partners, would stay for the season with First Nations bands, and make a "country marriage" with a high-status native woman. This woman and her children would move to live in the vicinity of a trading post, becoming "House Indians" [as they were called by the company men]. House Indians eventually formed distinct bands. Children raised within these "House Indian" bands often became employees of the companies in turn. (James Foster cites the legendary York boat captain Paulet Paul as an example). Eventually this second-generation group ended employment with the company and became "freemen" traders and trappers. They lived with their families raising children in a distinct culture based around free trading, buffalo hunting, and so on. He considered that the third generation, who were sometimes Métis on both sides, was the first true Métis. He suggests that in the Red River region, many "House Indians" (and even some non "House" First Nations) were assimilated into Métis culture due to the Catholic Church's strong presence in that region. In the Fort Edmonton region, many House Indians never adopted a Métis identity but continued to identify primarily as "Cree" and so on.

The Métis played a vital role in the success of the western fur trade. They were skilled hunters and trappers, and were raised to appreciate both Aboriginal and European cultures. Métis understanding of both societies and customs helped bridge cultural gaps, resulting in better trading relationships. The Hudson's Bay Company discouraged unions between their fur traders and First Nations and Inuit women, while the North West Company (the English-speaking Quebec-based fur trading company) supported such marriages. Trappers typically took First Nations women as wives, too, and operated outside company strictures. The Métis were respected as valuable employees of both fur trade companies, due to their skills as voyageurs, buffalo hunters, and interpreters, and their knowledge of the lands.

We cannot mention the Métis people of Canada without reporting on Louis David Riel, whose grandfather was a personal friend of Charles Cholmondeley, and who had served as their leader for many years.

Chapter Three: Charles Cholmondeley (1684-1756)

According to *Peoples of Canada* by J M Bumsted (1992):

> Louis David Riel (22 October 1844 - 16 November 1885) was a Canadian politician, a founder of the province of Manitoba, and a political leader of the Métis people of the Canadian prairies. He led two resistance movements against the Canadian government and its first post-Confederation Prime Minister, Sir John A. Macdonald. Riel sought to preserve Métis rights and culture as their homelands in the Northwest that came progressively under the Canadian sphere of influence. Over the decades, he has been made a folk hero by the Francophones, the Catholic nationalists, the native rights movement, and the New Left student movement. Riel has received more scholarly attention than practically any other figure in Canadian history.
>
> His first resistance was the Red River Rebellion of 1869-1870. The provisional government established by Riel ultimately negotiated the terms under which the modern province of Manitoba entered the Canadian Confederation. Riel ordered the execution of a Protestant who annoyed him, Thomas Scott, and fled to the United States to escape prosecution. Despite this, he is frequently referred to as the "Father of Manitoba". While a fugitive, he was elected three times to the Canadian House of Commons, although he never assumed his seat. During these years, he was frustrated by having to remain in exile despite his growing belief that he was a divinely chosen leader and prophet, a belief which would later resurface and influence his actions. Because of this new religious conviction, Catholic leaders who had supported him before increasingly repudiated him.

Louis David Riel, President of the Provisional Government of Saskatchewan, courtesy of The University of Manitoba Press

The Delamere Saga: Part 1

He married in 1881 while in exile in Montana in the United States; he fathered three children.

In 1884 Riel was called upon by the Métis leaders in Saskatchewan to articulate their grievances to the Canadian government. Instead he organized a military resistance that escalated into a military confrontation, the North-West Rebellion of 1885. Ottawa used the new rail lines to send in thousands of combat soldiers. It ended in his arrest and conviction for high treason. Rejecting many protests and popular appeals, Prime Minister MacDonald decided to hang him. Riel was seen as a heroic victim by francophone Canadians; his execution had a lasting negative impact on Canada, polarizing the new nation along ethno-religious lines. Although only a few hundred people were directly affected by the Rebellion in Saskatchewan, the long-term result was that the Prairie Provinces would be controlled by the Anglophones, not the Francophones. An even more important long-term impact was the bitter alienation Francophones across Canada showed and anger against the repression of their countrymen. After years of leadership and success, in 1884, Riel was involved in another armed uprising, but this was quickly crushed by the military might of the Canadian government, and Riel surrendered. Riel was found guilty of treason and hanged on November 16, 1885, in Regina, Canada.

Meanwhile, Charles Cholmondeley upon his return to his home; his loving family and the beloved estate at Vale Royal Abbey in late 1752, he now had to face the crucible of his life. Charles resumed his duties as Master of Vale Royal Abbey and MP for Cheshire with dignity, although thoroughly conscious of his severe infirmity and the pity plus compassion displayed by his loyal downstairs staff and his many close friends in the surrounding area of Cheshire. Charles Cholmondeley was so obsessed in keeping his war injury; the loss of his lower right leg from becoming general public knowledge; he also tried to prevent any parliamentary or any other records being made regarding his serious war injury received while in North America, as he was so paranoid about being shown pity or being felt sorry for by his friends, colleagues and associates. He spent most of the remaining few years of his life in isolation at his estate at Vale Royal Abbey as a recluse and very few people

Chapter Three: Charles Cholmondeley (1684-1756)

knew about his infirmity, but also in the loving care and support of his devoted wife Essex, until she eventually died on 7 March 1754.

During Charles's final two years of his life, now to be spent without the support, companionship, intellect and loving care of his late wife Essex, these proved to be very difficult and trying years, which tested his character intensely. One early spring day in 1756 when in his 72nd year, Charles was taking his usual daily, but now very difficult walk around the ruins of the old Vale Royal Abbey of Saint Mary the Virgin, the main structure having being totally demolished back in 1539, except for some remaining low walls covered in spring flowers and that were now part of the garden area adjoining the Great House at Vale Royal Abbey. Charles found that walking with the aid of his crutches was becoming more and more difficult each day and he could not walk very far, having only one useful leg as a result of his war injury while serving in America and Canada fighting the French armies. As he sat down on the low stone wall his gaze fell across the large expanse of the grounds and gardens of his treasured home at Vale Royal Abbey.

It wasn't a warm spring that year but it was at least dry and the snowdrops and clumps of daffodils against the green lawns made a beautiful sight indeed, and so did the yellow primroses alongside the long curved gravel driveway leading up to the Great House. Charles closing his eyes and enjoying the warm sun on his face and closed eyelids, his mind floated back to the couple of years he spent in America and Canada, when he served in the Cheshire Regiment whilst resisting the French armies and their attempted domination in that part of the world. He reflected; if only he could be young again and with a complete body, he would have loved to have joined the many hundreds of adventurous young men, women and their young families who left their homes and friends in England and relocated across the vast Atlantic Ocean to settle in the "New World"; the now quickly developing nations of North America. Charles could still vividly remember the beautiful fertile Ohio and Mississippi River basins, the Allegany Mountains, Shenandoah Valley and the Blue Ridge Mountains beyond, and what a sight that was to behold!

Snapping back to reality, Charles quickly opened his eyes and reminded himself that being the heir to the Cholmondeley family

The Delamere Saga: Part 1

name and property, plus now being the current legal owner of one the largest private estates in the whole of England, could be either a blessing or a curse, as being responsible for this grandiose estate of Vale Royal Abbey in one of the most beautiful parts of England; in the luxurious Cheshire countryside was indeed a blessing, but to carry the burden of controlling the destiny and future of this treasured, national possession and now being the custodian of its continued growth and survival, also brought tears to his eyes and a heavy load to his mind and heart.

Charles had never really felt in his heart that he and his family actually owned Vale Royal Abbey, but the estate rightfully belonged to the people of glorious England and only by destiny had he and his family been given the grave responsibility, as custodians, in taking the best care possible of this valued possession; a national treasure. He was also fully aware that his son and heir Thomas, who was now 38 years, did not have the same sentiments as he himself had, and they argued often about this issue on a regular basis, plus neither did Thomas his son show the love and commitment that Charles would have wanted regarding taking care of Vale Royal Abbey the way he personally did, especially so after his death, and this knowledge tormented his soul. It appears that his son and heir Thomas spent many weeks each year with his gentlemen friends visiting the taverns and brothels of Manchester and London, he being very often away from the treasured, peaceful, and yes, Charles thought to himself, also the "spiritual atmosphere" of this lovely tranquil salubrious estate in beautiful Cheshire.

Snapping back to reality indeed; and trying not to be too worried or concerned about the future of Vale Royal Abbey, he knew in his heart of hearts that the 'Lord in His Wisdom' would take of that, and Charles was at least satisfied and also very grateful that he had been blessed with the time and the skills to record the past intriguing history of Vale Royal Abbey for future posterity with the tremendous help and support of his late beloved, dear wife Essex. In addition, we too today must also be grateful that while Vale Royal Abbey was the refuge and beloved home of Charles Cholmondeley for 72 years and for the loving care he rendered. We thank him also for his dedication to this vitally important task of taking care of this treasured historical estate, plus the extremely valuable library, envied by many, that he and his dear wife Essex

Chapter Three: Charles Cholmondeley (1684-1756)

had expanded and cared for during his lifetime.

We must also remember that Charles Cholmondeley had taken a great deal of interest in the past history of Vale Royal Abbey and the Great House throughout his whole lifetime and in his journals are recorded many interesting, important historical facts and details, most of which have been preserved to this day for our enjoyment and enlightenment.

His carefully recorded journals now form the basis for modern scholars in their writings and research about the county of Cheshire and Vale Royal Abbey in particular. Charles was also a brilliant scholar of English history, so it would be amiss for us not to include some of these fascinating historical details listed and recorded by Charles for our reader's edification, in addition to the other details already listed in previous chapters of our story. Charles Cholmondeley was well-known throughout the land for his prowess and skill in creating many fine records of historical events and locations in England, and will be remembered for his honesty, frankness and candor in his reporting and recording of these historical manuscripts. Charles had also left his record of a life of unimpeachable rectitude and integrity.

Charles Cholmondeley had a very busy and full life, as he also served as the Parliamentary Representative for the County Palatine of Chester for 40 years and is described in Parliamentary Records as a man, "who never bought a vote, nor sold his own." He had also shown a laudable devotion and sterling dedication to his duties as a trustworthy and honest politician, a rare example in politicians in these modern times and also in the days gone by.

In addition to this complimentary extract, these notes are also listed in the *Parliamentary Records* (Ref. Vol.1715-1754):

> Charles Cholmondeley, whose father had represented Cheshire in 1669 and in James II's 1685 Parliament, was returned for the county as a Tory at every general election, except that of 1715, from 1710 to his death. A member of the October Club, on the flight of the Duke of Ormonde in July 1715, Cholmondeley, Sir Henry Bunbury and Lord Barrymore met and drank together the Jacobite[8] toast: 'to

---

[8] A Jacobite was a member of a political movement in Great Britain and Ireland that aimed to restore the Roman Catholic Stuart King James II of England and Ireland (as James VII in Scotland) and his heirs to the thrones of England, Scotland, France and Ireland.

The Delamere Saga: Part 1

our absent friends and that they may return with honour, prosperity and glory.' (*Prescott Diary*, 24 Aug. 1715, also published in *The Cheshire Sheaf*, 27 May 1936) In 1721 his name was included in a list of leading English Jacobites sent to the Stuart court in Rome. After his re-election in 1722 he voted regularly against the Government, speaking against them on the repeal of the *Septennial Act*, 13 Mar. 1734.

Much has been written in the annals of English history regarding this momentous "General Election of 1715", with some reports making unwarranted and uncalled for criticism of the conduct and parliamentary record of the Tory candidate for Cheshire, Charles Cholmondeley, especially regarding his moral turpitude and character that he displayed before and during this very important and critical general election being held throughout England from 22 January to 9 March 1715. Plus other implausible, scurrilous and unsupported allegations were also made against Charles, but these were mainly from just angry discontented people hurling epithets at Charles Cholmondeley, claiming he was 'spineless' and because he was a Tory with no 'backbone'.[9]

The unpredictable and peculiar reason why Charles Cholmondeley lost this vital election as the Member of Parliament for Cheshire in 1715 is recorded in the book, *Cheshire Election of 1715*, currently held in the archives of Rylands Library, Manchester, England, and in addition was also reviewed by the in-depth report *Preferring a Whig to a Whimsical—The Cheshire Election of 1715 Reconsidered* (pp. 140-158). Also published in *The Bulletin, John Rylands Library*) this document is also currently held in the Manchester University Library, part of the *National Research Libraries Archives* of England.

We quote portions of these records, as extracted from the above, by courtesy of researchers Steven Baskerville, Peter Adman and Katherine Beedham, all past members of the History Department of Hull University in England. Plus we include supporting quotations from the *History of Parliamentary Records*, 1715-1754, courtesy of the *History of Parliamentary Trust*.

The information presented in all of these records clearly establishes beyond all doubt the upright and moral character of the

---

[9] In those days and time in history, elections did not take place at the same date and time in every constituency as exists today. The returning officer in each county or parliamentary borough fixed the precise date within a predetermined period set down by Parliament.

Chapter Three: Charles Cholmondeley (1684-1756)

esteemed, honourable Charles Cholmondeley of Vale Royal Abbey and that he was not just a "whimsical, capricious, unapproachable recluse", as claimed in one report by a leading parliamentarian of the day. These records further confirm:

> By the middle decades of the eighteenth century county election contests were rare and expensive affairs, infrequently characterized by any coherent or sustained partisan rivalry. Coalitions of country squires and city merchants might occasionally challenge some dominant aristocratic interest under the conveniently vague banner of 'independence', but otherwise little stirred. During the initial third of the eighteenth century Cheshire was among the most fiercely contested constituencies in the country, with local party fortunes managing to mirror the national swing at all general elections held prior to the Hanoverian Succession.

Queen Anne died on 1 August 1714, aged only 49 years, having been plagued by ill health throughout her life. This meant that elections for a new parliament would have to be held within six months, and so the business of fixing interests for the forthcoming contest began almost at once. Queen Anne, the last of the Stuarts died childless, and reigned from 1702-1714. In *The Kings & Queens of England* (1976), Allen Andrews said:

> The central focus of her entire life was not politics but her marriage to George of Denmark, a "kindly nincompoop" of whom King Charles II said, "I have tried him drunk and I have tried him sober, and either way there is nothing in him." George, a constant man, gave Queen Anne 17 pregnancies, but because of a constitutional defect only five were born alive and only one survived for any appreciable time, dying at 11 years of age.

> During her 12-year reign, Queen Anne favoured moderate Tory politicians, who were more likely to share her Anglican religious views than their opponents, the Whigs. Amid this seemingly inexorable progression towards Tory hegemony in Cheshire, the general election of 1715 stands out as something of an aberration; for in that year a serious attempt was made to end the bitter rivalry so long extant between the political parties.

The Delamere Saga: Part 1

Portrait of Queen Anne by Michael Dahl (1705), courtesy of the National Archives

In Cheshire, the sitting Tory members, Charles Cholmondeley and Sir George Warburton, quickly wrote to their 'Particular Friends in every hundred' to assess their chances of being re-chosen as their party's representatives. Sir George Warburton, who sat alongside Charles Cholmondeley in the House of Commons for most of their time in Parliament, was a bespectacled, softly spoken and garrulous man, plus he tended to mix freely with the local voters, whereas, Charles on the other hand tended to keep himself to himself and was reluctant to fraternise with the local voters, plus he was not liked because of his plummy accent.

The initial response to their overtures was decidedly lacking in enthusiasm, however. It is quite clear, nevertheless, that John Ward III (local Chester lawyer and Tory politician) had little sympathy for the received opinion regarding the correct lessons to be drawn about Cholmondeley's character and principles from his recent political conduct:

> His not being free to be security for some of the late Ministry when such a vote was desired & not answering blindfold to some after such demands, give me full satisfaction he is an upright man & if a man may be in any case allow'd to use his own judgm[en]t I'm sure ye particulars he can be charged with may easily be justified & he may remain as true a friend to the establishm[en]t in church and state, as ever he was.

Chapter Three: Charles Cholmondeley (1684-1756)

The stumbling block it appears was Charles Cholmondeley himself, whose voting record in the previous parliamentary session had been less than a model of partisan consistency, and whose recent marriage to Essex Pitt in 1714, thereby joining the very powerful, influential and wealthy Pitt family, which was currently the talk and gossip throughout the county of Cheshire. Whereas his colleague, Sir George Warburton was regarded by the Cheshire backwoodsmen as a man of the soundest Tory principles, Cholmondeley by contrast had come to enjoy the dubious reputation of being a 'whimsical'. In stark contrast to his unopposed return in 1713, unbeknownst to Charles Cholmondeley at that time was that he had been abandoned by a number of his Tory supporters and their political shenanigans in the Cheshire election of 1715. Ostensibly because of the loss of the support of a number of local magnates and a desire to prevent further conflict, a compromise was reached between Whig and Tory interests, to exclude Cholmondeley, and had been agreed at the county meeting of August 1714. It appears that Charles Cholmondeley was unfairly traduced in many quarters, but Charles was certainly not a querulous sort of man and the ongoing reputation of Charles as a sound, honest politician was sacrosanct.

Surely, he [i.e. John Ward III)]urged, 'it is reasonable to let him, when he has applied to you, know what he is to expect or depend upon'. Cholmondeley, he reported, was perfectly willing to stand down if Sir Francis Leicester would agree to offer his own services, and might easily be brought in for a borough seat by his influential Pitt relatives. Yet even John Ward was a little uneasy about the wisdom of forcing their neighbour into a still closer dependence on the whiggish 'Governor' Thomas "Diamond" Pitt, (As noted earlier, the self assured and arrogant Thomas Pitt claimed that he had been appointed as the Governor of Fort St George in India (Fort St George is the name of the first English fortress in India, founded in 1644 at the coastal city of Madras, the modern city of Chennai) by the new East India Company on behalf of the Stuarts. Pitt also claimed he was the President of Madras in India on 7 July 1698 and remained in this (so-called) post till 1709.)

Thomas Pitt, confessing to his colleague Peter Legh (Leigh) of Lyme Park in Cheshire, who was MP for Newton, Warrington, that Charles Cholmondeley was the best choice for the Member of Parliament to represent Cheshire. The report includes these remarks by Pitt about his son-in-law, Charles Cholmondeley,

> that he had rather he came in any other way then to create that obligation to family tho there is among them in the eldest son ye greatest instance I know of a son voting against his father & I verily believe Ch[arles] Ch[olmondeley] is as like to make another as any man & on ye Schism bill he gave a full proof.

But while Cholmondeley and Warburton both remained in some doubt about how they ought to proceed, the latter at least contrived to make effective use of his time; whereas his erstwhile colleague Charles Cholmondeley, spent the greater part of December (1714) languishing at his estate at Vale Royal Abbey, and agonizing over the problem of how best to construct a viable electoral interest. In Cheshire, however, the air of gloom and uncertainty was almost palpable, as well into January 1715; Cholmondeley continued to dither about the merits of pressing his candidacy. Sir Francis Leicester had again refused to join with him on a straight Tory ticket. Charles, calmly stroking his now greying beard, he decided to reflect and cogitate about his future as a politician, and was it really worth all this stress and anxiety that was increasing on a daily basis upon himself and his family?

John Ward, for one, seems to have regarded this call for a county meeting as being in some way connected with the earlier efforts of certain unidentified Tories to get rid of Charles Cholmondeley in order to make room for a sounder candidate; for barely twenty-four hours after receiving the sheriffs summons, he was offering to stand down.

The poll for knights of the shire opened in the Shire Hall at Chester on 16 February 1715 and lasted three days before it became clear that Charles Cholmondeley's best efforts had been in vain. The Hon. Langham Booth, (brother of George Booth, the 2nd Earl of Warrington of Dunham Massey Hall, also known as Baron Delamere (Delamer) of Dunham Massey (see Chapter 5) was returned at the head of the poll, with Warburton just behind,

Chapter Three: Charles Cholmondeley (1684-1756)

and the disgruntled squire of Vale Royal Abbey still some 550 votes short of the tally needed to win the second seat."

> As the returns came in from other constituencies as well, it became obvious that, in spite of their earlier optimism, the Tories had been disastrously beaten in the country as a whole. The Tory party was now firmly in a period of steep declivity at this time in history and to put it more bluntly, the Tories were given a real pasting by the Whigs!
>
> In Cheshire, despite only one net loss, the divided state of the Tory ranks was clear for all to see. Like many another defeated Tory, Charles Cholmondeley was not so much the victim of royal disfavour, or of crude external manipulation by agents of the Whig ministry, as of defections within his own party, the self-interested machinations of local magnates, the apparent volatility of the electorate, and, above all else, of his own fatal indecision."
>
> His 'whimsical' voting record appears to have counted against him with a number of the county's Tories, and the perception of his reported unreliability would not have been lessened by his marriage in the summer of 1714 to the daughter of his fellow 'whimsical' Thomas (Diamond) Pitt. Despite assurances that he 'remain[ed] a true friend to the establishm[en]t in Church and State', Charles Cholmondeley was defeated at the poll in February 1715.

On hearing this depressing news; unfortunately not totally unexpected in view of the results coming in from adjoining constituencies, the face of Charles Cholmondeley looked even more lugubrious than usual, not just for himself but for the Tory party as a whole. Charles now reflected to himself that as he was now unfettered of his responsibilities and duties as a long standing MP for Cheshire, he once more could concentrate on his primary duties at his beloved estate, Vale Royal Abbey, also in caring for his dear wife Essex and family plus his dedication to the ever expanding very valuable private library. Most of the Tory voters in Cheshire expressed the opinion that the political career of Charles Cholmondeley was now 'kaput' but this view proved to be premature as Charles was back in Parliament as MP for Cheshire a few years later. Charles Cholmondeley of course felt like lambasting his critics and the underhanded scheme of attempting to have his name removed as a Tory candidate in this critical 1715 election. However Charles kept his private feelings to himself, plus he was now simply resigned to the trickery and chicanery of British politics of the time and that still continues to this day. The imperturbable Charles Cholmondeley was not totally discouraged by this loss of his seat as MP for Cheshire and neither did it thwart his future career as a brilliant politician. Charles Cholmondeley had been accused by fellow parliamentarians that he was aloof and had viewed the local people of Cheshire as a group of 'gormless' (an English idiom meaning lacking intelligence or vitality; stupid or dull and stupid) fools, and that this attitude also contributed to the loss of his seat as MP for Cheshire. This claim recorded in the archives of British Parliament was not true of course, as other records indicate that Charles was a very compassionate and understanding person plus he viewed his neighbours in Cheshire as dignified and intelligent individuals, certainly not as adversaries.

And if the reason why so many Cheshire Tories chose to support a Whig in 1715 rather than a 'Whimsical' Tory remains, in the end, a matter for informed speculation. Or was it simply a case of, "the pot calling the kettle black"? [English proverbial idiom, used by a person who is guilty of the very thing of which they accuse another.]

Notes from the *Encyclopedia Britannica* about the Whig political party:

> The Whigs were a political faction and then a political party in the parliaments of England, Scotland, Great Britain, Ireland and the United Kingdom. Between the 1680s and 1850s, they contested power with their rivals, the Tories. The Whigs' origin lay in constitutional monarchism and opposition to absolute monarchy. However the Whigs eventually joined the Liberal Party. The Liberal Party (the term was first used officially in 1868, but had been used colloquially for decades beforehand) arose from a coalition of Whigs, free trade Tory followers of Robert Peel and free trade Radicals, first created, tenuously under the Peelite Earl of Aberdeen in 1852 and put together more permanently under the former Canningite Tory Lord Palmerston in 1859. Although the Whigs at first formed the most important part of the coalition, the Whiggish elements

Chapter Three: Charles Cholmondeley (1684-1756)

1601. Although Essex's execution had been necessary and just in Elizabeth's mind, she mourned him after his death. She lamented that he had kept her feeling young, and she missed her favorite. It took three strokes of the axe to sever his neck and the headsman held the head aloft by its long, fair hair, saying 'God save the Queen!' Elizabeth would only reign for a short time afterwards, as she would die in 1603." Thus came to an end the Tudor Monarchy that had ruled from 1485 to 1603.[5]

Queen Elizabeth will also be remembered by one of her most famous quotes: "I know I have the body of a weak and feeble woman, but I have the heart and stomach of a King and of a king of England too." To quote from the script of the BBC documentary:

> Despite pressure from her advisers, particularly Lord Burghley, Elizabeth always refused to marry and provide an heir. She had a close relationship with Robert Dudley, Earl of Leicester, and was not averse to using the promise of marriage for diplomatic purposes, but asserted her independence until the end of her life. She insisted that she was 'married' to her country.

As suggested by David Nash Ford in *Royal Berkshire History* (as extracted from the *Dictionary of National Biography of 1896*), Thomas Pitt always had a grandiose view of himself and his family, plus he also boasted that he was a distant relative of the Tudor royal family through his Welsh roots. The most famous descendant of his was his great-grandson, William Pitt the Younger (1759-1806) who eventually became the Prime Minister of the United Kingdom in 1804, during the reign of King George III.

Based on this superior education received from her father and her tutors, Essex Cholmondeley (nee Pitt) was adequately and capably qualified in supporting and assisting her husband Charles; helping him to acquire numerous books, manuscripts and records

---

[5] This tumultuous relationship between Queen Elizabeth and the Earl of Essex is dramatically portrayed in the brilliant, 1939 award winning film, **The Private Lives of Elizabeth & Essex**, staring Bette Davies and Errol Flynn. Also the excellent film **Young Bess**, which is a 1953 Technicolor biographical film made by Metro-Goldwyn-Mayer about the early life of Elizabeth I, from her turbulent childhood to the eve of her accession to the throne of England. It stars Jean Simmons as young Lady Elizabeth and Stewart Granger as Thomas Seymour, with Charles Laughton as Elizabeth's father, Henry VIII. Both of these films are strongly recommended for students of Elizabethan history.

of the new party progressively lost influence during the long leadership of the former Peelite William Ewart Gladstone and many of the old Whig aristocrats broke from the party over the issue of Irish home rule in 1886 to help form the Liberal Unionist Party, which in turn would merge with the Conservative Party by 1912. However, the Unionist support for trade protection in the early twentieth century under Joseph Chamberlain (probably the least Whiggish character in the Liberal Unionist party) further alienated the more orthodox Whigs. By the early twentieth century "Whiggery" was largely irrelevant and without a natural political home.

The frustration of Charles Cholmondeley in 1715, which was with his political friends and the Tory party in particular, was repressed, but later re-emerged through a cathexis in relation to his desire to continue and loyally serve his fellow neighbours, the great forward looking people of Cheshire, as their Member of Parliament. He was very loath to give way to the negative effect of losing this important general election of 1715. Charles regained this honourable position as MP for Cheshire seven years later in 1722, when he was re-elected to the House of Commons, a position he held until his death on 30 March 1756. The 1722 election was the 6th Parliament of Great Britain under the ruling monarch, King George I and this was the fifth such election since the merger of the Parliament of England and the Parliament of Scotland in 1707. Thanks to the Septennial Act of 1715, which swept away the maximum three-year life of a parliament created by the *Meeting of Parliament Act 1694*, it followed some seven years after the previous notorious election, that of 1715.

According to the *Encyclopedia Britannica*:

> The *Septennial Act of 1715* was an Act of the Parliament of Great Britain. It was passed in May 1716. It increased the maximum length of a parliament (and hence the maximum period between general elections) from three years, as mandated by the *Triennial Act* of 1694, up to seven years. Sir Robert Walpole, "First Minister" [This title became "Prime Minister" from the early 20th century] presented the motion in 1734 to try and repeal the *Septennial Act of 1715*. The original *Septennial Act of 1715* was eventually amended on 18 August 1911 by section 7 of the *Parliament Act 1911*

to reduce the maximum term of parliament to five years as exists today.

It is of interest to note that the Cholmondeleys' of Vale Royal Abbey and their distant cousins, the Cholmondeleys' of Cholmondeley Castle in Cheshire were all indirectly related to Sir Robert Walpole, who was a British politician and statesman and who is generally regarded as the de facto, first Prime Minister of Great Britain plus also the longest-serving British prime minister in history, with an uninterrupted run of over 20 years of service from 1721-1742.

On 30 July 1700, Robert Walpole had married Catherine, daughter of John Shorter of Bybrook in Ashford, Kent. She was described as "a woman of exquisite beauty and accomplished manners". Her £20,000 dowry was, according to her brother-in-law Horatio Walpole, spent on the wedding, christenings and jewels. Together Robert Walpole and his wife Catherine had two daughters and three sons. Mary Walpole, his second daughter married George Cholmondeley, 3rd Earl of Cholmondeley, on 14 September 1723 and they had three sons. Lady Mary Cholmondeley (nee Walpole) later died in Aix-en-Provence in the South of France in 1731 at the young age of 27 years as a result of consumption due to the damp climate in England, and was later buried at Malpas.

Robert Walpole was a Whig from the gentry class, who was first elected to Parliament in 1701 and he held many senior positions. He was a country squire and looked to country gentlemen for his political base. Historian Frank O'Gorman says in *The Long Eighteenth Century: British Political And Social History, 1688-1832* (1997):

> that Walpole and his leadership in Parliament reflected his "reasonable and persuasive oratory, his ability to move both the emotions as well as the minds of men, and, above all, his extraordinary self-confidence.

Julian Hoppit, in *A Land of Liberty?- England 1689-1727*, says Walpole's policies sought moderation, he worked for peace, lower taxes, and growing exports plus he allowed a little more tolerance for Protestant Dissenters. He avoided controversy and high-intensity disputes at all costs, as his middle way attracted moderates from both the Whig and Tory camps. Historian H. T. Dickinson in *Walpole and the Whig Supremacy* (1973) sums up Walpole's historical role:

Chapter Three: Charles Cholmondeley (1684-1756)

Walpole was one of the greatest politicians in British history. He played a significant role in sustaining the Whig party, safeguarding the Hanoverian succession, and defending the principles of the Glorious Revolution (1688) ... He established a stable political supremacy for the Whig party and taught succeeding ministers how best to establish an effective working relationship between the Crown and Parliament.

No. 10 Downing Street in London, a world famous and illustrious address, represents another part of Walpole's legacy. King George II offered this home to Walpole as a personal gift in 1732, but Walpole accepted it only as the official residence of the First Lord of the Treasury, taking up his residence there on 22 September 1735. His immediate successors did not always reside in Number 10 (preferring their larger private residences) but the dwelling has nevertheless become established as the official residence of the Prime Minister (in his or her capacity as First Lord of the Treasury). The portrait of Robert Walpole still hangs today in the cabinet room of No.10 Downing Street, immediately behind the seat of the current Prime Minister.

Lord Chesterfield (1694-1773), a fellow politician, writes in his journal regarding Robert Walpole:

> In private life he was good natured, cheerful and social, but inelegant in his manners, loose in his morals. He had a coarse wit, which he was too free of for a Man in his Station, as it is always inconsistent with dignity. He was very able as a Minister, but without a certain Elevation of mind... He was both the ablest Parliament man, and the ablest manager of a Parliament, that I believe ever lived...Money, not Prerogative, was the chief Engine of his administration, and he employed it with a success that in a manner disgraced humanity...When he found any body proof, against pecuniary temptations, which alas was but seldom, he had recourse to still a worse art. For he laughed at and ridiculed all notions of public virtue, and the love of one's Country, calling them the Chimerical school boy flights of Classical learning; declaring himself at the same time, no Saint, no Spartan, no Reformer. He would frequently ask young fellows at their first appearance in the world, while their honest hearts were yet untainted, well are you to be

an old Roman or a Patriot? You will soon come off of that, and grow wiser. And thus he was more dangerous to the morals, than to the liberties of his country, to which I am persuaded that he meant no ill in his heart. ... His Name will not be recorded in History among the best men, or the best Ministers, but much, much less ought it to be ranked among the worst.

Portrait of Robert Walpole (1676-1745) in No.10 Downing Street, London, courtesy of the Parliamentary Office

One of Robert Walpole's most famous, controversial quotes was:

> The very idea of true patriotism is lost, and the term has been prostituted to the very worst of purposes. A patriot, sir! Why, patriots spring up like mushrooms!

An amusing story related to Robert Walpole is that the ancient children's nursery rhyme "Who Killed Cock Robin?" (1774) may allude to the fall of Walpole from political power in 1742, as he carried the popular nickname 'Cock Robin'. [Contemporaries satirised the Walpole regime as the "Robinocracy" or as the "Robinarchy."] 'Robinocracy' is now an accepted, although very rarely used, established word (noun) in the English language.

To quote a few lines from this historic nursery rhyme

> Who killed Cock Robin?
> I, said the Sparrow,
> with my bow and arrow,
> I killed Cock Robin.
> Who saw him die?
> I, said the Fly,
> with my little eye,I saw him die.....
> Who caught his blood?
> I, said the Fish,
> with my little dish,

Chapter Three: Charles Cholmondeley (1684-1756)

> I caught his blood.
> Who'll make the shroud?
> I, said the Beetle,
> with my thread and needle,
> I'll make the shroud.
> Who'll dig his grave?
> I, said the Owl,
> with my little trowel,
> I'll dig his grave....

In *Eighteenth-Century Britain – Walpole and the Rise of Robinocracy*, Paul Langford (2000) describes the establishment of the Hanoverian regime and the Whig system. The failure of the Jacobite rising of 1715 left the new dynasty secure and able to forge a partnership with the Whigs. When the South Sea Bubble (see Appendix 3) burst and collapsed, it brought a financial crisis in Britain, out of which Walpole came to power. Walpole's reign came to symbolise the corruption in politics and society that along with demographic crisis, blighted the age. Nonetheless, Walpole was successful in managing parliament and building a broad, stable coalition that gave some Tories a stake in the Whig system.

We now change the topic from his political life to another fascinating account regarding Charles Cholmondeley of Vale Royal Abbey and the reference of his birth in 1684 [some records state 1685] being prophesied by a local Cheshire prophet called Robert Nixon, who probably lived in the 15th or 16th century. In *Prophecy & Politics of Early Modern England* by Timothy Thornton (2006), pps. 135-136, reference is made to the records of "Nixon's Prophecies" (see also Chapter 10):

> Since the birth of Charles Cholmondeley on 12 January 1684, which coincided with the accession to the throne by King James II it must have seemed obvious. Nixon had prophesied, 'When an eagle shall sit on top of the house, then an heir shall be born to the Cholmondeley family.' According to Sarah Cowper, the eagle, 'the biggest bird she ever saw', sat in one of the windows all the time her sister Ann Cholmondeley was in labour. She confirmed that when the child Charles was born the eagle had flown to a nearby tree and stayed there for 3 days before it disappeared into the night.

> The rumour surrounding these events related to this saying in "Nixon's Prophecy" regarding the eagle had been fulfilled and also the prophecy had stated that England would have a foreign King, and James II was that King, as he had been born in Scotland and was a devout Roman Catholic. The prophecy also stated that the heir to Vale Royal Abbey, (Charles Cholmondeley, only son of Thomas and Ann Cholmondeley) would be born, but the prophecy also went on to say that this male heir to Vale Royal Abbey would be involved in the many great wars facing England especially in the 'west and north', and he would live to fight bravely for his king and country.

Was Robert Nixon, this humble, somewhat befuddled ploughboy, viewed by many as the local 'village idiot'? Did he uncannily and mysteriously foresee the English war in North America and Canada against the French, with which Charles Cholmondeley became intricately involved in the "west and north", namely North America and Canada during 1751 and 1752, when Charles fought in the King's service as a Colonel in the Cheshire Regiment with a great personal sacrifice?

Of course, history now records that King James became King of England and Ireland as James II, plus he was also King of Scotland as James VII, from 6 February 1685 until he was deposed in the Glorious Revolution of 1688. He was the last Roman Catholic monarch of England, Scotland and Ireland. James II did not remain as the English monarch for any length of time as he abdicated the throne within three years and fled to France at which time William of Orange and his wife Mary; devout Protestants, were invited in 1688 by Parliament to occupy the throne of England.

According to the BBC's History Channel:

> Early in 1689, the English Parliament formally offered William and Mary the throne as joint monarchs, an event known as the 'Glorious Revolution'. William III of Orange was now William III of England and Ireland and William II of Scotland. The new monarchs could not rule with the same direct power as their predecessors. They accepted Parliament's 'Declaration of Rights', later called the 'Bill of Rights'. This restricted the king's power and marked an important transition towards the system of parliamentary rule that still exists to this day.

Chapter Three: Charles Cholmondeley (1684-1756)

Nixon's prophesies regarding these future events that took place in Cheshire and England were based mainly on oral tradition but a full written record was eventually published by a Samuel Terry and printed by a local Liverpool newspaper, probably the *Liverpool Courant*, published from 1712-1736, which was the earliest Liverpool Newspaper on record, according to *Smith's Strangers Guide to Liverpool, Its Environs & Parts of Cheshire*, published in 1843 [and currently held in the archives of the British Museum]. This record of the prophecies of Robert Nixon was printed and published in 1715 in the form of a "chapbook" [mostly small paper backed booklets].

Read more about this intriguing account of these myths and legends connected to Robert Nixon, the "Cheshire Prophet" and especially those events directly related to Vale Royal Abbey in Chapter 10. But before we leave the life chronicles of Charles Cholmondeley and the important contribution he made to the historic records of Vale Royal Abbey, we provide the following:

Selected Information and Reports of the History of Vale Royal Abbey based on the archived Journals & Manuscripts of Charles Cholmondeley (1684-1756). [This information forms the basis of most records and articles produced by scholars today.]

Note: An additional record also exists today that is known as the *Vale Royal Ledger-Book* (also known as the *Green Book*) that is based on the records of the Cistercian Monks and was created in 1662. These records were no doubt extensively consulted by Charles Cholmondeley in his research and writing of his manuscript regarding the "History of Vale Royal Abbey". This 259 page book was later edited by John Brownbill in 1914 and is now contained in the archives of the Library of the University of Illinois at Urbana-Champaign.

The original *Ledger-Book* or *Green Book* is a chronicle of the foundation of the Abbey of Vale Royal and of the progress over the years of this Cistercian abbey of Vale Royal, in Delamere Forest, near Winsford in Cheshire. It comprises a contemporary history of the abbey, pleas and evidences, and a collection of Bulls granting privileges to the Cistercian order. It forms volume 68 of the publications of the Record Society of Lancashire and Cheshire. It is believed to have been started by the 5th Abbot of Vale Royal

Abbey named Peter in 1338. In 1662 this original manuscript was held by Sir Thomas Mainwaring, MP (1623-1689) at his residence in Peover Hall, Over Peover, Cheshire. It appears from records that a heated dispute arose over the actual ownership of this manuscript but we now know at least that by 1732 it thankfully ended up in the large Library at Vale Royal Abbey under the direct control and protection of Charles Cholmondeley (1684-1756). The motto of Charles Cholmondeley during his lifetime was "Cherish the past and you will protect the future."

The original 1662 copy of the *Ledger-Book*, which was held in the Library at Vale Royal Abbey for many years and once thought to have been destroyed, is now fortunately held in the archives of the British Museum in London, England and is recorded as the 'Harl. MS.2064'. A copy is also held in the archives of Rylands Library in Manchester, England, where students today can read and research these records by private appointment.

Extract from the notes by Charles Cholmondeley.

> The original abbey to be built on the site at Vale Royal was founded in 1270 by Edward the First for monks of the austere Cistercian order. The king intended the abbey to be on the grandest scale, even larger than Westminster Abbey in London, however, financial difficulties meant that these ambitions could not be fulfilled and the final building was considerably smaller than planned. The project ran into problems in other ways also; the abbey was frequently grossly mismanaged, relations with the local population were so poor as to result in large scale violence on a number of occasions and internal discipline was frequently bad. (The 14th century Cistercian Abbey of Vale Royal is located 3km north of Over. It was once the largest Cistercian monastery in England but it suffered at the Dissolution and little of the abbey survives. The large Vale Royal House was built in the 17th century, utilising the west and south ranges of the cloisters.)

Vale Royal Abbey itself was closed in 1538 by Henry VIII as part of the Dissolution of the Monasteries. Much of the abbey, including the church, was demolished but some of the cloister buildings were incorporated into a mansion known as the Great House by Thomas Holcroft, an important government official,

Chapter Three: Charles Cholmondeley (1684-1756)

during the 1540s. Over subsequent centuries this house was considerably altered and extended by successive generations. The building remains habitable and contains surviving rooms from the medieval abbey, including the refectory and kitchen. The foundations of the church and cloister have also been excavated. [Today it is a scheduled ancient monument and recorded in the National Heritage List for England as a designated Grade II listed building.]

The abbey we now know as Vale Royal was founded by Prince Edward, the future Edward I, prior to his accession to the throne. In 1263 the prince was undertaking a sea voyage from France when his ship was caught in a terrible storm. He then personally made a vow that if he came safe to land he would found an abbey of unprecedented size and grandeur as a thanksgiving to God for saving him. Political problems and civil war meant that the vow could not be fulfilled immediately, but by 1266 negotiations were in hand for the establishment of a monastery of Cistercian monks in the secluded location of Darnhall in Cheshire. In August 1270, Edward granted a charter to his new abbey along with an endowment of lands and churches.

As so often in the history of the abbey things did not go smoothly; preparing the site took considerable time and the first monks, led by Abbot John Chaumpeneys, did not arrive at Darnhall from Dore Abbey until 1274. The foundation of the new abbey provoked anger, resentment and strong resistance from the people of the area and the Darnhall site itself was found to be unsuitable for the huge buildings planned. In 1276 Edward, by now king, agreed to move the abbey to a better site and a location was chosen in nearby Over on the edge of the Forest of Mondrem (Delamere Forest). With its foundation, the new ecclesiastical site was named Vale Royal. In 1277 the King and Queen Eleanor and numerous great nobles arrived at Over to lay the foundation stones of the new abbey. In 1281 the monks moved from Darnhall to temporary accommodation on the Vale Royal site while the abbey started to rise around them.

King Edward had tremendous ambitions for Vale Royal. It was intended to be an abbey of the first importance, to surpass all the other houses of its order in Britain in scale and beauty and provide a fitting symbol of the wealth and power of the English monarchy and Edward's piety and personal greatness. The plans for the buildings reflected this. Royal masons under the leadership of Walter of Hereford, one of the foremost architects of his day, started work on a huge and elaborate High Gothic church the size of a cathedral. It was to be 116 m. long and cruciform in shape with a central tower. The east end was semi-circular with a chevet of 13 radiating chapels, some square, some polygonal; each of the transepts also had a row of three chapels on its eastern side. South of the church stood a cloister, 42m square, surrounded by the domestic buildings of the house, which were to be of a scale and grandeur to match the church.

At first matters went well. The king greatly expanded the initial endowment and made large donations of cash and materials toward the work. Soon, however, things began to go seriously wrong. As the 1280s progressed the royal finance first got into arrears then dried up. King Edward needed money to pay for his numerous wars and workmen to build the great castles such as Harlech he put up to cement his conquest of Wales. He took not only the money that had been set aside for Vale Royal but also conscripted the masons and other labourers to build his Welsh fortifications and in 1290 announced that he was no longer interested in the abbey and would have nothing more to do with it. The monks were left struggling to pay to complete the vast project and provide the running costs of it all by themselves, a task that would prove beyond their means, despite a substantial income, and incurring huge debts to other church institutions, royal officials, the building contractors and even to the merchants of Lucca. Work stopped for at least a decade after 1290 and was resumed only on a much reduced scale thereafter. Nevertheless, by the 1330s the monks had managed to complete the east end of the church (the rest remained a shell) and sufficient of the cloister buildings to make the place habitable, though far from complete In the 1350s there was cause for renewed hope.

Edward the Black Prince took an interest in completing the abbey and donated substantial funds to the job. Work began on completing the shell of the nave and making the east end even grander. However, in October 1360 disaster struck yet again. A hurricane swept across Cheshire and brought the arcades of the unfinished nave crashing down in ruins. This set the seal on things.

Chapter Three: Charles Cholmondeley (1684-1756)

It was subsequently agreed under the patronage of Richard II to finish the abbey on a much reduced scale from what was originally planned.

As well as the burden of trying to finish the abbey buildings, Vale Royal faced many other serious problems. From the beginning the monks' relationship with their tenants and neighbours was usually poor and sometimes abysmal. As previously noted, the initial foundation was resented by the people of Darnhall and Over, who found themselves under the lordship of the abbey. The monks proved harsh and oppressive landlords and the people responded fiercely, sometimes going to law, sometimes resorting to violence. The people of the area attacked monastic officials on many occasions (even killing the abbot in 1339), and more than once rose in arms against the abbey. Relations with the gentry were no better and they too often came to blows with the monks. The abbey was involved in feuds with a number of the prominent local families and these frequently ended in large scale violence. Vale Royal was often beset by scandal of other kinds too. Many of the abbots proved to be incompetent or venal, and the house was frequently grossly mismanaged. As time went on discipline became lax and in the fourteenth century and early fifteenth century there was much disorder at the abbey, with reports of serious crimes including attempted murder being committed by Vale Royal monks."

Another abbot, Henry Arrowsmith, a man with a reputation for lawlessness, was hacked to death in 1437 by a group of men including the vicar of Over. This abbot was slain in revenge for a rape he was alleged to have committed. The abbey was taken under royal supervision in 1439, but there was no immediate improvement: in the 1450s the scandalous doings of the monks of Vale Royal were still attracting the attention of the government and even the General Chapter, the international governing body of the Cistercian order who, in 1455, ordered senior abbots to investigate the abbey, which they described as "damnable and sinister". Thereafter things improved somewhat and the last years of Vale Royal were fairly peaceful and well ordered.

In 1535 the abbey was valued in the Valor Ecclesiasticus as having an income of £540, a very comfortable sum, which leads one to wonder how many of the abbey's financial problems were due to bad management. This figure meant that Vale Royal escaped being dissolved under the terms of the First Suppression Act, King Henry VIII's initial move in the Dissolution of the Monasteries. The last abbot was John Hareware (elected 1535), who had previously been abbot of Hulton Abbey. He pursued a two-pronged policy of attempting to ensure the survival of his abbey and, should that fail, the security of himself and his brethren thereafter. He bribed courtiers, influential nobles and in particular chief minister Thomas Cromwell with money and property in the hope of gaining respite; he also leased out most of the abbey lands to friends and associates of the monastery to keep them out of royal hands should the abbey fall (many of these leases had a clause which stated that they should be void if the abbey survived). He also began to realise the other assets such as livestock and timber for cash.

The great plans for Vale Royal Abbey, upon which the early prosperity of the village of Over depended, came to an end when first the great castle-building programme of Edward I stripped it of funds and then the Black Death killed half of the local population. When the plague cleared, there were empty spaces to be used up and ambitious men took advantage of this. This caused friction with the Abbot leading to several incidents culminating in a revolt when the local peasants took their case to the Justice of Chester and even to the Queen herself, asking for her to plead their case to the King. The King, however, decided in favour of the Abbot and all the men (and one woman) who had taken over lands had to give them up. The rebels were imprisoned at Weaverham. In 1545 Vale Royal Abbey and its lands were sold during the Dissolution of the Monasteries, with the land being purchased by Thomas Holcroft[10] for £466.10s.1d, who sold it almost at once to Edmund Pershall. Pershall was a London merchant who saw his purchase as a long term investment. He got regular rents and hoped the properties would increase in value. Much of the this land was sold in the middle of the 17th century to Thomas Cholmondeley, son of Lady Mary Cholmondeley who had purchased Vale Royal Abbey in 1615.

However the process of dissolution at Vale Royal Abbey was begun in September 1538 by Thomas Holcroft, one of the king's

---

[10] Holcroft's heirs lived at Vale Royal until 1615, when the abbey came into the hands of the Cholmondeley family (subsequently Lords' Delamere). The widowed Lady Mary Cholmondeley (1562-1625), a powerful woman with extensive properties in the area, had bought the abbey as a home for herself.

commissioners, and occurred in very shady, suspect circumstances. Holcroft claimed that the abbey had surrendered to him on 7 September, however, the abbot and convent strongly denied that they had done so and questioned Holcroft's authority. To defend himself, Holcroft then alleged that the abbot had attempted to take over the abbey for himself and had tried to conspire with Holcroft to engage in land fraud involving the abbey estates. The Vale Royal monks petitioned the government, in particular Thomas Cromwell who, in his role as Vicar General was in charge of church affairs under the Royal Supremacy. Abbot John appealed to Cromwell in person and in the course of his journey to London to see the chief minister wrote to him: "My Good Lord, the truth is, I nor my said brethren have never consented to surrender our monastery not yet do, nor never will by our good wills unless it shall please the King's grace to give us commandment to do so."

There must have been some disquiet in governmental circles as to whether the surrender of Vale Royal was in fact legitimate, so steps were taken to put the matter beyond doubt. A special court was held at the abbey on 31 March, 1539, with Cromwell himself as judge. However, instead of investigating the circumstances of the surrender, the court charged the abbot with treason and the murder of a monk who had committed suicide in 1536, serious crimes that would have earned the death penalty. The abbot was found guilty and Vale Royal was declared forfeit to the crown because of his crimes. However, Abbot John was not executed; instead he was given the substantial pension of £60 per year and the abbey's plate, indicating that the trial was a method of putting pressure on him to acquiesce to the wishes of Cromwell and Holcroft regarding the fate of his monastery. The rest of the community was also pensioned off. Pension records indicate that Abbot John lived until at least 1546.

After these transactions, Thomas Holcroft was now in charge at Vale Royal Abbey. In 1539 he demolished the church, telling King Henry in a letter that it was "plucked down". On 7 March 1544 the king confirmed Holcroft's ownership by granting him the abbey and a great deal of its estates for the sum of £450. Holcroft then took down many of the abbey's domestic buildings, retaining the south and west cloister ranges including the abbot's house and the monks' dining hall along with their kitchen as the core of his very large mansion on the site.

There is a legend that a secret tunnel leads from the Abbey to the Nunnery at Winsford. The monks and nuns would use this tunnel to meet in secret. Bodies of babies have said to have been found in this tunnel. This is all that remains of a grave and monument to a particular Nun called Ida. It is suggested that this monument, that can still be seen today on the Vale Royal estate, was erected by the Cholmondeley family to try and possibly add credence to this legend, but that is unconfirmed from our research.

A little knowledge of the background of the village of Over will enlighten our students of Cheshire History as it figures prominently in the records of Charles Cholmondeley and Vale Royal Abbey. In 1643, Royalists escaping from Nantwich 'sacked' the small village of Over. The situation during the English Civil War was very dangerous to everyone and proof of this was discovered when workmen in Nixon Drive found a little black ale mug full of silver coins, with a date range from Queen Elizabeth I (1593 to 1643). The coins were declared treasure trove and are now at the Grosvenor Museum in Chester. Daniel King, who published his history of Cheshire in 1656, described the village of Over thus: "tis but a small thing, but I place it here because of the great prerogative that it has, for it had a mayor". He included it in the list of boroughs of Cheshire for, despite being a tiny village, its mayor was of equal rank to the mayor of the City of Chester.

The Salt industry became firmly established in the Winsford area of Cheshire from the 1830s, bringing with it massive pollution. As the wind usually blew away from the village of Over, it became the popular place for more wealthy people in the town to live. However, people who worked on the barges and other people working in Winsford started to develop along the old Over Lane, now the High Street. The old Borough tried to keep itself separate but had been connected by the 1860s. In 1869 Abraham Haigh built a cotton mill at the end of what would become Well Street. He used the water supply trapped in the sand enclosed by clay on the Over Ridge to power steam engines. However, almost as soon as the building was completed most of it was destroyed, killing some of the workers who were then buried in a communal grave at St John's Church in Delamere Street, where a monument records their names. A town fire engine, although ordered, had not yet been delivered by the time of the fire. The last mayor of Over was Edmund Leigh who held office during the Diamond Jubilee of 1897. The mayoral status of Over was by then a purely ceremonial affair as the right of the mayor to sit in court as a magistrate had by then been removed.

The Government gave permission for artificial improvements to be made to the River Weaver in 1721 to allow large barges to reach Winsford from the port of Liverpool. At first, this was the closest that barges carrying china clay from Cornwall could get to the Potteries (Stoke and Stafford in the midlands). The clay was then taken overland by pack horses, which in turn would bring back the finished china products to be sent for export through the docks of Liverpool. In 1744, the manager of the wharf, George Wood, took control of the trade between Winsford and Stoke. He made a reasonable fortune and built Oak House, which remained a farm just off Beeston Drive before the land was purchased to build the Over Housing Estate and the house was demolished. That trade ended in the 1780s when the Trent and Mersey Canal carried the goods through Middlewich and bypassed the town. The canalised Weaver River was, however, the inspiration for the Duke of Bridgewater's canals and later the engineer for the Weaver Navigation, Edwin Leader Williams, designed and built the prestigious Manchester Ship Canal.

Charles Cholmondeley often recounted with pride, not only regarding his role in compiling the historical records of Vale Royal Abbey for posterity, which we can enjoy today, but also his role in the history of Canada and the way that the English military forces had driven the French into the local controlled area of Quebec, and eventually Canada (Previously known as New France) that in due time became a British protectorate in 1763 and ultimately today a proud member of the British Commonwealth.[11]

When Charles died in 1756, aged 72 years, his official obituary recorded that he was endeared and respected by his tenants and a large circle of friends, especially for his unostentatious virtues. He had showed the eternal verities of honor, love, and patriotism. Out of all the 'owners and masters' of Vale Royal Abbey over the past centuries, Charles Cholmondeley was remarkably outstanding and he was the one who made the greatest contribution to the

---

[11] The Commonwealth of Nations, formerly the British Commonwealth, also known as simply the Commonwealth, is an intergovernmental organisation of 53 member states that are mostly former territories of the British Empire.

expansion of its extensive library, but alas his brilliant work accomplished during his lifetime was eventually destroyed in the early 20th century. Charles proves to be an inspiration to all of us who love history, especially the history of Cheshire and our beloved Vale Royal Abbey. But, unofficially, we must also respect and honor Charles Cholmondeley of Vale Royal Abbey for the major contribution and sacrifices he personally made toward what is today, the well-established and very prosperous nation of Canada. [Vive le Canada]

Chapter Four: Thomas Cholmondeley (1726-1779)

Upon the death of his much loved and respected father Charles in 1756, Thomas, his fourth son and only living heir, quickly accepted his new position as master of Vale Royal Abbey and of course he was also personally thrilled that he could now thrive on the power and benefits that such a prominent role gave him, plus he also, as tradition dictated, became the MP for Cheshire. This required his absence from Vale Royal Abbey for many months of the year, but unfortunately he very soon fell into the same unsavory, disreputable routine and life style that his Grandfather Thomas had also displayed, and owing to his esteemed reputation, being now the owner and master of one of the largest private estates in the whole of England, he was soon mixing with the nobility and the aristocracy of the day, including members of the royal family of King George III. Thomas of course did not have the same dedication toward the Vale Royal Abbey as his late father Charles, and in due time this negative, indifferent attitude began to display itself.

Thomas had meantime married Dorothy Cowper in October, 1764 at St. James Church in Westminster, London. Dorothy was sole heir of Edmund Cowper, Esq. of Over Leigh near Chester and who had been born in the town of Colne, 25 miles north of Manchester in Lancashire; she was a true, genuine Lancashire lass! Thomas and Dorothy Cholmondeley (nee Cowper) had five children, the eldest daughter being named Hestor (1762?-1802), Dorothy (1765-1853), Thomas (1767-1855) who later became the 1st Lord Delamere of Vale Royal Abbey, Charles (1770-1846) and the Reverend Hugh Clolmondeley (1772-1815).

Reflecting on the life of Thomas Cholmondeley and his involvement with the family of King George III, it is expedient that we expand on this unusual and intriguing relationship with the Monarchy of Great Britain.

The Delamere Saga: Part 1

George William Frederick (4 June 1738 - 29 January 1820) was King George III of Great Britain and Ireland from 25 October 1760 until the union of the two countries on 1 January 1801, after which he was King of the United Kingdom of Great Britain and Ireland until his death in 1820. He was concurrently Duke and prince-elector of Brunswick-Lüneburg ("Hanover") in the Holy Roman Empire until his promotion to King of Hanover on 12 October 1814. He was the third British monarch of the House of Hanover, but unlike his two predecessors, King George I and King George II, he was born in Britain, spoke English as his first language and never ever visited Hanover in Germany.

His life and reign, which were longer than any other British monarch before him, were marked by a series of military conflicts involving his kingdoms, much of the rest of Europe, and places farther afield in Africa, the Americas and Asia. Early in his reign, Great Britain defeated France in the Seven Years' War, becoming the dominant European power in North America and India. However, many of Britain's American thirteen colonies were soon lost in the American Revolutionary War (1775-1783), also known as the American War of Independence. A further war against France from 1793 concluded in the defeat of Napoleon at the Battle of Waterloo in 1815.

Battle of Waterloo (1815,) painting by William Sadler, courtesy of the British Museum

Chapter Four: Thomas Cholmondeley (1726-1779)

In the later part of his life, King George III had recurrent, and eventually permanent, mental illness. Although it has since been suggested that he had the blood disease porphyria [a group of disorders caused by an over accumulation of porphyrin, which helps hemoglobin, the protein that carries oxygen in the blood]. Symptoms vary depending on the specific type. Acute porphyrias affect the nervous system and other organs) the real cause of his illness remains unknown to this day. After a final relapse in 1810, the Regency was established and King George III's eldest son, George, ruled as Prince Regent.

It is of interest to our readers that HRH, Charles, Prince of Wales and Earl of Chester, was interviewed by the *Guardian* newspaper regarding King George III:

> But the Prince of Wales[12] has disclosed that George III is the king he most respects, describing him as a good man who was simply misunderstood. The Prince was grilled by a group of teenagers, as he visited a London school. Marilyn Goncalves and Joshua Ashworth, both 14 years, took the opportunity to pick his brains as they entered a history lesson whilst showing him around Pimlico Academy. Marilyn said: we asked him the question: "Which monarch do you most respect?" And he said George III because he thought he was a really good man. People thought he was mad, but really (the Prince said) that the people misunderstood and that he just had an illness. He thought that he was a really good king.'

In 1788, King George suffered his first bout of what doctors diagnosed as insanity, an illness that plagued him for the rest of his life. After trying to smash his eldest son George's head against a wall he was placed in a straitjacket and after further wild outbursts, an iron chair was designed to restrain him.[13]

---

[12] The Prince of Wales on 2 August 1975 was awarded a Master of Arts degree from Cambridge University, in accordance with the university's practice Doctorate in History by submitting his excellent thesis regarding 'King George III'.

[13] We further recommend that our readers view the brilliant documentary by the BBC, *King George III: Genius of the Mad King*. An official review of this documentary reveals, "After 200 years under lock and key, all the personal papers of one of our most important monarchs are for the first time seeing the light of day. In the first documentary to gain extensive access to the Royal Archives, Robert Hardman sheds fascinating new light on George III, Britain's longest reigning king. George III may be chiefly remembered for his madness, but these private documents reveal a monarch who was a political micromanager and a restless patron of science and the arts, an obsessive traveller who never left southern England yet toured the world in his mind and a man who was driven (sometimes to distraction) by his sense of duty to his family and his country."

Thomas Cholmondeley and his personal life in the City of London was very complex to say the least. Not only was his relationship with one of the daughters of King George III, namely Princess Augusta Sophia (1768-1840) being criticized by his political colleagues, he also was still involved with additional illicit affairs with other prominent women in London, many who were amazingly, actual wives of his fellow Members of Parliament; unknow to them of course! The voracious Thomas always had a large appetite for sexual indulgence!

Who was this daughter of King George III, Augusta Sophia, who Thomas Cholmondeley was privately and secretly involved with? Records of the time provide some enlightening information. Since she and her sister were quickly approaching a marriageable age, Augusta Sophia, daughter of King George III, and the Princess Royal were given their first lady-in-waiting in July 1783. Augusta frequently wrote to her elder brother William, who was in Hanover for military training. She was a good correspondent, telling him family news and encouraging him to tell her what was happening in his life. She reveled in his attention and in the little gifts he sent her, even though the Queen tried to discourage William from taking up his sister's valuable time. Though their academic lessons were nearly over, the Queen was loath to have her daughters waste time, and made sure that the Princesses spent hours studying music or art, learning many types of specialty work from different masters.

The Princesses did not 'dress' until dinner in the evening, wearing morning gowns nearly all day. Even when 'dressed', the Royal Family often wore plain clothes, far removed from the ornate splendor of other courts. As there were six Princesses, the Queen's expenses even for these clothes were enormous, and she tried to keep costs down and within the allowance she was given. Moving into this new phase of life meant that the amount of money the Queen was spending on her three eldest daughters was rapidly increasing. The Princesses constantly needed dresses, hats, trimmings, fans, and other items. The quarterly expense for their clothes was estimated to be £2000 (an enormous cost in today's terms), and the expense of all their servants and tutors added to that. Yet it all paid off in one way especially, as the Princesses were quickly becoming a familiar sight to the public. When their group portrait was exhibited to the people, it was marveled at for the porcelain impersonal beauty they

Chapter Four: Thomas Cholmondeley (1726-1779)

displayed. They were dressed the same, and only their accessories hinted at the very different personalities that lay underneath the painted masks.

By 1785, Augusta and her sister Charlotte were reaching an age where they could be considered as potential brides for foreign Princes. In that year the Prince Royal of Denmark (later King Frederick VI) indicated to King George III that he would break off every other discussed proposal for the hand in marriage of a British Princess. He was also supposed to prefer Augusta to her older sister. However, the King declared that after the horrible treatment of his younger sister by the Prince Royal's father, King Christian VII, he would never send one of his daughters to the Danish court.

Painting of the Coronation of King George III, courtesy of the British Museum

As their friends and ladies of the court began to get married, the Princesses wondered when their turn would come. In 1797, she received a proposal from Prince Frederick Adolf of Sweden, a proposal given without the approval of the Swedish royal house. A British Princess, especially from so fertile a mother, was a prize, but Augusta's father seemed increasingly unwilling to allow his daughters to marry.

Augusta Sophia, daughter of King George III, of course never did marry and she unfortunately wasted most of her young adult life being pursued, conquered, sexually used and abused by Thomas Cholmondeley of Vale Royal Abbey, who lasciviously and wantonly used their relationship to satisfy his bestial lusts while he was living in London as the so-called esteemed Member of Parliament for Cheshire. Augusta was tall, willowy and ethereal but the poor hapless girl, despite being a member of the Royal Family was like putty in the hands of the ruthless and avaricious Thomas Cholmondeley.

The Delamere Saga: Part 1

Portrait of Augusta Sophia, courtesy of the National Archives, London

Cheshire meanwhile had a history of wars and rebellions. In August 1655, England had been placed under military rule and Cheshire, Lancashire and North Staffordshire were governed by Charles Worsley.

Charles Worsley was an English soldier and politician. He was also an ardent supporter of Oliver Cromwell and was an officer in the Parliamentary army during the English Civil War and the Commonwealth of England. He sat in the House of Commons in 1654 and governed this district of England during the Rule of the Major-Generals. Riots were planned, even by Parliamentarians, notably Sir George Booth of Dunham Massey near Altringham in Cheshire, though these were eventually quashed and most of the leaders executed. Finally military rule ended in 1658 and the monarchy was restored with King Charles II of England.

In 1689, Henry, Duke of Norfolk, raised a regiment on the Little Roodee in Chester (in those days an open field on the opposite side of the River Dee from Chester Castle, currently used as the Chester Racecourse, which is known as the oldest and smallest racecourse in England) in an effort to resist any attempt by King James II to re-take the English throne. This regiment became the Cheshire Regiment and now forms part of the 1st Battalion, Mercian Regiment (Cheshire).

At the end of the 18th century, land enclosure and district reorganizations took place. Also the local industries, industrialization of the Lancashire and Manchester area mill towns was growing rapidly, which saw and experienced the Cheshire farms abandoned as workers sought a better living in the industrial towns. These remaining lands were absorbed into bigger estates culminating in 98% of Cheshire land belonging to only 26% of the population. However, industrialization also bought many benefits to Cheshire. The completion of the Trent and Mersey Canal in 1777 and

Chapter Four: Thomas Cholmondeley (1726-1779)

innovations such as the Anderton Boat Lift, allowed the Cheshire cheese and salt industries to become major county exports.

Thomas Cholmondeley meanwhile was forced, because of serious illness, to return Vale Royal Abbey after spending most of his time during the year of 1779 desperately trying to take care of his duties as Member of Parliament and also of course satisfying his lusty male pleasures and other forms of moral turpitude with the young Augusta Sophie, daughter of King George III. Unfortunately the health of Thomas (1726-1779) was deteriorating at such an alarming rate, probably as a result of his lascivious, depraved life style. Thomas eventually died of an 'unspecified' disease on 2 June, aged only 53 years; and by this time in his life he was an abandoned, forlorn and disillusioned man.

His loyal, stalwart wife Dorothy died 7 years later in 1786, and, because their children had all now grown up to be adults with their own personal ambitions and interests, they showed very little feeling or compassion for their dying, now disgraced father Thomas Cholmondeley. His wife Dorothy also had little compassion or leniency regarding his fall from grace, as she being a true, solid Lancashire lass took it in her stride and stoically rose above her husbands gross misconduct, as she was completely and fully aware of his scandalous affairs and his immoral life style while he was residing in London. She had accepted this fact and actually had forgiven him; she reasoned that he was simply the unfortunate victim and a casualty of being born with a 'silver spoon' in his mouth. [This is an expression synonymous with wealth, especially inherited wealth; someone born into a wealthy family.]

An interesting event worth noting in the life of Thomas Cholmondeley (1726-1779) is that he and his wife Dorothy Cowper, had five children. Their eldest daughter called Hester (1770-1802) had married into the famous Scottish family, the Drummonds. Hester. Her husband John Drummond (1766-1833) had several children and the youngest daughter named Charlotte Drummond (1791-1876) married Robert Hibbert (1790-1829) of Birtles Hall in Cheshire in 1823, and he was also the owner of a notorious slave trading station in Jamaica. Robert Hibbert died in 1829 aged only 39 years of age. In our research we also discovered that the grandfather of Charlotte, Thomas Cholmondeley was also a major investor in the slave trade business of Robert Hibbert and as a result added more wealth to the family assets of the Vale Royal Abbey. This account of the slave trade and events related to the scandalous slave ships is covered in *The Birth, Life & Death of King Cotton*. We quote from the opening chapter of this excellent book:

> Our current story begins with the life of Elijah Hobbs, his birth name being Zimbi (meaning inspiration and hope) from the village of Salaga in Ghana, Africa. His new name Elijah was assigned to him by Elizabeth Hobbs the wife of the slave master James Hobbs, who was the manager of the slave trading estate called 'Albion' located fifteen miles east of Kingston in what was St. David parish but is now modern day St. Thomas. Albion Estate was owned by Englishman Robert Hibbert who lived a lavish lifestyle of a wealthy slave owner and trader at his palatial home, Birtles Hall located in Over Alderely, Cheshire.

Chapter Five: Thomas Cholmondeley, 1st Lord Delamere of Vale Royal Abbey (1767- 1855)

Thomas Cholmondeley, son of Thomas (1726-1779) took over the reigns as "lord and master" of Vale Royal Abbey upon the death of his pathetic, disgraced father in 1779. Thomas Cholmondeley, according to family tradition also took over the political duties in 1796, after his appointment as Member of Parliament for Cheshire, plus his duties as Sheriff of Chester. Thomas had also recently married Henrietta Elizabeth, youngest daughter of Sir Watkin Williams-Wynn of Wynnstay, Denbighshire, Wales, plus she was an outstandingly beautiful woman, according to portraits of the time. They married at Ruabon, Wales, on 17 December, 1810 and were blessed with five sons and one daughter.

18th-century engraving of Vale Royal manor house, courtesy of *Creative Commons* and G. Ormerod, *History of Cheshire* (1819)

Henrietta Elizabeth Williams-Wynn, the new wife of Thomas was well-known as a local landscape and portrait artist, a skill that appears to have been passed onto her descendants today, plus she was an avid, knowledgeable and skilled collector of antiques. In our research we also discovered some very revealing, interesting letters and documents from Henrietta Elizabeth Williams-Wynn, which are in the collection of manuscripts belonging to a family called Osborne, currently held in trust at Yale University.

The Osborn Manuscript Files contain single, unbound manuscripts and small groups of documents and private letters acquired for the Osborn Collection from various sources at various times, which the Library has chosen to describe in finding-aid style lists rather than as discrete entries in Yale University Library's on-line public access catalog (*Orbis*). The materials in the Osborn Manuscript Files include literary and historical manuscripts, individual and small groups of private letters, and single documents, as well as some 'unprocessed' material such as engraved portraits and bibliographic information. (see Appendix 4, regarding the Osborne Collection)

The Williams-Wynn family was a major landowner in north and mid-Wales and also across the English border. For centuries they had a great influence on the political, cultural, social and literary life of Wales. Although the family owned several houses throughout Wales, the main seat of the family was at Wynnstay in Ruabon. The fifth baronet became so powerful locally that he was given the unofficial title of 'The Prince IN Wales'.

Wynnstay had passed into the possession of the Wynn family (as they were then known) through marriage. The estate, originally known simply as Rhiwabon, was owned by the Eyton family who later changed its name to "Watstay". On inheriting the estate, Sir Watkin Williams-Wynn took on the additional surname of Wynn and commissioned the building of a new mansion, to be known as Wynnstay, to replace the original building. The coat of arms of the Williams-Wynn family show an eagle with the Welsh motto "Eryr Eryrod Eryri", which translates into English as "The Eagle of Eagles of the Land of Eagles", the "Land of Eagles" being Snowdonia and reflecting the family's origins in that part of the scenic and beautiful Wales.

Chapter Five: Thomas Cholmondeley, 1ˢᵗ Lord Delamere of Vale Royal Abbey

Painting of Wynnstay in Wales (1793) by John Ingleby, courtesy of the National Library of Wales

Thomas Cholmondeley (1767-1855) is distinctly noted in English history as being the individual and member of the Vale Royal family line who in 1821 purchased the title of Baron (Lord) Delamere from the British Crown. This title had previously belonged to the well-known and locally established Booth family of Dunham Massey, Cheshire.

The first recorded use of the title "Lord [Baron] Delamere" [some records indicate Delamer] referring or related to an English family is in 1661, when King Charles II, who reigned from 1660 to 1685, had created this title for Sir George Booth (1622-1684) in return for his loyalty to the English Crown, because Sir George was well-known as a staunch Royalist during the Cromwell era. According to *The English Civil War*, Peter Gaunt (2014) informs us that:

> In April 1660, Booth was elected to the Convention Parliament. He was one of twelve MPs appointed to convey Parliament's invitation to Charles II, who was residing in The Hague in the Netherlands at the time, to return as King. On 13 July 1660, the House of Commons awarded Booth £20,000 as a reward for his services. This was reduced to £10,000 at his own request.

At the King's coronation in April 1661, Booth was made Lord Delamere with a license to create six new knights. The same year he was also appointed 'custos rotulorum' (principal justice of the peace in an English county who is also keeper of the rolls and records of the sessions of the peace) of Cheshire." According to this extract from *Encyclopedia Britannica,* regarding George Booth, 1st Baron Delamere of Dunham Massey in Cheshire:

> He was an English politician who led an abortive Royalist revolt against the Commonwealth government in August 1659. His insurrection foreshadowed the Royalist upsurge that resulted in the restoration of the Stuart monarchy in 1660.

This extract from the archives of the North Cheshire History Society reveals the following details about the Booth family:

> The Booth family of Dunham Massey can trace their ancestry back to early medieval times when their name appears in several different forms, including Bouth, Booths and Bothe. Around 1275 William de Booths had married Sibel, daughter of Sir Ralph de Brereton, in 1474 John Legh of Booths was married to Raufe Egerton, and by Tudor times, the family had married into most of the neighbouring aristocratic families. For example, Sir William Booth (1540-1579) married Elizabeth Warburton of Arley, and yet another George Booth (1515-1543) was married to Elizabeth de Trafford.
>
> One daughter of the family also married into the Grey family - it was of that same family that the unfortunate Lady Jane Grey came, before she fell prey to Henry VIII's axeman. Thus the family extended their influence and power base in the county. Certainly the Booths held many lands in the area around this time, as evidenced in the *House of Commons Journal* of the 30th July 1660, which passed "...a Bill to enable Sir George Booth Baronet to lease and sell Lands, for Payment of his Debts, and raising Portions for Advancement of his younger Children".
>
> This same Sir George Booth had fought for the Parliamentarian cause during the First Civil War and was elected MP for Cheshire in May 1645. He was also elected

Chapter Five: Thomas Cholmondeley, 1st Lord Delamere of Vale Royal Abbey

to the First Protectorate Parliament in 1654 and was commissioned to assist the Major-Generals in Cheshire. However, he appears to have fallen out of favour when he described them as 'Cromwell's hangmen' and by 1659 was plotting with Royalists to bring about the Restoration.

Sir George Booth lived in the area north of Chester, England, at Dunham Massey Hall, Dunham Massey in Cheshire. Sir George had a son and heir named Henry.

Dunham Massey Hall, Cheshire now owned by the National Trust, courtesy of Mike Peel

Henry Booth, (1652-1694) 2nd Lord Delamere and Earl of Warrington, was the son of Sir George who became the second Baron Delamere of Dunham Massey, was also created by King William, as the Earl of Warrington in 1690. Henry also had a son whom he named George (1688-1758) who also upon the death of his father Henry became 2nd Earl of Warrington and 3rd Lord (Baron) Delamere, but the Earldom became extinct in 1758 upon the death of George who had no male heir. [Earldoms can only pass to a direct male descendent, although legal steps are currently underway in 2018 to change this rule and government legislation.]

George's brother Nathaniel had taken up the title 4th Lord Delamere but this title also became extinct in 1770 upon the death

The Delamere Saga: Part 1

of Nathaniel, as the son of Nathaniel, also named Henry (1710-1784) refused to take up the title for personal and private reasons. This latter Henry Booth was legally entitled to the designation of "Lord Delamere", but not having any child born in wedlock he refused to claim the title, and the "Barony of Delamere" terminated in the person of Nathaniel the 4th Baron in 1770; and ownership of this esteemed title reverted back to the English Crown. From Parliamentary records and also detailed in *The History of the County Palatine and City of Chester* by George Ormerod (1882):

> This Henry Booth was Lord Delamere, but not having any child born in wedlock he refused to claim the title. A certain Miss Orrill of South Elkington lived with him to his death. She bore him two sons, John who lived and died at Louth and Henry Jnr, who is named upon his grave stone, who was killed by a fall from his Horse. The Father lived many years at Thorpe Hall.

The gravestone of the Booth family, records the following:

> Here lieth the Body of Henry BOOTH, Esqr, who died Feby the 13th 1784, aged 74. Also of Henry BOOTH, Junr who died May the 21st 1772 aged 24.

For our history addicts, this report was also submitted:

> It now appears that Sir George Booth (1622-1684) son of a Sir William Booth was created a Baronet (the lowest hereditary titled British Order. See report below called "The Peerage-Barons") and he was given the title 'Lord Delamere' on 20 April 1661 by King William of Orange.
>
> Sir George had a son named Henry (1652-1694) who eventually became 2nd Lord Delamere, but was also created Earl of Warrington in 1690 as a reward for his contributions toward the Crown. Henry was allowed to take over the title Lord Delamere by King William of Orange (1688-1702) in addition to being the Earl of Warrington. It is this Lord Delamere (Henry) who apparently accompanied King James the second (1685-1688) when he fled England and went to live in France on 23 December 1688, (they must have had catholic leanings) Henry Booth had also been arrested for being accused of being part of an 'anti-royalist

Chapter Five: Thomas Cholmondeley, 1ˢᵗ Lord Delamere of Vale Royal Abbey

plot' but was acquitted during the reign of King James the second (1685-1688) be royal influence.

This report also shows the bias of King James and the Court regarding this incident (*History of England, Book 4*, Chapter 18):

> Hundreds of the common people were sent to the gallows by common juries for the Rye House Plot and the Western Insurrection. One peer, and one alone, my Lord Delamere, who was brought at that time before the Court of the Lord High Steward; and he was acquitted. But, it is said, the evidence against him was legally insufficient. Be it so. So was the evidence against Sidney, against Cornish, against Alice Lisle; yet it sufficed to destroy them. But, it is said, the peers before whom my Lord Delamere was brought were selected with shameless unfairness by King James and by Judge Jeffreys (The Hanging Judge). Be it so. But this only proves that, under the worst possible King, and under the worst possible High Steward, a lord tried by lords has a better chance for life than a commoner who puts himself on his country."

The full details of this incident and resultant trial are revealed in *The Tryal of Henry Baron Delamere for High Treason* by George Lord Jeffreys (1685). Also read this revealing extract from the *Warrington Times* of 1659:

> Sir George Booth began his own unsuccessful attempt to restore the Stuart monarchy by declaring Charles II the king at Warrington.

One of our researchers points out that some incidents and events related to the life of a Lord or Baron Delamere are inaccurately recorded by some historians, linking them to the lives of the Cholmondeley family, Lords' Delamere of Vale Royal Abbey, when in fact these incidents should have been recorded and attributed to the Booth family members of Dunham Massey Hall, who also held this esteemed title, Lord (Baron) Delamere from 1661-1770, thus causing some confusion to students of Cheshire history.

For example, here are some brief accounts uncovered by our researchers. In *Floyd County, Virginia. A History of Its People and Places* by Amos D. Wood (1986), pps. 19-21:

George Booth, "The Settler". George Booth, the first of the family in America, was born in England about the year 1745, the son of an English earl. (His father must have been Henry (1710-1784) son of Nathaniel who refused to take up the title Lord Delamere at the death of Nathaniel in 1770) for reasons clarified in this archived report from St Andrews Church in Utterby, Lincolnshire, England.

The tradition in the family is that he was secreted on board a ship and sent to America as a teenage boy to save his life. When still at home in Cheshire, he and some neighbour boys were trying their strength, lifting a stone on the bank of a creek in which they had been bathing. George Booth moved the stone. It was learned later that this stone was a cornerstone to a plot of land. At that time in England it was a capital offense to move a "corner to land." He was often heard to say to his friends in America that he was born with a "silver spoon in his mouth," but it would never do him any good. He was a man of great energy, often making the trip on horseback from his home on Little River in Canton, New York, to the old family home further south in the State of New York, bringing back many droves of horses, which he turned out on the "range." He lived in the present county of Floyd, Virginia for many years and is buried on the land he took up. The names of only three of his children are known. They were: 1. Obadiah (this has not been verified). 2. Isaac. 3. Daniel.

We also discovered some interesting reports that fill out the life of Sir George Booth (1622-1684), his son Henry (1652-1694) and Grandson George (1688-1758). These documents are filed in the Archives of Rylands Library in Manchester, England and include the following.

> 1850–WINNINGTON is a township and pleasant village, containing several genteel residences in the Eddisbury Hundred, forming a suburb on the north west side of Northwich and extending about a mile from that place. It contains 597a, 1r. 16p. of land, and at the last census had 68 houses and 321 inhabitants; population in 1801: 196; in 1831: 256.
>
> For some time previous to the reign of Henry VIII, this

Chapter Five: Thomas Cholmondeley, 1ˢᵗ Lord Delamere of Vale Royal Abbey

place was held by a family that assumed the local name; in the latter part of which reign it passed in marriage with the heiress of Richard de Wynnington to Sir Peter Warburton, at a subsequent period, it passed in like manner to Richard Pennant, Esq., created Lord Penrhyn of the kingdom of Ireland, on whose death (1808), the estate was sold to the present proprietor, Sir J T Stanley-Bart. Winnington Hall, a large, stuccoed mansion, has nothing particularly striking in its appearance; the situation, however, is delightfully picturesque and romantic. The Hall is now the seat of Edward John Stanley, Baron Eddisbury.

A magnificent and costly poultry house, erected by Lord Penrhyn, is perhaps the most remarkable feature about the hall. During the lifetime of Lord Penrhyn, upwards of 600 head of poultry were usually kept. Winnington Bridge over the Weaver was the scene during the Civil War of a sharp conflict between the Parliamentary troops under Major-Gen. John Lambert, and the Royal forces, commanded by Sir George Booth, in which the latter were defeated.

Further records in the archives of Rylands Library in Manchester revealed the following about the Booth family:

We have a very large collection of papers of the Grey family, Earls of Stamford, and their predecessors from Dunham Massey Hall near Altrincham, Cheshire. The Grey family inherited Dunham Massey in the mid-18th century from the Booths, Earls of Warrington, who are also represented. The collection contains the personal papers of the Booth and Grey families; title deeds and settlements; important manorial records from the courts leet of the barony of Dunham Massey and the borough of Altrincham, the court leet with court baron for the manor of Bollin cum Norcliffe (Wilmslow), courts baron for the manors of Dunham Massey, Carrington and Ashton upon Mersey, and Altrincham fair court; household records including 18th- and 19th-century accounts and inventories, and correspondence relating to the restoration of Dunham Massey Hall; papers relating to local schools and charities; and large quantities of estate papers, principally from the 19th and 20th centuries, including deeds, leases, rentals, valuation books, rent ledgers, cash books, income and expenditure accounts, invoices and vouchers, plans and correspondence files. The deeds and other papers relate to properties in Altrincham, Ashley, Ashton upon Mersey, Bollin Fee (Wilmslow), Bollington, Bowdon, Carrington, Dunham Massey, Hale, Hattersley, Matley, Millington, Partington, Pownall Fee (Wilmslow), Sale, Stayley (Stalybridge), Thornton-le-Moors and Timperley in Cheshire, and Ashton-under-Lyne and Warrington in Lancashire.

Among the personal papers of the Booth family is an account roll of Sir Robert Booth as sheriff of Cheshire, c.1445-1450; a detailed compendium of family and estate accounts of Sir George Booth, 1648-1651/2; personal correspondence and accounts of George Booth, 2nd Earl of Warrington, 1693/4-1758; and papers of his daughter Mary, Countess of Stamford, relating to the construction of the Bridgewater Canal, 1758-1767. The personal papers of the 5th and 6th Earls of Stamford contain material relating to the lord lieutenancy of Cheshire, the magistracy and local militia, the defense of the county against possible French invasion and internal security measures in the late 18th and early 19th centuries, including printed matter relating to the Peterloo Massacre of 1819. (St. Peter's Square in Manchester) [see Appendix 8 regarding the Peterloo Massacre]. Among the papers of the 6th Earl of Stamford are colourful letters written by his son while on the Grand Tour in the 1820s.

There are also interesting manuscripts of, and papers pertaining to, the naturalist Gilbert White of Selborne (1720-1793) and other members of the White family who were relatives of the Booth family. Gilbert White, FRS (18 July 1720 - 26 June 1793) was a 'parson-naturalist', a pioneering English naturalist and ornithologist. He remained unmarried and a curate all his life. He is best known for his book, Natural History and Antiquities of Selborne. White is regarded by many as England's first ecologist, and one of those who shaped the modern attitude of respect for nature. For example he said of the lowly earthworm: 'Earthworms, though in appearance a small and despicable link in the chain of nature, yet, if lost, would make a lamentable chasm. Worms seem to be the great promoters of vegetation, which would proceed but lamely without them.'

Chapter Five: Thomas Cholmondeley, 1st Lord Delamere of Vale Royal Abbey

Additional papers are also archived, especially of the Lumsden family of Cheshire, related to the Booth family, concerning service in the East India Company and colonial life and administration before and during the Indian Mutiny; and papers of the Rev. William Grey, a missionary in Newfoundland, Canada, 1849-1853. There are other papers belonging to and relating to James Grant Lumsden, a civil servant in the East India Company who held various administrative and judicial positions within the Bombay presidency. These items contain many references to Indian affairs, including the Indian Mutiny. The majority of other papers concern purely family and personal matters, but they contain detailed descriptions of life in India in the 1830s and 1940s, and of the administrative structure of the Bombay Civil Service:

> The Grey family; Earls of Stamford, were related to the Lumsden family by the marriage in 1834 of Mary Grey (d. 1885), daughter of Rev Harry Grey (1783-1860), to James Grant Lumsden, son of Lieutenant Colonel James Lumsden. Mary Grey was the sister of Rev William Grey (1819-1872), the father of the 9th Earl of Stamford.
>
> The Lumsdens were descended from the ancient Lumsden family of Cushnie in Aberdeenshire, Scotland, whose pedigree appears in Burke's Landed Gentry (London: Harrison & Sons, 1898), vol. 1, p. 948. Several members of the Lumsden family served with the East India Company in India. John Lumsden, son of John Lumsden of Cushnie, was a director of the Company. His brother David Lumsden (1765-1823) rose to the rank of Lieutenant Colonel in the Company's Bengal Army, and another brother, Matthew (1777-1835), had charge of the East India Company's press office in Calcutta. A fourth brother, James (d. 1822), was Lieutenant Colonel of the 55th Regiment of Foot in the British Army. His sons, David (1812-1842) and John Richard (1808-1841), held the ranks of Lieutenant and Captain respectively in the Bengal Army. Their brother James Grant Lumsden (1807-1863) served the E.I.C. for over thirty years, holding various administrative and judicial positions in the Bombay presidency.
>
> Biographical information on members of the Lumsden family, who served in the East India Company, has kindly

been provided by Mr David Blake, European Manuscripts Curator, and British Library Oriental and India Office Collections, whose assistance is gratefully acknowledged.

Additional records archived at Rylands Library reveal that Sir George Booth was also very involved with James Scott, 1st Duke of Monmouth, and also known as 1st Duke of Buccleuch who was an English nobleman. Originally called James Crofts or James Fitzroy, he was born in Rotterdam in the Netherlands, the eldest illegitimate son of Charles II of England, Scotland and Ireland, 1660-1685, and his Welsh mistress Lucy Walter. The following account reveals these facts.

'The whole county is disloyal,' said the rector of Whitchurch, as James Scott, Duke of Monmouth, rode like a conqueror through Cheshire towns and villages in the autumn of 1682. Over 300 years ago it must indeed have seemed to many Cheshire folk that the spirit of Protestant rebellion was rising and that Monmouth, first-born of Charles II several illegitimate sons, might well be the next king. Traditional hostility to Popery had focused itself on the fact that the King's heir, James, Duke of York, was a Catholic.

Monmouth, a staunch Protestant, a gentleman and an idealist but not a very clever conspirator, had allowed himself to be manipulated by the scheming Lord Shaftsbury who dreamed of Protestant rebellion and the establishment of a new monarch with himself as the eminence grace. It was Shaftsbury who persuaded the Duke to embark on a tour of Cheshire to test popular feeling in the country—a tour which was to lead, ultimately, to Monmouth's exile, rebellion and execution as he was beheaded for treason on 15 July 1685. He rode into Nantwich to the ringing of church bells and accompanied by the Earl of Macclesfield with many aristocratic followers, all well mounted on horses with the finely embroidered saddles which showed them to be men of quality and substance. In the narrow streets and the market square of Nantwich people flung hats into the air and shouted 'Monmouth, Monmouth!'

The Duke was acknowledged by all who knew him to have been a personality of great charm. Samuel Pepys described him as 'A most pretty spark'. His darkly handsome features

Chapter Five: Thomas Cholmondeley, 1st Lord Delamere of Vale Royal Abbey

made him look remarkably like his father and added to his crowd appeal. In the square by the church several children said to be suffering from the 'King's Evil' (scrofula) were brought forward and he gently laid his hand on them. History does not record the results.

From Nantwich he progressed to Wallasey where he entertained himself in the local races and won the 12-stone plate. In the streets his victory caused some local disturbances when his supporters lit celebratory bonfires and his enemies promptly poured water on them. Monmouth excelled at several sports and knew well the popularity that this gained him with the crowd, so the next day he ran in foot races and played bowls. From Wallasey he went to Dunham Hall, near Altrincham, there to stay the night with Lord Delamere. The party dined with the doors of the hall wide open so that the populace might see him. From the crowd beyond the doors there were frequent shouts of 'A Monmouth, A Monmouth!'

This archived report in the *History of Parliament* also connects Sir George Booth, Baron Delamere with Sir Gilbert Ireland:

In 1654, Ireland was elected Member of Parliament for Lancashire in the First Protectorate Parliament, and was re-elected in 1656. In 1659, he was elected MP for Liverpool in the Third Protectorate Parliament. Gilbert Ireland was re-elected MP for Liverpool in April 1660 for the Convention Parliament. He was also knighted at the restoration to the throne of Charles II on 16 June 1660. In 1661 he was re-elected MP for Liverpool for the Cavalier Parliament and sat until his death in 1675. Gilbert Ireland was also Mayor of Liverpool in 1674 and in the same year he moved into Hale Manor House in Halton, Cheshire. During the turmoil of the mid 17th Century, Hale Manor was under the control of Gilbert Ireland, a Presbyterian and personal friend of Oliver Cromwell. The Irelands were a well-established Lancashire family of ancient descent having been involved in campaigns as far back as King John and several branches of the family held Manors at Lydiate, Garston, Warrington, Bewsey and elsewhere.

His father died when he was just 7 years and he was 18 when hostilities broke out in Manchester in 1642. Although the Hundred of West Derby, in which Hale was situated, initially supported the King, Gilbert was firmly behind the Parliamentarians. He married Margaret Ireland of Bewsey at Hale in 1646. A sundial, the pedestal of which remains in Hale Churchyard, was set up by him in this year, bearing his initials and date 1646 on the dial plate.

Gilbert Ireland began a successful career in Parliament under Cromwell. In 1646, when the Presbyterian classes had been established in Lancashire, he became a lay elder of several Lancashire Parishes and was appointed High Sheriff of Lancashire in 1648 at the relatively young age of 24. In 1654, after the dissolution of the Barebones or Little Parliament, Gilbert was elected as a member for Lancashire in the new Parliament and a year later was appointed Governor of Liverpool, a difficult task in a time when opinions were divided as to the continuance of Cromwell's Government. In Parliament he made his voice heard over the arrears of the Cheshire Brigade, which had joined the fight at Worcester in 1651 and had only been given a part of their pay. The issue was successfully resolved. In 1657 Gilbert supported the proposal to make Cromwell King, but the following year Cromwell was dead and his son Richard became Protector. By 1659 there was growing discontent with Richard Cromwell's Government and Gilbert was involved in a debate concerning the restoration of the Monarch. On 20th August of the same year, Gilbert marched with Sir George Booth to Winnington in Cheshire where a battle ensued against government forces. The outcome was a disaster for Gilbert who was imprisoned in Chester Castle."

Our researchers also uncovered this archived report regarding the *History of Colonel Robert Dukinfield*, who came from Dukinfield in North East Cheshire. During the Civil War he was one of the leading parliamentarians in the Civil War. He defended Stockport Bridge against Prince Rupert and conducted the siege of Wythenshawe. He became High Sheriff of Cheshire in 1625. In 1650, during the Commonwealth period he was made the Governor of Chester. The following year he was a member of the court martial that sentenced the Earl of Derby, a Royalist Commander, to death who had been taken prisoner at Nantwich in 1651 and later beheaded

Chapter Five: Thomas Cholmondeley, 1st Lord Delamere of Vale Royal Abbey

at Bolton, Lancashire. Lord Derby had estates in the Isle of Man and Robert Dukinfield was sent out as the head of an expeditionary force to the island against Charlotte Stanley, widow of the Earl of Derby, where the Countess of Derby and her staff had been evacuated. She surrendered the island after receiving a letter from the Earl noting "that the Colonel (Dukinfield), being so much of a gentleman born, will doubtless, for his own honour, deal fairly with you." "Towards the end of the Commonwealth, there was a rebellion against Richard Cromwell, led by Sir George Booth of Dunham Massey. Booth had also been a leading supporter of the parliamentary cause but became disillusioned with the new dictatorship. Robert Dukinfield was the main commander involved in suppressing this rebellion. He lived to see the Restoration and the Glorious Revolution of William and Mary. His son, also Robert, was made a baronet shortly after the Restoration. Colonel Robert Dukinfield died at Dukinfield Hall in 1689, aged 70.

One additional fascinating story was discovered in the local archives of the *Stalybridge and District Chronicle*:

> Once a handsome medieval home in Stalybridge, Staley Hall has been left a pitiful wreck by red tape and recession.
>
> If there were an equivalent of the European Court of Human Rights for buildings, the case of Staley Hall, in Greater Manchester, would be one of its 'causes célèbres'. Wander on to a scraggy foothill of the Pennines a mile north of Stalybridge and you can hardly fail to be moved by the horror of the scene. You have to approach quite close before you realise that this blackened outcrop of hell was once a house. Roofless and windowless, its gables half-crumbled and its north-west wing all but vanished; it looks as if it has just suffered a sharp kick in the groin from the storm trooper of a pylon which stands yards away. Brave the threat of falling masonry to wander inside and it becomes obvious that the building only stands at all thanks to the maze of joists and telegraph poles that has been erected to hold it up. Every so often you come across a lump of soggy clay: the dissolved remains, it turns out, of a section of wattle and daub wall. Between the stumps of bramble bushes lie crisp packets and the odd condom left behind by local youths.

The Delamere Saga: Part 1

The building started out as a medieval hall house erected in 1343 by Sir Ralph de Staveley, in what would then have been a lush and rural part of Cheshire. It was remodeled and faced with stone and mullion windows in the mid-17th century under the ownership of Sir George Booth, a parliamentarian who had become disillusioned with Cromwell and led the failed Cheshire Rebellion of 1659. A stone tablet on the front elevation commemorates the visit of John Wesley on November 7, 1745. Wesley stayed the night and, according to the tablet, succeeded where the Church of England had failed: "His preaching so inclined the hearts of the people towards religion, that in it, can be traced the beginnings of Public Worship in Staleybridge."

Thereafter, however, the importance of the building declined. In the 18th century, the Booths married into the Grey family, who had a grander home on the other side of Manchester, and Staley Hall fell from being an ancestral pile to a tenanted farmhouse. By the mid-19th century, the building appears to have developed structural problems. The tenant farmers moved into an adjoining cottage and the hall was propped up with brick pillars. At the same time, it appears that its flagstone floor was removed, and the hall was turned into a barn.

From the church records of the village of Stretton-on-Dunsmore located just outside Coventry, Warwickshire, the following is also recorded regarding a Lord Delamere [also confirmed in the records of the *History of Cheshire* by George Ormerod (1785-1873) published in three volumes in 1819]:

> The Dunsmore remained desolate and sparsely populated for centuries. Until the middle of the 18th century, maps show little more than a track across the heath. John Booth's survey carried out in 1763 for Lord Montagu refers to it as the Chester Road. With little habitation, the area developed a bad reputation as the scene of much highway robbery. A traveller's journal in 1650 records 'passing through robbers to Dunchurch, with its townsfolk of plundering and gluttonous fame'. In 1686 one Jonathan Simpson robbed Lord Delamere (This must have been Henry Booth (1652-1694), also Earl of Warrington) of 350 guineas, together with 'innumerable drovers, pedlars and market people' along the road and was executed the next year aged thirty two.'

Chapter Five: Thomas Cholmondeley, 1st Lord Delamere of Vale Royal Abbey

Jonathan Simpson was the son of a very wealthy inhabitant of Launceston, in Cornwall, and his father put him as apprentice to a linen-draper in Bristol when he was about fourteen years of age. When he had served out his time, which he did with reputation, the same indulgent father gave him fifteen hundred pounds to set up with in the city, where he was free, and where he soon fell into great business and got money apace. No sooner had Simpson wasted all his substance but he was apprehended and condemned at the Old Bailey for a robbery on the highway, and he must certainly have swung for it if some of his rich relations had not procured him a reprieve from above. It came when he was at Tyburn, with the halter about his neck, and just ready to be turned off in company with several others. As he was riding back to Newgate behind one of the sheriff's officers, the officer asked him if he thought anything of a reprieve when he came to the gallows. "No more," said Simpson, 'than I thought of my dying day.' A very pretty expression at that time!

When he was brought to the prison door, the turnkey refused to receive him, telling the officer that, as he was sent to be executed, they were discharged of him, and would not have anything to do with him again, unless there was a fresh warrant for his commitment; whereupon Simpson made this reflection: 'What an unhappy cast-off dog am I, that both Tyburn and Newgate should in one day refuse to entertain me! Well, I'll mend my manners for the future, and try whether I can't merit a reception at them both the next time I am brought hither.' He was as good as his word; for it was believed he committed above forty robberies in the county of Middlesex within six weeks after his discharge.

Another time he had robbed the Lord Delamere on Dunsmoor Heath of three hundred and fifty guineas, persuading his lordship first to send away all his attendants, on sham pretence of two highwaymen that were just before who had robbed him of forty pounds. This action made his lordship swear never to do a good-natured deed again to a stranger. The robberies he committed on drovers, pedlars, market-people, etc., were almost innumerable. He stopped in one day nineteen of those people between London and Barnet, and took from them above two hundred pounds.

He even ventured to attack the Duke of Berwick, natural son to King James II., and take from him his watch, rings and money, amounting in all to a great value. The report concludes he was a 'Highwayman who was witty with a Halter round his Neck and, being reprieved, found that Newgate would not have him. He was finally executed on the 8th of September, 1686.'

It is of interest to note that the Booth family name in later years became world famous, as it was a later descendant of the Booth family of Cheshire, namely William Booth, who established in 1865 the world famous 'Salvation Army'. Today the Salvation Army boasts almost two million members and performs extraordinary charitable work world-wide. The title and designation, Baron (Lord) Delamere, relinquished by the Booth family in 1770, was revived again in 1821 by the Vale Royal Abbey, branch of the Cholmondeley family.

Portrait of Thomas Cholmondeley, 1st Baron (Lord) Delamere (1767-1855) astride a dappled grey hunter with Vale Royal Abbey in the background, courtesy of the National Archives, London

Chapter Five: Thomas Cholmondeley, 1ˢᵗ Lord Delamere of Vale Royal Abbey

Thomas Cholmondeley (1767-1855) acceded to the title of Baron [Lord] Delamere (of Vale Royal Abbey) by purchasing the Barony Title, forfeited by the Booth family in 1770 from the English Crown for £5000 in 1821 [which, by the way, is the equivalent of over £5 million today in 2018] he actually overpaid for the title as it was originally offered at only £1200, but other prominent wealthy individuals in the regions of Cheshire and Lancashire were also bidding for this title because of its influential and very useful connotation related to the far-reaching and very well-known Delamere Forest area of Cheshire; known and admired throughout the whole of England, plus its important connection with the Norman conquest of 1066 [this was the 11th-century invasion and occupation of England by an army of Norman, Breton, and French soldiers led by Duke William II of Normandy, later styled William the Conqueror], and also because of the great prestige and power this prominent, esteemed title Lord Delamere would carry. But Thomas Cholmondeley, being who he was; an indomitable character, enterprisingly thought the title was truly worth the price he had paid, and he was indeed proved to be right in his perception.

Although the archived family records do not reveal the precise motive of Thomas Cholmondeley behind his decision to purchase this title, Baron Delamere, from the British Crown in 1821; but it would seem reasonable to assume that because he had inherited and now owned the Great House and Estate at Vale Royal Abbey, plus all the surrounding land, including the vast prestigious Delamere Forest, and now also being one of the most prominent and wealthiest land owners in Cheshire; if not the whole of England, perhaps also because his distant cousins, the Cholmondeley family of Cholmondeley Castle had a title. They had also recently built the very impressive (although somewhat incongruous) mock-gothic Castle in 1801-1804, likewise, why should not he—being Cheshire's leading citizen, the "one and only" Thomas Cholmondeley of Vale Royal *Abbey*—also now be titled? Let us remember that at this time in history he was also the Sheriff of Chester and MP for Cheshire.

The Delamere Saga: Part 1

The Coronation of King George IV at Westminster Abbey on 19 July 1821, courtesy of the British Museum, London

Thomas Cholmondeley thus became the 1st [Baron] Lord Delamere of Vale Royal Abbey on 19 July 1821 and had his name entered into the list of British Peers [House of Lords] at the coronation of King George IV of the United Kingdom, which was one of the most magnificent, illustrious and also the most expensive coronation in English history. This great, historic event and the extravagant related ceremony would have perfectly suited Thomas Cholmondeley and his taste for being a celebrity, plus this event would permanently establish his claim as an outstanding, notable, titled character in the whole of England.

Regarding this great and magnificent event when Thomas Cholmondeley accepted the title of "Lord Delamere" in 1821 from King George IV, read the report from the "Georgian Index Files" of Cambridge University and *Anecdotes of John Manders*: Book No. 7, 1820-1829, pps. 964-967:

> George Augustus Frederick Hanover became King George IV of England on the death of his father George III on

Chapter Five: Thomas Cholmondeley, 1ˢᵗ Lord Delamere of Vale Royal Abbey

January 29th 1820. His Coronation was not held until July 19th 1821. George IV greatly enjoyed planning events. His Coronation would be his grandest. He wished to outshine Napoleon's coronation. The new king selected costumes for all the participants that were inspired by Tudor styles. He spent £24,000 on a Coronation robe of crimson velvet with gold stars and ermine trim costing £855 with a train that stretched 27 feet. George IV was determined to have a magnificent Coronation that would outshine Napoleon's Coronation of 1804. Parliament had voted £100,000 for the costs in 1820. An additional sum of £138,238.0s.2d paid 'out of Money received from France on Account of pecuniary Indemnity, under Treaty, Anno 1815', made a total £238,238. 0s. 2d, which amounted to the most expensive coronation ever held in British History.

The Coronation Banquet for three hundred guests at Westminster Hall was served by a procession of household Officials and Gentlemen Pensioners. Some of the dishes served were: soups including turtle, salmon, turbot, and trout, venison and veal, mutton and beef, braised ham and savoury pies, daubed geese and braised capon, lobster and crayfish, cold roast fowl and cold lamb, potatoes, peas and cauliflower. There were mounted pastries, dishes of jellies and creams, over a thousand side dishes, nearly five hundred sauce boats brimming with lobster sauce, butter sauce and mint. The peers and bishops having had nothing to eat since breakfast turned to their plates with relish. The guest's wives and children could only look on from the galleries built for the occasion. One peer at least tied a capon in his handkerchief and tossed it up to his famished family.

This acquisition of the title Lord Delamere, in 1821, from the Crown was not without protest, as many thought the choice of the recipient, Thomas Cholmondeley of Vale Royal Abbey was inappropriate. Read this extract from *Peerage for the People* by William Carpenter (1837):

> This is a branch of the same family as the Marquis of Cholmondeley, and the Marquis and the Baron are kindred in politics as well as in blood. The Peerage was conferred upon the present Baron by Lord Liverpool, in 1821; and he has uniformly justified the selection made by the Minister, in

an uncompromising opposition to every measure of reform and political amelioration.

Thomas Cholmondeley (1st Lord Delamere of Vale Royal Abbey, 1767-1855) also after his success of achieving his new position in the English aristocracy, apparently spent massive amounts of the family funds inherited from the Holford family through his Great, Great, Grandmother, Mary Cholmondeley (nee Holford); funds that he used to extravagantly refurbish, buy more works of art, antiques and valuable books for the ever increasing extensive library and to also further renovate and extend the Great House and Great Hall at Vale Royal Abbey. These family funds he used with an honest, honorable purpose and also with a pure motive, according to the records and private letters at that time. The wife of Thomas, Henrietta Elizabeth was also an expert, plus an avid collector of antiques and she also played a vital role in this field of expertise, assisting her husband Thomas in his quest to enrich the family acquisitions to be proudly displayed at Vale Royal Abbey. The reputation and grandeur of Vale Royal Abbey was increasing by the day, and was now enjoying pride of place as being known throughout the land as the prime locale to be invited as a special guest.

One regular special guest and visitor to Vale Royal Abbey at this time was the flamboyant George Bryan Brummell, more well-known by his nickname, 'Beau' Brummell (1778-1840), a personal friend of Thomas Cholmondeley. Beau Brummell was an iconic figure in Regency England and the arbiter of men's fashion, plus he was also a personal friend of the Prince Regent, the future King George IV, but was very nonchalant in his attitude toward the British aristocracy. He goes down in history as having established the mode of dress for men that rejected the overly ornate fashions for one of understated, but perfectly fitted and tailored bespoke garments. This look was based on dark coats, full-length trousers rather than knee breeches and stockings, and above all immaculate shirt linen and an elaborately knotted cravat.

Brummell was born in London, the younger son of William Brummell, a politician, of Donnington Grove in Berkshire. The family was middle class, but the elder Brummell was ambitious for his son to become a prominent gentleman, and young George was raised with that clear understanding. George Brummell was of

Chapter Five: Thomas Cholmondeley, 1st Lord Delamere of Vale Royal Abbey

course appropriately educated at the prestigious Eton College in Windsor near London and personally knew the Cholmondeley boys for many years, who also had attended Eton, and he made his precocious mark on fashion when he not only modernised the white stock, or cravat, that became and was eventually the mark of the Eton college boy.

Brummell's friendship with, and influence over, the Prince Regent, George, the son of King George III, known as the Prince of Wales, continued for a number of years. His simple yet elegant and understated manner of dress, coupled with his natural wit, gained him entry to the Prince's society and his personal friends.

George Bryan (Beau) Brummell by Richard Dighton in (1805), courtesy of the National Archives, London

The life and the daily routine of most aristocratic men of the time included making one's toilette and shopping in the morning; riding in Hyde Park or making the round of gentlemen's clubs in the afternoon; followed by the theatre, then gambling at Almack's (Almack's was the name of a number of establishments and social clubs in London between the 18th and 20th centuries, privately financed by many leading politicians of the day) or perhaps a private party, or maybe, if so inclined, visiting the brothels, also patronised by many leading politicians in the evening. These contacts and connections also greatly benefitted Thomas Cholmondeley, 1st Lord Delamere, based on their long-standing mutual friendship.

In 1816, "Beau" Brummell, owing thousands of pounds, had fled to France to escape debtor's prison. Usually Brummell's gambling obligations, as "debts of honor", were always paid immediately, by who still remains a mystery to this day and our intense research revealed absolutely nothing. The one exception to this was the final wager, dated March 1815 in White's betting book, which was marked "not paid, 20th January, 1816".

White's is the oldest gentleman's club in London, founded in 1693, and is widely considered to be the most exclusive private club in the world, plus being the 'unofficial' headquarters of the Tory political party and both Beau Brummell and Thomas Cholmondeley were prominent members. It is well-known, especially in London, because in the past it operated and controlled what was known as its "Betting Book".

To quote from *Regency Wagers* by Liz Hanbury:

> The men at White's not only betted on anything and everything, but registered their transactions in black and white. Members of the club betted on births, deaths, marriages, the length of life of their friends, on the shock of an earthquake or anything else that took their fancy. Gambling was a passion in Regency times. It dominated society in London (and elsewhere) from Queen Anne's time until the start of the Victorian era. Gambling for high and sometimes ruinous stakes was at its zenith in the late eighteenth century, but it continued into the Regency period. Men and women indulged in gambling and not only for fun. For many, it was a serious business and a very serious addiction. Gambling was made illegal in the 18th century, as was the act of keeping a house or establishment for prohibited gaming, in practice, however, the wealthy and influential clientele of the clubs, assisted by their very clever lawyers, ensured that they were protected from the law.

Brummell lived the remainder of his life in French exile, spending ten years in Calais without an official passport before acquiring an appointment to the consulate at Caen in Normandy, France, through the influence of Lord Alvanley, who was a prominent Regency buck and member of the Prince Regent's circle, and was a friend of Beau Brummell) and the Marquess of Worcester. [Henry Somerset, who was also known as 7th Duke of Beaufort, was also a personal friend of Beau Brummell and Thomas Cholmondeley.] This appointment provided him with a small annuity but lasted only two years, when the Foreign Office in London accepted Brummell's recommendation to abolish the consulate. He had made this recommendation in the hope of being appointed to a more remunerative position overseas, but no new position was forthcoming to the now very distressed and worried

Chapter Five: Thomas Cholmondeley, 1ˢᵗ Lord Delamere of Vale Royal Abbey

Beau Brummell.

Rapidly running out of money and he had grown increasingly slovenly in his dress, Brummell was forced into debtors' prison by his long-unpaid Calais creditors; only through the charitable intervention of some of his friends in England [probably including Thomas Cholmondeley, 1ˢᵗ Lord Delamere, from records of the time] was he able to secure release. In 1840 Brummell died penniless and insane from syphilis at Le Bon Sauveur Asylum on the outskirts of Caen in France; he was 61 years.

Another outstanding, well-known visitor to Vale Royal Abbey in 1814 was George Gordon Byron, 6ᵗʰ Baron Byron, commonly known simply as 'Lord Byron'. Lord Byron was regarded as one of the greatest British poets and writers that ever lived; his works still remain widely read and are influential even to this day. Among his best-known works are the lengthy narrative poems, "Don Juan" and "Childe Harold's Pilgrimage", and especially the outstanding short lyric poem, "She Walks in Beauty".

Lord Byron travelled extensively across Europe, especially in Italy, where he lived for seven years in Venice, Ravenna and Pisa, where he also had a chance to frequently visit his friend the famous poet Percy Bysshe Shelley. Later, Byron joined the Greek War of Independence fighting the Ottoman Empire, for which Greeks even today revere him as a national hero. He died in 1824 at only 36 years from a fever contracted while in Missolonghi, Western Greece.

Often described as the most flamboyant and notorious of the major Romantics, Byron was both celebrated and castigated in life for his aristocratic excesses, including huge debts, numerous love affairs—with men as well as women, as well as rumours of a scandalous liaison with his half-sister, and of course his self-imposed exile in 1816.

From old archived letters and records of Vale Royal Abbey, it appears that the invitation for Lord Byron to spend a few days at the Great House in Cheshire was at the request of Henrietta Elizabeth the wife of Thomas Cholmondeley [eventually to become the 1ˢᵗ Lord Delamere in 1821], as she, through her father, Sir Watkin Williams-Wynn, personally knew the late father of Lord Byron, namely John (Mad-Jack) Byron, a British Army Officer, and Henrietta Elizabeth was so full of admiration for the early works of

Lord Byron, plus what she had read and heard about his exciting, flamboyant lifestyle. As they were also of a similar age, she wished to meet him and exchange notes, plus other private notional and mutual ideas.

On his visit in 1814, it appears that Lord Byron presented Henrietta Elizabeth with a hand written copy of his latest poem, "She Walks in Beauty" and although it is said to have been inspired by another event in Byron's life earlier that year, while at a ball in London, where Byron had met Anne Beatrix Wilmot, his cousin by marriage through Robert Wilmot. She was in mourning, wearing a black dress set with spangles, as described in the opening lines of his poem.

She Walks in Beauty

She walks in beauty, like the night
Of cloudless climes and starry skies;
And all that's best of dark and bright
Meet in her aspect and her eyes:
Thus mellow'd to that tender light
Which heaven to gaudy day denies.

One shade the more, one ray the less,
Had half impaired the nameless grace
Which waves in every raven tress,
Or softly lightens o'er her face;
Where thoughts serenely sweet express
How pure, how dear their dwelling-place.

And on that cheek, and o'er that brow,
So soft, so calm, yet eloquent,
The smiles that win, the tints that glow,
But tell of days in goodness spent,
A mind at peace with all below,
A heart whose love is innocent!

(Courtesy of the Lord Byron Trust)

Chapter Five: Thomas Cholmondeley, 1st Lord Delamere of Vale Royal Abbey

During those five days in 1814 when Lord Byron made a private visit to Henrietta Elizabeth Cholmondeley at Vale Royal Abbey, apparently at the personal request of Henrietta, it is also rumored that Lord Byron personally signed a hand written copy of his new poem, "She Walks in Beauty" and especially noteworthy is that he had privately dedicated it to Henrietta, also expressing and endorsing in his own handwriting, his personal sentiments regarding her outstanding beauty. If this is so, then whoever owns this hand written copy today, containing the signature of Lord Byron and his personal sentiments for his now close intimate friend, Henrietta Elizabeth Cholmondeley, written in his own hand, is truly blessed and very fortunate, as this document once held 'pride of place' amongst the many other valuable books and manuscripts held in the Vale Royal Abbey library.

Portrait of Lord Byron (1788-1824), courtesy of the Poets Foundation, USA

This valuable, precious copy of this world famous poem by Lord Byron, which was once displayed prominently in a glass case, according to records, was, along with all the other assets held in this expansive, impressive library, sold off in the early 1900s, when a later descendant of the Cholmondeley family, broke up, cleared out and disposed of this valuable private library. All its contents at Vale Royal Abbey were sold off in 'job lots' at a public auction. This original hand written copy of Lord Byron's poem, if it still exists, was sold, possibly being unnoticed for what it truly was, during this 'no-reserve' clearance auction. Today, it would be truly priceless.

Although Lord Byron kept a detailed journal in which he recorded most of his travels and adventures, there is no mention of these special five days that he stayed at paradisaical Vale Royal

Abbey estate in the intimate companionship of his lifetime friend and admirer, Henrietta Elizabeth Cholmondeley. The most likely explanation for this omission is that the husband of Henrietta, namely Thomas, the future Lord Delamere, who was absent in London for the whole of these five days, taking care of his duties as Member of Parliament for Cheshire, plus his other distractions of course, wished to avoid possible embarrassment for Henrietta, who was later to become the famous 'Lady Delamere', when her husband purchased this honoured title in 1821 from the British Crown.

Lord Byron, in view of his questionable reputation with women, especially women belonging to the aristocracy, may also have sought to protect the honour of Henrietta and her position in society by omitting any mention of this in his journals. We will probably never know the full truth

However on reflection, with romantic incidents like this in its history, possibly involving Lord Byron and Henrietta it is no wonder that today, Vale Royal Abbey is now well-known as a place and location of romance and love, and this aurora still permeates the atmosphere of the place even today, as demonstrated by the numerous weddings that now take place at the privately owned Vale Royal Abbey today. Quoting from the current website of the Vale Royal Abbey Golf Club: "Flower clad walkways, formal gardens, panoramic views and a serene lake all help to create a truly picturesque setting that speaks of romance."

When Byron's great-uncle, William the 5th Lord Byron, died on 21 May 1798, the ten-year-old boy, George Gordon Byron, became the 6th Baron Byron of Rochdale (the name of a town adjacent to Royton in Lancashire), and he also inherited the ancestral home, Newstead Abbey, in Nottinghamshire, a partial ruin according to records of 1798. The young Lord Byron very soon moved to Newstead Abbey with his mother and he was greatly impressed by the large estate, according to records of the time. No doubt the scale and size of the estate contributed to Byron's extravagant taste and sense of his own importance. However, we remind ourselves, no less impressive was the scale of the many problems that needed attention at Newstead Abbey, where the yearly income had fallen to just about £800 and many urgent repairs to the main dwelling house were desperately needed. He and his mother, after realizing

Chapter Five: Thomas Cholmondeley, 1ˢᵗ Lord Delamere of Vale Royal Abbey

the scope of the work and major improvements required, very soon moved to the nearby city of Nottingham and neither of them ever lived permanently at Newstead Abbey for any extended period. The Abbey today, ironically still a partial ruin, is now publicly owned by Nottingham City Council, and houses a small, somewhat limited museum containing some Byron memorabilia (see Appendix 5).

Royton Hall in Lancashire is approximately three miles from the much larger town of Rochdale (see Appendix 6) and had been the home for over 400 years of 12 generations of the Byron family, but they sold the Hall in 1622, according to the 'Royton Local History Society', by which time Lord Byron had now inherited the large estate at Newstead Abbey in Nottinghamshire. The vibrant, historic town of Royton today still echoes with the name of Byron, for example, Byron Street, Byron School, and Byron Gardens (see Appendix 7).

The Poetry Foundation commented on Lord Byron and his death in 1824:

> On 9 April, having been soaked by a heavy rain while out riding, Byron suffered fever and rheumatic pains. By the twelfth he was seriously ill. Repeated bleedings, which he initially resisted, further debilitated him. On Easter Sunday, he entered a comatose state. At six o'clock on the evening of Easter Monday, 19 April 1824, during a violent electrical storm, Byron died.
>
> In memorial services throughout the country, he was proclaimed a national hero of Greece. His death proved effective in uniting Greece against the enemy and in eliciting support for its struggle from all parts of the civilized world. In October 1827 British, French, and Russian forces destroyed the Turkish and Egyptian fleets at Navarino, assuring Greek independence, which was acknowledged by the sultan in 1829.
>
> Byron's body arrived in England on 29 June, and for two days lay in state in a house in Great George Street, London. On Friday, 16 July 1824, Lord Byron was buried in the family vault beneath the chancel of Hucknall, Torkard Church near Newstead Abbey.

Returning to Vale Royal Abbey and its intriguing history we are reminded that the most outstanding contribution made by Thomas,

The Delamere Saga: Part 1

1st Lord Delamere, to the Vale Royal Abbey and the surrounding land, was especially beautifying and improving Delamere Forest, which is now a living permanent record of his skillful horticultural management and today, Delamere Forest is listed as one of the most desirable natural areas to visit in the whole of England. For this outstanding dedication and hard work by Thomas Cholmondeley, as related to Delamere Forest in Cheshire, we must be forever grateful.

To quote from the article "History of Delamere Forest" in the *National Geographic*:

> Delamere Forest had been donated by the crown to the grandson of Lady Cholmondeley, who was Charles Cholmondeley, MP (1684-1756) father of Thomas Cholmondeley, MP (1726-1779). The reason for the gift to the family was because of the support to the crown as Royalists, and the then King William the Third (William of Orange) (1688 - 1702) made rewards of this kind for loyalty.

Delamere Forest today is a large wooded area near the small market town of Frodsham, and adjacent to the Vale Royal Abbey. The woodland, which is carefully managed today by the Forestry Commission, covers an area of 972 hectares (2,400 acres) making it the largest area of woodland in the county. It contains a mixture of deciduous and evergreen trees.

'Delamere', which means "forest of the lakes" is all that remains of the great Forests of Mara and Mondrem, which covered over 60 square miles (160 km^2) in this part of the beautiful county of Cheshire in England. Established in the late 11th century, they were the hunting forests of the Norman Earls of Chester. Order was maintained under forest law. However this governance limited the agricultural potential of the area for centuries. It was not until ownership passed back to 'The Crown' in 1912 that the ancient ordnances were abolished. In 1924 the woodland thankfully came under the direct control of the Forestry Commission.

Being of French origin, the name basically means "of the water". The earliest record of use is by a French (Normandy) family "De Le Mere" and records exist of a Norman De La Mere, a French Baron who lived in Castle De La Mere (the castle still exists but is now a ruin in France) and was referred to as the "Castle

Chapter Five: Thomas Cholmondeley, 1st Lord Delamere of Vale Royal Abbey

on the Lake". The surname is still used today, plus its derivations and slight modifications, i.e. De La Mare, Delamere, Delamore and Delemerc.

The area of Delamere Forest includes Old Pale Hill, the high point of the northern mass of the Mid Cheshire Ridge, and Blakemere Moss, a lake approximately 1 km (0.62 of a mile) in length. Black Lake, a rare example of quaking bog or 'schwingmoor', has been designated a 'Site of Special Scientific Interest (SSSI)' and forms part of an international Ramsar site; Linmer Moss has also been designated an 'SSSI' for its fenland habitat. The white-faced darter, a species of dragonfly rare in the UK, and marsh fern and white sedge, wetland plants that are rare in Cheshire, are found here in Delamere Forest.[14]

Delamere Forest also encompasses broadleaved and mixed woodlands, blocks of coniferous plantation, as well as grassland and wetland. The area provides a habitat for numerous woodland bird species, including nuthatches, tree-creepers, crossbills, pine siskins, tawny owls and great spotted and green woodpeckers. Dragonflies such as the 'southern hawker' can be seen in the wetland areas; the nationally scarce 'white-faced darter' has been observed at several sites within the forest, including Black Lake. Butterflies such as the small tortoiseshell are common in the Old Pale area. Adders have been observed in the woodland, and mammals seen here include badgers, foxes and bats.

Quoting from the *Local Rural Cheshire Magazine* we read:

> Delamere takes its name from the ancient 'De la Mara', which means Forest of the Meres. The forest, which is managed by the Forestry Commission, comprises over 1000 hectares of mixed broadleaf and conifer woodlands, interlinked with a mosaic of open meres, mosses and heaths. The diverse nature of the area, ranging from mature woodlands through young plantations to open areas provides a haven for wildlife with diverse habitats for a wide variety of species.

---

[14] A Ramsar Site is a wetland site designated of international importance under the Ramsar Convention. The Convention on Wetlands, known as the Ramsar Convention, is an intergovernmental environmental treaty established in 1971 by UNESCO, named after the city of Ramsar in Iran, and coming into force in 1975. It provides for national action and international cooperation regarding the conservation of wetlands, and wise sustainable use of their resources. Ramsar identifies wetlands of international importance, especially those providing waterfowl habitat.

The Delamere Saga: Part 1

A view of Delamere Forest, courtesy of the *Chester Chronicle*

This report from a local Cheshire newspaper about "Wicken Tree Farm" is also of interest to the background of Delamere Forest:

> The property of Wicken Tree Farm dating in parts from 1711 and earlier times, is set within the Delamere Forest, Vale Royal area of Cheshire, which has long been regarded by many visitors as some of the most scenic in the county, much favored by tourists, visitors and home buyers wishing to view, walk and live in Delamere, an area of prestigious outstanding natural beauty, yet extremely accessible to Chester, Manchester, Liverpool and the airports, including all the commercial centre's of the North West via the motorway links.

The clearing at Wicken Tree was one of the first to be formed in this area of the ancient Delamere Forest, although the recent road sign denotes Hatchmere, it is actually part of the village of Norley. Wicken Tree Farm is in Blakemere Lane. Delamere Forest in Cheshire once stretched from Liverpool in the north to Wolverhampton in the south and was used originally as royal hunting grounds, the Donn family in particular ruled as the head foresters for approximately 500 years. A detailed account of the lives and fortunes of 16 generations of the Donn Family of Cheshire

Chapter Five: Thomas Cholmondeley, 1st Lord Delamere of Vale Royal Abbey

from Richard de Donne (1190-1240) to Mary Donn (1604-1690) exists in the archives at Ryland's Library in Manchester. As Master Foresters of Delamere Forest, Commanders of the famed Cheshire Archers, Knights of the Shire, plus Sheriffs and Constables of Chester, they played an important role in the history of Cheshire and of England during the 500 years from the Early Middle Ages to approximately 1690. We quote from an extract from the book by R. M. Bevan, *The Donnes*:

> 'Forest de la Mare' (Delamere Forest) was a Royal hunting ground, jealously guarded through harsh and cruel laws introduced by William the Conqueror to ensure that all hunting and game preservation remained vested in the Crown. Miscreants, normally the peasantry, were dealt with severely and anyone caught in the act of poaching faced short shrift on the end of a rope.
>
> The Crown's representative in the forest and holding almost exclusive powers over life and death was the hereditary Master Forester and Chief Bowbearer, the first of whom was Ralph (Ranulph) de Kingsley who was granted the title in 1123 by the 3rd Earl of Chester. The symbol of his authority was a black horn that came to be known as the 'Delamere Horn'.
>
> Through marriage and inheritance, the office of Master Forester passed to Henry Donn, of Utkinton, and remained in the Donn family for over four-hundred years. Sir John Donn (1577-1629), the 19th Master Forester, was actually knighted at Utkinton Hall, in 1617, by King James I, following a day's hunting in the forest. 'Arise Sir John—a gentleman very complete in many excellencies of nature, wit and ingenuity.'
>
> The last of the true Donnes associated with the Master Forestership was Mary Donn who married into the influential Crewe family. Her son, Sir John Crewe, became the 23rd Master Forester. Through the female line the title and estates then passed into the Arden family whose best known son was Richard Pepper Arden, Chief Justice of the Court of Common Pleas, who, in 1801, became Baron Alvanley, of Alvanley.

Within this area of Norley, Cheshire, there were cheese-rolling contests held on Cheese Hill. The gallows, being on an adjacent mound, are now known as Gallows Clough Lane. If you were caught poaching, the royal head forester would have hung you there. Adjacent there is also Gads Bank, being a derivative of God's Bank, where poachers prayed just prior to hanging, and there were indeed many.

To quote from a local record:

> For an early period of time an evil monk ruled the area from the ancient Vale Royal Abbey, he on holding a function or at whim would raid the local farms for livestock and produce. He was eventually taken to London and executed by King Edward the 1st for his atrocities. The area where he lived within the Abbey was demolished and some of the old stones from the Abbey can be seen within the structure of Wicken Tree buildings.

Read also this report from Norley Town Council:

> The name Delamere derives from the French language, "of the mere". It was named in Norman times after the many meres that are a feature of the area, a legacy of the retreating glaciers of the ice age 10,000 years ago. The Romans cut a road through the Forest to connect the Fortress town of Chester and the salt town of Northwich and on towards Manchester, but other than this, the area remained relatively unchanged until after 1066.
>
> At the time of the Norman conquest in 1066 AD, the Forest was much larger than it is today, stretching from Nantwich in the south, to the banks of the River Mersey in the north, and encompassing the two Norman forests of Mara and Mondrum.
>
> The Norman Kings claimed the area for private hunting. Areas were fenced off to protect the Royal deer - the legacy of which still lives today in local names Old Pale and New Pale.
>
> The area known as Blakemere Moss was drained in Napoleonic times and planted for commercial forestry. Recently, however, The Forestry Commission, current

Chapter Five: Thomas Cholmondeley, 1ˢᵗ Lord Delamere of Vale Royal Abbey

trustees of the forest, have felled the trees and re-flooded the area to once again create a boggy wildlife sanctuary.

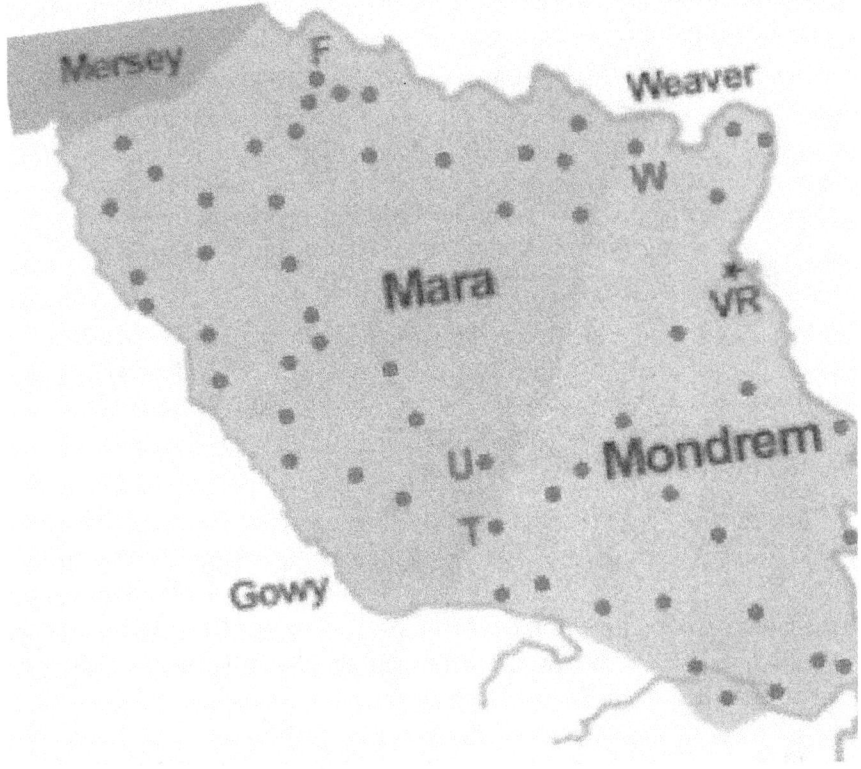

Layout of Delamere Forest (~1200 AD), courtesy of Rylands Library [the initials VR indicate Vale Royal Abbey; note also the River Mersey at the top and also the River Weaver]

A report of 1656 from the Archives of Kelsall Civil Council reads:

> It is believed that the ancient woodland may well have been a hunting ground long before the advent of the Normans in 1066. But it was they who, with characteristic efficiency, put the seal of their authority on the extent and administration of the area. To them the territory earmarked for hunting should be protected by law, which would mark it out as a game reserve, for the sport was their addiction. It was a vast area stretching cross-country from the River Gowy

southwards to the outskirts of Nantwich. The northern half was known as la Mara; the southern as Mondrem, a fact remembered in the name of a village close to Nantwich, Aston-juxta-Mondrem.

In early and mediaeval times this forestland was an uncharted wilderness of self-seeded woodland, mainly birch, ash and oak interspersed with areas of heath, marsh, bog and meres, usually referred to as waste but teeming with wild life. There was herbage and meat under the trees providing food and natural cover for the animals of chase and warren. The meres were full of fish.

Evidence of the occupation of Kelsall men in the 13th century is to be found in the Ledger Book of Vale Royal Abbey, well entitled as the interesting accounts of the organization and costing of the building of this great Abbey Church are therein detailed.

Today the Delamere Forest in Cheshire is once again "Crown Land" and is managed by the "Forest Enterprises" on behalf of the "Forestry Commission", which is part of the "Crown Estates". The forest also is the supplier of most of the natural Christmas trees sold in England, according to the report (2016) from the Forestry Commission.

Thomas Cholmondeley became 1st Lord Delamere of Vale Royal Abbey in 1821. He completed the greatest achievements and renovations of the Great House of Vale Royal Abbey, plus he refurbished it in magnificent Georgian style, and he also created an additional wing, which later became known as the Great Hall, which was very impressive according to paintings and records of the time, using large amounts of the family fortune in undertaking this work. This was also in addition to his loving care and attention to the development and protection of Delamere Forest.

Thomas Cholmondeley recruited workers and tradesmen from a wide surrounding area, including Royton, Rochdale, Crompton, Shaw and Oldham, in the County of Lancashire. Stonemasons were in great demand to work on the Great House. There were over 100 rooms at Vale Royal Abbey, including the Great Hall. The ceiling of the Great Hall is covered with the coats of arms of the Cholmondeleys and the families they married into. Today, this is

Chapter Five: Thomas Cholmondeley, 1st Lord Delamere of Vale Royal Abbey

one of the most impressive displays of skill and art in the whole of England. All this work required a large staff of skilled workmen to handle the ongoing upkeep and maintenance.

Amongst those recruited by Thomas Cholmondeley was an expert master mason named Walter Green (1835-1886), who was assigned to work on the roof of the Abbey. Walter had been born in Cowlishaw Village or Hamlet [no longer in existence, only the name Cowlishaw Lane survives; see Appendix 8] in Crompton, Lancashire, which was based in the area of Lancashire on the lower Pennines that later developed into a prominent centre for the cotton and textile industries. Walter very quickly settled into his new employment and also the pleasant, lifestyle as a resident of the beautiful Cheshire countryside. It was not too long before Walter met a very attractive local Cheshire girl named Margaret Delamore (1835-1908), who lived in Chester. She was the daughter of a local grocer and after a brief courtship they married in 1853. Walter and Margaret produced a healthy family and Margaret was also employed in the Cholmondeley household, joining the downstairs staff in about 1854. Her initial primary duty was to serve as the chambermaid for the only daughter of Thomas Cholmondeley, 1st Lord Delamere, Henrietta Charlotte, born on 3 June 1823 and who eventually died in distressing circumstances on 13 August 1874.

The bond between Henrietta Charlotte Cholmondeley and her supportive chamber maid Margaret Green very soon developed into one of confidentiality and secrecy, as poor Henrietta had been promised in marriage by her domineering father, to the elderly Lord Berners, Henry William Wilson, who was at least 30 years older than Henrietta, which was an attempt by her father to acquire more funds into the Vale Royal Abbey bank account. Lord Berners was a long standing personal friend of Thomas, 1st Lord Delamere and they often met to discuss mutual ideas, especially for promoting and advancing their private estate projects and ambitious ways of making more money. The prospects of this marriage left poor Henrietta Charlotte panicky and breathless, as Henry Wilson was well-known as a sexual pervert. Arranged marriages, also known as "Marriage à-la-mode", were very common throughout the world until the 18th century, and, despite our repulsion to this practice today, they were often used for mercenary purposes in bygone days.

One of the most extreme cases of an arranged marriage in the European community was that of Princess Marie Adélaïde of Savoy (1685-1712), who, aged only 12 years, became the wife of Louis, Dauphin of France, Duke of Burgundy. She was the eldest daughter of Duke Victor Amadeus II of Savoy and of Anne Marie d'Orléans. Her betrothal to the Duke in June 1696 was part of the Treaty of Turin (August 1696). On 6 December 1697, on her twelfth birthday, Princess Marie Adelaïde was married to the Duke in the Palace of Versailles. The event took place after the signing of the Treaty of Ryswick, which ended the Nine Years' War of Europe.

Fortunately, Henrietta Charlotte managed to calm down her feelings of dread with the help of her confidential, supportive chambermaid Margaret Green, and she was also more mature and philosophic about her future prospects, being already 35 years old. She was thus eventually compelled to leave her comfortable home at the Vale Royal Abbey and leave behind the protective company of her eldest brother Hugh, who she dearly loved and who was more of a father to her than her biological father, Thomas, 1st Lord Delamere. Henrietta also had to leave behind her personal chambermaid and close companion, Margaret Green to the depressing, melancholic house of Lord Berners at Ashwellthorpe Hall in Norfolk, until he eventually died on 27 June 1871. [The story goes, based on rumours from the local public house of the Crown Inn, located in Uppingham, Norfolk, where most of Lord Berners estate workers spent their time in the local bar, that Lord Berners died of a heart attack while trying to have sex with a goat on his farm]. But his timely death did not eliminate the misery and heartache that Henrietta Charlotte had to endure for those years living away from the Abbey; time that she could have enjoyed associating with younger, 'normal' men of her own age and to share the joys of youth along with her peers and contemporaries.

Prior to her marriage, a serious matter that was of great concern to Henrietta Charlotte and more so to her brother, Hugh, was that Mary Leticia Crump, the late wife of Henry William Wilson, had been incarcerated and committed to an insane asylum at the Norfolk County Asylum in about 1850. It is reported that Mary Leticia Crump died there in 1857, and her condition was that of a dithering, trembling wreck of a woman, who could neither speak,

Chapter Five: Thomas Cholmondeley, 1ˢᵗ Lord Delamere of Vale Royal Abbey

hear or even communicate, and she was confined in isolation to a padded cell. What this once normal woman had seen, experienced and endured during the many years she was dominated and abused by this man, one can only imagine, but it was enough to drive her to insanity. Being Catholic, Henry William Wilson could not divorce his insane wife, but, within three weeks of her welcomed death, he rushed over to Vale Royal Abbey to claim his new virginal bride, Henrietta Charlotte Cholmondeley. The wedding took place in Vale Royal Abbey on 21 July 1857. After taking his new bride back to Ashwellthorpe Hall in the remote marshes of Norfolk, God knows what Henrietta Charlotte had to endure and survive in those few years of marriage to Henry Wilson, until his death in 1871.

During the years that the 1ˢᵗ Lord Delamere, Thomas Cholmondeley, held control at Vale Royal Abbey, his family had to endure an almost dictatorship by this 'lord and master' of the household. Henrietta had suffered much emotionally during this time, but so also had her eldest brother Hugh Cholmondeley, the first-born son of Thomas and future heir to the estate of Vale Royal Abbey.

Hugh had meanwhile married the love of his life, Lady Sarah Hay-Drummond, daughter of Thomas Hay-Drummond, 11ᵗʰ Earl of Kinnoull, Scotland, in 1848. She joined Hugh to live on the estate at Vale Royal Abbey, but the remainder of this story must wait until Part Two of our narrative. It was during this time that Margaret Green, the humble chambermaid became an integral part of the Cholmondeley family, and as a result became almost like a sister to Henrietta Charlotte and also a great comforter and personal friend to Hugh and his wife, Lady Sarah.

Upon the death of Lord Berners, Henry Wilson, Henrietta Charlotte quickly vacated Ashwellthorpe Hall and returned to live at Vale Royal Abbey where she spent the last remaining few years of her life secluded from all outside association and companionship, with the exception of her very close dear friend and confidant Margaret Green, who was now like the younger sister she never had. Although dearly loved by her brother Hugh and Margaret Green, she slowly deteriorated in health. She gave the clear impression to onlookers as though she wanted to die. Indeed her wish was granted on 13 August 1874, when she was only 51 years.

The Delamere Saga: Part 1

Thomas Cholmondeley, 1st Lord Delamere, who had to relinquish his role as Member of Parliament for Cheshire, assumed his new role in the House of Lords in 1821, but he very rarely attended the pre-arranged sessions and according to archived records, his seat in the House of Lords was empty 95% of the time. Thomas was more interested in building up his inheritance and enhancing the prestige of Vale Royal Abbey, now being personally viewed as his private "empire".

Extract from the *Welsh Parish Records* of Denbigh:

> Henrietta Elizabeth Williams-Wynn, married in 1810, Thomas Cholmondeley, of Vale Royal, Cheshire, created in 1821, Lord Delamere, and had issue, Hugh, (1812) Thomas Grenville, (1818) Henry Pitt, (1823) Charles Watkin (1825) and Henrietta Charlotte (1835). On the death of 1st Lord Delamere in 1855 he was succeeded by his son Hugh Cholmondeley, second Lord Delamere, born 1812; educated at Eton. He has sat in Parliament for Denbighshire and Montgomeryshire in Wales.

How did Hugh Cholmondeley, eldest son and heir to Vale Royal Abbey, cope with this difficult situation of living under the same roof as his heavy handed, overbearing and controlling father, Thomas, 1st Lord Delamere?

What we do know from available records is that the daily life and circumstances were very difficult and complicated for Hugh. He was assigned mundane, earthy duties involving basically the management of the staff and estate at Vale Royal Abbey, but Hugh was also personally and privately very concerned about the serious structural issues that he had discovered—problems resulting from the renovations and extensions that had taken place in previous years with respect to the Great House and Great Hall. As a result Hugh was compelled to call in an associate of his, the local architect John Douglas who resided in the nearby city of Chester, to help and advise him.

Thomas Cholmondeley, 1st Lord Delamere, died on 30 October 1855, aged 88, having served as Member of Parliament for Cheshire from 1796 to 1821. The last occasion that Thomas appeared in public was in Chester at a county meeting on behalf of the Patriotic Fund, to which he was a liberal contributor, at Chester

Chapter Five: Thomas Cholmondeley, 1ˢᵗ Lord Delamere of Vale Royal Abbey

Castle in November of 1854, while speaking to the esteemed gathered audience he said his last farewell to public life. He had commanded a brigade in the Duke of York's expedition to Holland but was taken prisoner in 1793 but was returned to England as part of a prisoner exchange the same year.

Thomas Cholmondeley 1ˢᵗ Lord Delamere of Vale Royal Abbey had the pleasant experience of seeing some of his children and grandchildren become successful citizens of the world. For example, his third son, Henry Pitt Cholmondeley (1820-1905) had nine children, one of whom was named Lionel Berners Cholmondeley and, like his father the Reverend Henry Pitt Cholmondeley, Lionel became an ordained Anglican priest. He was also an educator, historian and Rector of St. Barnabas' Church at Ushigome in Shinjuku, Tokyo. For thirty years he served as a minister in the Anglican Church in Japan, and variously as a lecturer at Waseda University and honorary chaplain to the British Embassy in Tokyo. Lionel made his father, Henry Pitt Cholmondeley especially proud, and who one day in a letter informed Lionel that Thomas, 1ˢᵗ Lord Delamere, would also have been very proud of his accomplishments, had he lived to see his grandson's success in Japan.

As a fellow historian, Lionel Cholmondeley published the first English-language history of the Bonin Islands, now known as the *Ogasawara Islands in the Pacific Ocean*. This 178 page book, although taking many years to write and complete was eventually published in 1915 as *The History of the Bonin Islands from the Year 1827-1876*, and the *Story of Nathaniel Savory, One of the Original Settlers*. [An additional supplement was later added to the book dealing with the Islands after their occupation by the Japanese]. To further expand on Lionel Berners Cholmondeley's book, our research revealed:

> Nathaniel Savory (1794-1874) was one of the first American colonists who is said to have settled on the Bonin Islands. (These are an archipelago of over 30 subtropical and tropical islands, some 620 miles directly south of Tokyo, Japan.) He eventually became governor of the Islands, and played an active role in government before and during the colonization by Japan. Nathaniel Savory was born in Bradford, Massachusetts, USA and later in life relocated to Hawaii. In 1830 he headed out for an adventure expedition,

> led by Matteo Mazzaro (of Italian-British descent), and accompanied by a small group of Americans, British, and Hawaiians, a total of 25 people who all eventually settled in Ōgiura, Chichi-jima. These first settlers were Richard Millichamp of Devon, England; Matteo Mazzaro of Ragusa/Dubrovnik, Austrian Empire (now in Croatia); Alden B. Chapin and Nathaniel Savory of Massachusetts; Carl Johnsen of Copenhagen; as well as seven other unnamed men and 13 women from the Kingdom of Hawaii.[15]

After a shift in power and the death of Matteo Mazzaro, Nathaniel Savory became governor of the islanders. In 1862 the islands were claimed by Japan, overruling the previous claim by the British Crown, but Savory was left in charge of the islanders and in 1875 the Japanese government renamed them the Ogasawara Islands. Today, the Ogasawara (Bonin) Islands have become a 'World Heritage Site'; in other words, they were designated by the World Heritage Committee of **UNESCO** as being of special cultural or physical significance.

Harpers Magazine of March 1856 reveals further material from Lionel Cholmondeley's book:

> Nathaniel Savory was born in Bradford, Massachusetts, the oldest son of Benjamin and Judith Burbank Savory of Bradford, (now Groveland) and he later became a resident of New Rowley (Georgetown). On arriving at his age of majority, he left the town to seek his fortune, declaring that he never would return until he could come back wealthy. He never returned to Georgetown, and for fifty years was believed to be dead. When discovered alive, the incidents of his wanderings became known to his relatives and friends in Georgetown.

Still connected with Lionel Berners, the grandson of Thomas Cholmondeley, 1st Lord Delamere, is an interesting extract from a

---

[15] Hawaii, previously known as The Sandwich Islands, a name chosen by Captain James Cook who discovered these Island in 1778 in honor of the then, 1st Lord of the Admiralty, John Montagu, 4th Earl of Sandwich. Also of interest is that today, the 'sandwich', a food typically consisting of vegetables, sliced cheese or meat, placed on or between slices of bread and is considered to have also been named after John Montagu, 4th Earl of Sandwich.

Chapter Five: Thomas Cholmondeley, 1ˢᵗ Lord Delamere of Vale Royal Abbey

letter written by a certain Captain Pitman in 1855, as he retrieved this information from the Journals of a Captain Beechy, of the *HMS Blossom*, who had originally discovered the Bonin Islands in 1827 and the year when he took formal possession on behalf of England. Captain F. W. Beechey took ownership of this Group of Islands in the Name of His Britannic Majesty, George IV, on the 14 June 1827. When Captain Beechey of *HMS Blossom* reached the island chain and claimed them as a British possession, a copper plate was removed from *Blossom*'s hull and left on a beach as a marker of the claim.

This fascinating extract of 1855 regarding Captain Beechey's experiences provides more information about the strange appearance and character of Nathaniel Savory who had been living in the Bonin Islands since 1830 [provided by courtesy of Georgetown History, taken from the notes and files as compiled by researcher, A. E. Meader]:

> On landing on the beach, as I looked up among the trees, and as I approached the house, I saw standing in the doorway an old white-headed man with a snow white beard reaching down to his waist. At first sight I made sure that the old man was a Scotchman. As the boy Horace and myself drew toward the man, the old fellow hailed us in this manner: 'Horace, who you got there?' and before the boy could answer I replied, 'No one that means any harm to you or yours, old gentleman.' He replied, 'Humph, the quickest way you can prove that to me is to go on board your vessel and be off out of this.' What a crusty old Scotchman he is I thought to myself. But I answered him: 'Well, old gentleman, I came on shore to look at this island, and as I do not think I can do it justice in one day, I propose to remain here until I do, if it takes a month. If this reception you have given me is a sample of your civility, there is no need of you and I becoming any better acquainted.'
>
> During this conversation we were standing within three feet of each other, he standing in the doorway of the house. The old gentleman eyed me very closely after that last remark for a number of seconds, he then turned, and with the words 'Come in', he led the way into the house. As soon as we were fairly inside the room I took off my hat and exclaimed, 'God bless all under this roof.'

After my return home (now America), one day I was sitting in the railroad station at Salem to take the train for Boston when I heard someone call me by name. I turned and was just going to exclaim, 'For mercy sake, old gentleman, how did you get here?' when the man said, 'Captain, I understand that you saw my brother at the Bonin Islands?' I answered at once, 'I did, sir, and there is no disputing that you are his brother, for I thought it was the old man himself.' He told me that he was but eight years of age when his brother left home. They were then old men long past three score and ten, and the Salem gentleman was a prominent citizen of that city. We held many conversations about the long-absent brother. Within recent years, both of these brothers have died.

A book was also published called *Narrative of a Voyage to the Pacific and Beering's Straits (To Co-operate with the Polar Expeditions: Performed in His Majesty's Ship Blossom, Under the Command of Captain F.W. Beechey ... in the Years 1825, 26, 27, 28.*) This 472-page (two volumes) book written by Frederick William Beechey (and his ghost writers) was published by Colburn and Bentley of Fleet Street, London, by authority of the Lords Commission of the Admiralty in 1831. This exhilarating account by F. W. Beechey is truly a delight to read and is strongly recommended for our fellow students of adventure and exploration.

Back in Cheshire, the youngest son of Thomas, 1st Lord Delamere, Charles Watkin Neville Cholmondeley (27 May 1826-18 March 1844) had died at the age of 17, apparently from a fatal accident at the Rugby School in Warwickshire, England. Thomas was so distressed over the death of his youngest son, that it caused regular attacks of severe depression during the final 11 years of his life.

Our researchers uncovered a major blot on the records of Thomas Cholmondeley, 1st Lord Delamere: his involvement in the slave trade of the 18th and 19th centuries, in which he, along with many other British politicians of the day, made a fortune on the blood of African slaves. Unfortunately the Cholmondeley family had a strong connection and major investment in a slave factory business in Kingston, Jamaica and this tainted their reputation. Mary Caroline Henrietta Cholmondeley (1803-1879) was the niece of Thomas Cholmondeley, MP (1767-1855), who later became 1st

Chapter Five: Thomas Cholmondeley, 1ˢᵗ Lord Delamere of Vale Royal Abbey

Lord Delamere in 1821 and Mary Coraline Henriette had married Thomas Hibbert, who owned Birtles Hall in Over Alderely, which was built in Cheshire in 1819 for Robert Hibbert (1750-1835).

Thomas Hibbert (1788-1879) was the eldest son of Robert Hibbert (1750-1835) and Letitia Hibbert (née Nembhard). Robert had been a partner of his uncle Thomas Hibbert (1710-1780) in the slave trade and Robert became very wealthy out of the trade as he was also a slave and plantation owner at Albion estate, fifteen miles east of Kingston in what was St. David parish but is now St. Thomas. Robert left the staggering sum of £250,000 in his estate, an enormous amount even in those days, as well as his "Jamaica estates with slaves, stocks etc." when he died. Birtles Hall appears to have gone out of the Hibberts' ownership around the time of Colonel Hugh Thomas Hibbert's [son of Thomas Hibbert] death in 1895. Birtles Hall remains a Grade II English Heritage listed building and the current ownership is listed as 'private and confidential'.[16]

This extract from the *Independent* of 15 February 2013 revealed the following about the slave trade and connection with many of the stately homes of England built on the back of slaves:

> Some of Britain's most illustrious stately homes were built or bought with money reaped from slavery, it can be revealed. More than 100 country houses and estates across the country benefited from the millions of pounds given in compensation to slave owners in the 19ᵗʰ century. Our reporter revealed that when slave ownership was abolished by Britain in 1833 the government paid out a total of £20m – the equivalent of £16.5bn today—to compensate thousands of wealthy families for their loss of 'property'. Some of the country houses clearly are built by the proceeds of slavery in a very direct way. Others are occupied by slave-owning families for a limited period. There is little doubt that a certain percentage of Britain's country homes were financed by money funneled into the UK from slavery.
>
> Now historical records have been released showing that many of those who received the windfalls ploughed at least some of the cash into buying, building or refurbishing

---

[16] More details of the Albion Estate, the slave trade station in Jamaica, owned by Robert Hibbert, plus the history of other slave plantations in the southern states of North America, will be covered in the soon-to-be published book, "The Birth, Life & Death of King Cotton".

The Delamere Saga: Part 1

some of the greatest properties in the British countryside. A number of the homes have since been lost to the ravages of time or destroyed in one of the world wars. But many are still standing (including Vale Royal Abbey) and have either been taken over by the National Trust or remain in private ownership.

So came to an end the most prosperous period of time in which Vale Royal Abbey under the management and tight control of Thomas Cholmondeley, 1st Lord Delamere of Vale Royal Abbey had experienced, and now featured as one of the leading, flourishing private estates in English history. So despite his unctuous and prickly personality, plus his blind spots, we today must still show gratitude to the 1st Lord Delamere, as he was primarily responsible for establishing without any doubt, the security and ongoing success of Vale Royal Abbey in the 19th century, plus of course the beautiful, exquisite Delamere Forest.

Chester Castle has also figured prominently in the lives and chronicles of the Cholmondeley family and knowing something of its history and background is enlightening.

Chester Castle is in Chester, Cheshire. It is sited at the southwest extremity of the area bounded by the city walls. The castle stands on an eminence overlooking the River Dee. In the castle complex are the remaining parts of the medieval castle together with the neoclassical buildings, designed by Thomas Harrison, which were built between 1788 and 1813. Parts of the neoclassical buildings are used today as Crown Courts and as a military museum. The museum and the medieval remains are still today a tourist attraction.

The castle was built in 1070 by Hugh Lupus, the first Earl of Chester. It is possible that it was built on the site of an earlier Saxon fortification but this has not been confirmed. The original structure would have been a motte-and-bailey castle.[17] In the 12th century, the wooden tower was replaced by a square stone tower, the Flag Tower. During the same century the stone gateway to the inner bailey was built. This is now known as the Agricola Tower and on its first floor is the chapel of St Mary de Castro. The chapel contains items of Norman architecture. In the 13th century, during the reign of Henry III, the walls of an outer bailey were built,

---

[17] A motte-and-bailey castle is a fortification with a wooden or stone keep situated on a raised earthwork called a motte, accompanied by an enclosed courtyard, or bailey, surrounded by a protective ditch and palisade with a wooden tower.

Chapter Five: Thomas Cholmondeley, 1ˢᵗ Lord Delamere of Vale Royal Abbey

Photo of Chester Castle, by John Allen

the gateway in the Agricola Tower was blocked up and residential accommodation, including a Great Hall, was built along the south wall of the inner bailey. Later in the century, during the reign of Edward I, a new gateway to the outer bailey was built. This was flanked by two half-drum towers and had a drawbridge over a moat 26 feet deep. Further additions to the castle at this time included individual chambers for the King and Queen, a new chapel and stables.

Part Two: Life & Chronicles of Hugh Cholmondeley, 2nd Lord Delamere (1811-1887)

Chapter Six: Hugh Cholmondeley, 2nd Lord Delamere (1811-1887)

The eldest son of the marriage between Thomas Cholmondeley, 1st Lord Delamere and Henrietta Elizabeth was named Hugh Cholmondeley (1811-1887) [Welsh Church records indicate 1812 as being the year of his birth] and he became the 2nd Lord Delamere of Vale Royal Abbey in 1855, as heir of Thomas Cholmondeley, upon the death of his powerful, heavy handed, domineering, headstrong and very influential father.

Hugh, 2nd Lord Delamere, who was a far more gentle, compassionate and understanding individual than his late father, had inherited not only the family title and the vast now well established estate, but also 'major headaches' and with some very serious legal issues because of the haphazard overspending of the family fortune previously inherited and directly controlled by his late father. Thomas had been extravagantly spending the family wealth, primarily on renovating the Great House and constructing the Great Hall at Vale Royal Abbey, using the funds that had been passed down through the Cholmondeley family from the Holford family.

How did Hugh handle these financial problems and difficulties that ensued, plus the complicated, complex legal affairs of the estate that he had now inherited and had to deal with and also try to resolve? Extracts from the family records and letters related

Pencil Drawing of Hugh Cholmondeley, by Frederick Sargent (c. 1860), courtesy of *Creative Commons*

to his personal and private life, plus various family issues, indicate that he had to care for and also handle additional serious personal problems, especially related to his first wife, Lady Sarah Hay-Drummond, whom he had married in 1848 and her subsequent death at the young age of 30 in 1859, which devastated Hugh, according to the family journals plus other records of that dreadful event and grievous related funeral.

Who was this person Hugh Cholmondeley had married in 1848 and with whom Hugh was very much deeply in love?

Lady Sarah was the second daughter of Thomas Robert Hay-Drummond, 11th Earl of Kinnoull (1785-1866), styled Viscount Dupplin between 1787 and 1804, and a Scottish peer. His titles were Earl of Kinnoull, Viscount Dupplin and Lord Hay of Kinfauns in the Peerage of Scotland; and Baron Hay of Pedwardine in the Peerage of Great Britain.

To quote from *Great Historic Families of Scotland* (James Taylor, 1880):

> The Hays of Kinnoull are descended from a common ancestor with the Earls of Errol. The titles of Earl of Kinnoull, Viscount of Dupplin, and Baron Hay of Kinfauns, were conferred, in 1633, upon Sir George Hay, second son of Peter Hay of Megginch. He was born in 1572, and studied for six years in the Scots College at Douay, under his uncle, the well-known Father Hay, who was Professor of Civil and Canon Law in that seminary. He returned to Scotland about 1596, and obtained the office of a gentleman of the bedchamber to King James, who bestowed upon him the commendam of the Charter-house of Perth, and the church lands of Errol. He was present with James at Gowrie House, Perth, when the Earl of Gowrie and his brother were killed, and obtained the lands of Nethercliff out of that nobleman's forfeited estates.
>
> In the year 1616 he was nominated Clerk Registrar, and was made a Lord of Session; and in 1622 he was raised to the office of Lord High Chancellor of Scotland. He was elevated to the peerage in 1627, by the titles of Viscount of Dupplin and Lord Hay of Kinfauns, and on the 25th May 1633, he was raised by Charles I. to the rank of Earl of Kinnoull, immediately before the coronation of the King. This mark of royal favour did not, however, render

Chapter Six: Hugh Cholmondeley, 2nd Lord Delamere

him unduly compliant to his Majesty's wishes. One of the objects which Charles had in view at his coronation was to increase the power and prominence of the hierarchy, and with this view he sent Sir James Balfour, Lyon King-at-Arms, to the Chancellor, to inform him that it was his Majesty's pleasure that he should give precedence for that day to the Archbishop of St. Andrews. Lord Kinnoull, however, replied to this order, with proper spirit and firmness, that 'since his Majesty had been pleased to continue him in that office, which by his means his worthy father, of happy memory, had conferred on him, he was ready, in all humility, to lay it at his Majesty's feet. But, since it was his royal will he should enjoy it with the various privileges pertaining to the office, never a stolid priest in Scotland should set a foot before him while his blood was hot.' When this courageous reply of the old Chancellor was reported to the King, he said, 'Well, Lyon, I will meddle no further with that old cankered, goutish man, at whose hands there are nothing to be gained but sour words.'

Hugh Cholmondeley and Lady Sarah probably first met and fell in love while Lady Sarah was staying at the family estate of Hardmead in Newport-Pagnell, Buckinghamshire, England. It is very likely that Hugh Cholmondeley personally knew George Hay-Drumond as they were both Members of Parliament (MP's) and both visited London regularly, and therefore it is quite probable that Hugh met Lady Sarah Ann Hay-Drummond either through her brother George who was the 12th Earl Kinnoull or even maybe her father the 11th Earl Kinnoull. The Earl of Kinnoull had later moved from Scotland to live in England and bought the mansion at Hardmead in Newport-Pagnell, Buckinghamshire.

Extracted from the Council records of Newport-Pagnell in England:

> Hardmead, in the hundred, and deanery of Newport, lies nearly six miles to the north-east of Newport-Pagnell. The manor was anciently in the families of Gifford and Reynes, afterwards for nearly three centuries in the Windsors: having been given to the crown in exchange, it was granted in 1544 to the family of Catesby, of whom it was purchased about the year 1675, by Serjeant Maynard. John Hobart, Earl of Buckinghamshire, whose father had married the serjeant's

grandaughter, sold this manor about the year 1751, to Alexander Small esq. of whose family it was purchased in 1792, by the present proprietor, the Earl of Kinnoull.

Hugh was now unfortunately still living under the 'shadow' of his famous father, the late Thomas, 1st Lord Delamere, who had been a high powered socialite and had left a legacy after his death of being a big spender, and also had been very extravagant with the family fortune, plus he had undertaken much lavish entertaining at his home at the Great House at Vale Royal Abbey, which had greatly enhanced his reputation. By the time Hugh 2nd Lord Delamere inherited the estate, the title and the Great House, in 1855, the funds in the estate had almost become depleted, making it very difficult for Hugh to maintain and continue the life style of a Lord of the British Peerage.

Hugh's marriage to Lady Sarah in 1848, also resulted in placing a great emotional burden on Hugh, as Lady Sarah, whom he loved so dearly, but she was a very weak, delicate girl and was sick for most of her life up until her death on 17 February 1859. Without the help and support of Margaret Green, the chambermaid of his much younger only sister Henrietta Charlotte, Hugh could not have coped with the situation that faced him each and every day, as he diligently tried to play and fulfill the important role and related responsibilities of now being the new 'lord and master' of Vale Royal Abbey.

After his sister, the much loved Henrietta Charlotte was forced to leave Vale Royal Abbey in 1857 to marry the elderly Lord Berners, this event also took its toll on Hugh. He was feeling personally responsible, as he could do nothing in his desperate efforts to try and cancel or revoke the legally binding contracts that had been drawn up many years earlier. Hugh also had to cope with the knowledge of the reputation of Lord Berners, so with a sad heart he had to bid farewell to Henrietta Charlotte as she moved away to live in Norfolk.

Two years later, adding to his already depressing situation, his very ill wife, Lady Sarah, also left him. She died after feeling the strength of her husband's devotion, and had desperately tried to hold onto life despite her medical prognosis. Since moving into the Great House at Vale Royal Abbey in 1848, Lady Sarah had found inner peace and contentment there. She so wanted to live! Lying in her sick bed, she tightly clasped Hugh's hands, but alas during the evening of 17 February 1859, she passed away with an angelic smile on her face, as Hugh held her in his arms.

The only real woman now left in the life of Hugh Cholmondeley and his lonely existence at Vale Royal Abbey was Margaret Green, who had by this time been promoted to housekeeper. Their relationship soon developed into one of intimate close friends and confidants. But, given their differences in position, and both being god-fearing Christians, they never allowed their relationship to develop into anything more serious or involved.

On one rare occasion in 1860 Hugh Cholmondeley, 2nd Lord Delamere held a social function at his estate at Vale Royal Abbey, respectfully sometime after the death of Lady Sarah. Hugh invited most of his remaining family members and a few selected friends to Vale Royal Abbey to enjoy some of the summer glory of the Cheshire countryside. Amongst the guests invited were Sir George Hamilton Seymour and his wife Gertrude (nee Trevor), along with their precocious daughter, Augusta Emily Seymour. Augusta was still unmarried at the age of 24 and, as her two younger sisters had already become betrothed, Augusta was urgently on the hunt for a suitable husband and as Hugh Cholmondeley was now a single man, plus he now had also recently inherited the esteemed prominent title, Lord Delamere. This was a pre-condition related to any man that Augusta Emily Seymour would even consider marrying, so she thus saw the chance of a lifetime and the opportunity of capturing the somewhat naïve, gullible Hugh Cholmondeley. It was just a matter of time before the vulnerable Hugh was entwined in a situation that Augusta and her mother had manipulated. On 27 December 1860, Hugh Cholmondeley and Augusta Emily Seymour were married at St. James's, Westminster, London, England.

However, meanwhile, Hugh Cholmondeley and Margaret Green grew ever closer. Hugh explained in confidence to Margaret Green that he had an ambition to create a permanent memorial to his late wife, and he carefully explained his plans for the building a new local church in the village of Over, nearby to Vale Royal Abbey. Margaret wholeheartedly agreed and using her skillful discretion and knowing Hugh intimately and also his current confused state of mind, she knew in her heart that this would prove a great outlet, diversion and distraction for her now very dear friend away from his recent impetuous decision of marriage to Augusta Emily Seymour as Margaret Green had already clearly observed and foresaw that this forthcoming marriage would not prove to be a happy, contented one for Hugh.

We have all heard the saying 'that opposites attract'; well, in this case it did not prove to be true with Hugh Cholmondeley, 2nd Lord Delamere and Augusta Emily Hamilton-Seymour, as Augusta, after their marriage, being an outgoing, flamboyant and ostentatious individual, very soon viewed Hugh as a boring introvert, lacking vitality and ambition. Thus Augusta soon preferred that she spend most of her personal, private time with her socialite friends in London and also Bournemouth on the south coast of England, to enjoy and be adulated in her new role as Lady Delamere, and she very rarely visited or spent any time at Vale Royal Abbey, an 'extremely boring place she now despised', according to her private letters.

Augusta also had very soon realized, after moving into the Great House at Vale Royal Abbey after her marriage, that the property in Cheshire was beginning to look very run down, dowdy and in desperate need of renovation and major ongoing repairs, with no prospects in sight of any substantial improvements ever being undertaken because of the shortage of funds in the family estate. Augusta no doubt reflected to herself that this dwelling and so-called 'Great House' in Cheshire was not up to the required standard she was used to, being the daughter of a very wealthy, successful politician and businessman from London, whose family fortune had been built on the scandalous slave trade from Africa, "one of the greatest atrocities of civilization", according to the book *John Wesley & Slavery*, published by George Fox University.[18] The incompatible marriage between Hugh and Augusta was therefore an unfruitful one and for a number of years they had little or no intimacy, or even personal communication.

As the years slowly passed, Lady Gertrude Hamilton Seymour (nee Trevor), the mother of Augusta, who was now the wife of

---

[18] According to this report about the slave trade, from the Social Sciences & Humanities Research Council of Canada, the following facts are revealed. "During the nineteenth century, a number of individuals and organizations from around the globe advocated abolishing slavery and the international slave trade. Between 1808 and 1896, international authorities began to seize and detain ships suspected of participating in the slave trade. Once these ships were seized or detained, a network of international courts "decided the fates of the survivors." These courts secured the freedom of 250,000 enslaved Africans — approximately 6% of the number of Africans forced into slavery during this time period.

Chapter Six: Hugh Cholmondeley, 2nd Lord Delamere

Hugh, 2nd Lord Delamere, was acting under very firm direct instructions from Augusta's father, Sir George Hamilton Seymour. One day she took her daughter Augusta to one side and clearly and carefully explained, also putting undue pressure upon her, that it was about time that she produced an heir for Hugh, 2nd Lord Delamere, in order to keep the Cholmondeley family line of Vale Royal Abbey and the title 'Lord Delamere' intact, which of course would prove to be of tremendous, immense value and of great benefit to her and her future as his legal wife, especially as she was now the esteemed "Lady Delamere".

Photograph of Augusta Emily Seymour before she married Hugh Cholmondeley, 2nd Lord Delamere in 1860, courtesy of National Portrait Gallery, London

Based on this motivating knowledge and the realization of these facts pointed out to her by her manipulative mother, plus also being discreetly promised a very substantial financial personal reward in return for her cooperation with her shrewd parents, Augusta very quickly swallowed her pride and calculatingly decided to return to Vale Royal Abbey, a place she actually hated and despised, and to resume normal relations with her husband, in her opinion as expressed to her mother, to reunite again with her 'apathetic, subjective and easily manipulated' husband Hugh Cholmondeley. This calculated decision by Augusta, as a consequence resulted in the birth of a son being born in 1870, also named Hugh, the boy's name being cunningly selected and decided by Augusta or more likely her mother, to be named after his father, and also now being heir and entitled to the designation and title of the future "Lord Delamere" of Vale Royal Abbey. Either planned or by accident, a daughter named Sybil was born on the 29 December 1871.

The Delamere Saga: Part 2

Hugh Cholmondeley, 2nd Lord Delamere had received the gift of a beautiful solid gold snuff box from Sir George Hamilton Seymour, the father of Augusta Emily Seymour, based upon Hugh's marriage to Augusta, "Probably as a reward to Hugh, Lord Delamere, for taking his very difficult and headstrong daughter off his hands". This cryptic comment is based on an extract of a letter from a personal friend of Hugh, 2nd Lord Delamere. This gold box recently sold at auction in London to an undisclosed buyer for $6000 by Bonhams of New Bond Street, London and has the inscription on the underside of the cover with the words "Hugh, Lord Delamere, from George Hamilton Seymour 1866".

Photo of the 19th century Continental vari-coloured solid gold box, given by Sir George Hamilton Seymour to Hugh Cholmondeley, 2nd Lord Delamere, courtesy of its current owner in Saudi Arabia

In the following few short years after moving back to Vale Royal Abbey, Cheshire, from her luxurious house in London, Augusta very quickly grew restless again, finding her tumultuous and boring relationship with Hugh her husband difficult to handle and endure. She also intensely despised living in the now quickly deteriorating property; the neglected estate and the ("shabby", in the words of Augusta) Great House at Vale Royal Abbey. Plus she was of course by this time once again seriously missing the exciting atmosphere

Chapter Six: Hugh Cholmondeley, 2nd Lord Delamere

and opulent lifestyle of London and living on the very pleasant, mild south coast of England. She cuttingly and bitterly expressed in a letter to a friend that: "she found Cheshire a most boring place to live and hated the house at Vale Royal Abbey", so she made a personal decision, being determinably resolved and now being very disconsolate about living in Cheshire. Based on this and despite her husband's weak objections, she also decided that young Hugh, who was now approaching four years old, should be sent away to boarding school, firstly to Winchester School for boys and then on to Eton College in Windsor, and she also decided that her daughter Sybil, now three years, would accompany her as she resumed her lengthy yearly visits to London and Bournemouth to spend time with her socialite friends, both male and female. This was the pattern of her life style up until her eventual death on 25 February, 1911 in Boscombe, Bournemouth at the age of 75.

The locality of Boscombe, in which Lady Delamere spent most of her remaining life, is situated between the somewhat older village of Pokes Down and Bournemouth Square, and was part of the great heathland which covered much of western Hampshire, and extended well into eastern Dorset. From Norman times it was within the Liberty of Westover. From the beach and cliffs the whole of Poole Bay stretching from Hengistbury Head in the east to Poole Harbour entrance in the west, and on to Studland and Swanage bays to the south can be seen. Boscombe was originally an independent settlement, separated from Bournemouth by dense wood and moorland; it was incorporated into the boundaries of Bournemouth in 1876 (against the wishes of Boscombe residents). The coronation of King Edward VII and his Queen, Alexandra of Denmark was scheduled to take place on 26 June 1902. To mark the occasion, Bournemouth Council agreed on 20 May 1902 to rename common No 59 as "King's Park". Boscombe thrived with the growth of the English seaside holiday. Between the wars Boscombe was one of Bournemouth's wealthiest areas with many large Victorian and Edwardian family houses.

The continuous absence of Augusta from Vale Royal Abbey for these long periods did not concern Hugh Cholmondeley too much, as he now had his mind set and focused on building and completing this new church in Over village in Cheshire, to be built as a permanent memorial to Lady Sarah, which his second wife

151

The Delamere Saga: Part 2

Augusta had blatantly stated to Hugh "was an extreme waste of the family's money". Hugh fortunately also had by this time, the very positive support and up-building companionship and personal advice of his now highly discerning, loyal and faithful housekeeper, Margaret Green.

Hugh Cholmondeley, now fully motivated, ambitiously commissioned the building of this new church near Vale Royal Abbey. This must have been a very complex undertaking at the time, not only in monetary terms in view of his current financial restraints, but also consuming much of his time and energy, considering all the other problems he had to cope with related to the running of the large estate and the Great House and Great Hall at Vale Royal Abbey, which were still in need of more urgent restoration and ongoing maintenance, this being competently handled under the supervision of the local Cheshire architect and now Hugh's personal friend, John Douglas (1830-1911).

From records of the time:

> In 1860 Hugh Cholmondeley, 2nd Baron Delamere, commissioned his friend, the Chester architect John Douglas, to build a church in the centre of Over, on Delamere Street, which was then a village at that time separate from Winsford, this church was to be built as a memorial to his dear late wife, Sarah. At that time Douglas was at the start of his career and was working for Lord Delamere at his house and estate at Vale Royal Abbey. A new parish of St John the Evangelist was created out of the parishes of St Mary, Whitegate and St Chad, Over. The church was consecrated by John Graham, Bishop of Chester in June 1863. This was the first church designed by John Douglas.

The church of St. John the Evangelist in Over, Cheshire, is built in Runcorn sandstone with a grey slate roof. It is in decorated style. Its plan consists of a five-bay nave with a clerestory, north and south aisles, a chancel, a tower at the southwest corner, and a vestry at the northeast. The tower is in three stages with a spire and angle buttresses. In the third stage of the tower are two-light bell openings and clock faces on three sides. There is no clock face on the south side because when the church was built there were only

Chapter Six: Hugh Cholmondeley, 2nd Lord Delamere

fields on that side. The spire is 140 feet (43m.) high. On the spire are lucarnes [small gabled opening in a roof or a spire], and at the top is a wrought iron cross. A chimney stack rises from the gable of the vestry. Internally there is stone paneling at the east end with an alabaster model of the Last Supper. In the churchyard there are many memorials; these include one to those who died in a cotton mill fire in Over in 1874. This memorial is constructed in yellow sandstone and carries inscriptions, including a quotation from St Mark's Gospel, and the names of the four victims, which include a baby aged three months. Fortunately today the Church is listed as a Grade II building by the Historical Commission and will remain so as a tribute to Hugh Cholmondeley, 2nd Lord Delamere, his wife Lady Sarah and the brilliant architect John Douglas. The inscription above the main door into the church, reads, "To the Glory of God and the memory of his dearly beloved wife Sara Delamere. This Church was erected by Hugh, Lord Delamere."

North-east View of St. John the Evangelist Church in Delamere Street, Over, Winsford, Cheshire, courtesy of Peter Vardy

John Douglas figures prominently in the life of Hugh Cholmondeley. He was also intricately involved in trying to keep the Great House and Great Hall at Vale Royal Abbey in a decent, livable condition, and also diligently trying to stall or hold in abeyance the decay that was now rapidly taking place So we feel it is appropriate that some mention must be made regarding this brilliant but complex individual. Who was John Douglas, and what was he like as an architect and a person?

The Delamere Saga: Part 2

South wing of Vale Royal Abbey as designed by John Douglas, courtesy Peter I. Vardy and *Creative Commons*

John Douglas (1830-1911) was an English architect who designed over 500 buildings in Cheshire, North Wales, and northwest England, in particular in the expansion of Eaton Hall, the estate of the Grosvenor family, later to be known as the Duke of Westminster, perhaps the wealthiest family in the land. He was trained in Lancaster and practiced throughout his career from an office in Chester. Initially he ran the practice on his own, but from 1884 until two years before his death he worked in partnerships with two of his former assistants.

Douglas's output included new churches, restoring and renovating existing churches, church furnishings, new houses and alterations to existing houses, and a variety of other buildings, including shops, banks, offices, schools, memorials and public buildings. His architectural styles were eclectic. Douglas worked during the period of the Gothic Revival, and many of his works incorporate elements of the English Gothic style. He was also influenced by architectural styles from the mainland of Europe and included elements of French, German and Dutch architecture. However he is probably best remembered for his incorporation of vernacular elements in his buildings, in particular half-timbering, influenced by the black-and-white revival in Chester.

Other vernacular elements he incorporated include tile-hanging, pargeting, and the use of decorative brick in diapering and the design of tall chimney stacks. Of particular importance is Douglas's use of joinery and highly detailed wood carving.

John Douglas was born at Park Cottage, Sandiway, Cheshire, and baptized on 16 May 1830 at St Mary's Church, Weaverham. He was the second of the four children, and the only son, of John Douglas and his wife Mary née Swindley (1792-1863). John Douglas senior was born in Northampton about 1798-1800 and his wife was born in Aldford, a village on the Eaton estate in Cheshire. Her father was the village blacksmith at Eccleston, another village in the Eaton estate. John Douglas senior was by trade a builder and joiner, and also described himself as a surveyor and a timber merchant. In 1835 he acted as architect for a house at Hartford, a village between Sandiway and Northwich. By 1851 he was employing 48 men. He owned land in Sandiway, and a house and land in the neighboring village of Cuddington.

Douglas practiced on his own until 1884, when his son, Colin, became ill. He then took Daniel Porter Fordham into partnership and practiced as Douglas & Fordham. Fordham was born around 1846 and had been an assistant in Douglas's office since at least 1872. In 1898, having developed consumption, Fordham retired from the practice and went to live in Bournemouth where he died the following year. He was replaced as partner by Charles Howard Minshull, who had been born in Chester in 1858 and who became articled to Douglas in 1874; the practice became Douglas & Minshull. During the first decade of the 20th century, Douglas became less active but, for reasons unknown, the partnership was dissolved in 1909. The practice returned to the title of John Douglas, Architect. Minshull went into partnership with E. J. Muspratt in Foregate Street, Chester. When Douglas died, this partnership worked from the Abbey Square address as Douglas, Minshull & Muspratt.

According to *The Works of John Douglas* by Edward Hubbard (1991):

> Douglas designed some 500 buildings. He built at least 40 new churches or chapels, restored, altered or made additions to many other churches, and designed fittings and furniture for the interiors of churches. His buildings are

The Delamere Saga: Part 2

'anything but copyist' and they 'bear a highly individual and nearly always recognizable stamp'. The major characteristics of his buildings are "sure proportions, imaginative massing and grouping ... immaculate detailing and a superb sense of craftsmanship and feeling for materials". His work is 'architecture which can be enjoyed as well as admired'.

According to John Douglas's records, it was during his inspection of Vale Royal Abbey in 1875 that he became aware of the advanced state of dry rot[19] in the roof timbers of the Great House and that the dry rot was spreading rapidly. In the 19th century there were no powerful chemicals available to treat dry rot, so it was an ongoing problem that caused serious depression to Hugh Cholmondeley according to notes compiled by Margaret Green.

In a recent report, the organisation Save Britain's Heritage stated:

> Hundreds of historic buildings are standing empty and being allowed to decay. Prompt action by local people can not only prevent ultimate demolition, but also save thousands of pounds in repair costs. A blocked rainwater gutter leads very quickly to damp penetrating the walls. If the building is closed up and not properly ventilated, the perfect conditions for dry rot are likely to arise as soon as the weather gets warm.

Fortunately today the problem of dry rot appears to have been conquered at Vale Royal Abbey after it was reported in 1971 by well-known writer on historic buildings in England, Sir Nikolaus Pevsner (1902-1983), who also lectured at Cambridge University for almost 30 years. Pevsner along with his colleague Edward Hubbard[20]

---

[19] Dry rot is wood decay caused by certain species of fungi that digest parts of the wood, giving the wood strength and stiffness. It was previously used to describe any decay of cured wood in ships and buildings by a fungus that resulted in a darkly colored deteriorated and cracked condition. The life cycle of dry rot can be broken down into four main stages. Dry rot begins as a microscopic spore, which, in high enough concentrations, can resemble a fine orange dust. If the spores are subjected to sufficient moisture they will begin to grow fine white strands known as hyphae. As the hyphae germinate they will eventually form a large mass known as mycelium. The final stage is a fruiting body, which pumps new spores out into the surrounding air.

[20] Edward Horton Hubbard (1937-1989) was an English architectural historian who worked with Nikolaus Pevsner in compiling volumes of the *Buildings of England*. He also wrote the definitive biography of John Douglas. When they were preparing the Cheshire volume, Hubbard drove Pevsner around the county. In the introduction to the book, Pevsner says of Hubbard, '...his even temper and his psychological treatment of my moments of

Chapter Six: Hugh Cholmondeley, 2nd Lord Delamere

recorded that "Vale Royal Abbey is one of the best examples of dry rot in a country mansion in England." Pevsner is best known for his monumental 46-volume series of county-by-county guides, *The Buildings of England* (1951-74). If Hugh Cholmondeley were still alive today, he would be so pleased to know that this serious problem of dry rot at his much loved home at Vale Royal Abbey has eventually been cured, but according to records of the time, his physical health was seriously impaired as he struggled to cope with the severe deterioration of Vale Royal Abbey during his lifetime.

It was during 1866-1868 that Hugh Cholmondeley was forced to reduce the number of his staff working at Vale Royal Abbey, mainly due to the current and ever increasing difficult financial restraints, which included giving notice to his master stone mason, Walter Green. Because Walter was now without employment, he had to move back to his original home in Cowlishaw Village (Hamlet), Crompton in Lancashire. Walter had to take his wife Margaret Green and their five children—Marriel, Mary Ann, Sarah and Elizabeth, plus a young son named George. Hugh personally felt that Margaret would have stayed on in her position at Vale Royal Abbey, but, being a loyal and devoted wife and mother, she had no choice but to leave the Abbey.

It was a sad day indeed when the goodbyes had to be said. Walter Green did not seem to care too much, and he simply shrugged at the change of circumstances for his wife and his young family, as he expected that his life style would continue as usual—spending many hours after work each day away from his family, preferring the company of his mates and cronies in the local public houses. But for Margaret and Hugh Cholmondeley, it was a truly heart wrenching emotional experience as they had experienced that private and secret personal bond that would remain intact despite the distance that would now separate them.

What made the return to Cowlishaw Village for Margaret even more saddening and heart-wrenching was that, on their way, their son George was accidentally burned to death at only two years of age when his nightgown caught fire in the fireplace of the house where they were temporarily staying. Now with even greater sadness in their hearts, the Greens continued their disheartening journey back to Crompton after having to bury George in the public

---

despondency were invaluable.' In 1976 Hubbard was elected as a Fellow of the Society of Antiquaries.

The Delamere Saga: Part 2

cemetery of Salford in August 1868. George Green, however, today is still remembered by the engraving on the headstone of the Green family plot at the Holy Trinity Church in Crompton, Lancashire.

Soon after the return of Walter and Margaret Green to Cowlishaw Village, Walter had to move away again from this textile mill town area to find work and employment as a stonemason working on the new Town (Guild) Hall in the nearby town of Preston, also in Lancashire. Margaret very rarely saw Walter during the ensuring years and after 1873 was never to see Walter again until his emaciated body was delivered to her home in a coffin in later years, after drinking himself to death at the age of 49 years.

In the Green family Bible it records the birth of a second son to Walter and Margaret in 1872, probably conceived on one of the rare visits by Walter to Cowlishaw Village during the warm summer of 1871. This last child was born premature on 20 February 1872, and 'weighing only 3 lbs-8 oz.', according to Margaret's records. Margaret also named the young boy Thomas Herbert—Thomas after her late employer, Thomas Cholmondeley, 1st Lord Delamere of Vale Royal Abbey, who had died in 1855 and Herbert, after her late father from the city of Chester. This frail little boy died of pneumonia in February of 1873 during one of the most vicious winters in English history and was buried in the family grave in March. Apart from recording this depressing event in her beautiful, graceful handwriting, the eloquent, but now very saddened Margaret is reported to have said, "I also almost died, not of the very cold winter weather, but of a 'broken heart'."

As Margaret reflected forlornly on her life, little did she know how her circumstances were about to dramatically change, especially as related to Vale Royal Abbey.

Checking the archives of the *Weather History Journals*, based in the Meteorological (Met) Office in Exeter, Devon, England, a more detailed description of that terrible winter is provided:

> December 1872 followed in the same vein as most of the other months of 1872 did, i.e. it was damp and wet. The year of 1872 was exceptionally wet, the wettest on record for England and Wales. With low pressure dominating there was limited frost and snow during that month and this continued into the January of 1873. Then on the 20th, there was a slight change and the UK finally slipped out

of the South West air flow that it had been under almost constantly for nearly 4 weeks, as more of a polar maritime air-mass influence affected the UK.

The real change came on the 27th of January when the Siberian high crept closer to the UK as the Atlantic influence finally ran out of steam. The opening of February 1873 was cold with snowfalls and the first real wintry spell of the winter of 1872-73. With the heaviest snow fall in 25 years, and snow drifts up to 15 feet in the Pennines.[21]

To also quote from *History Today*:

> The week-long hurricane that struck the south of England and the English Channel at the end of the month was beyond anything in living memory. John Evelyn described it in his diary as 'not to be paralleled with anything happening in our age. Winds tore across the country, sending the roofs of houses flying, leveling barns and knocking flat thousands of trees, which lay prostrate in rows like regiments fallen in battle. It was reported that 4,000 oaks perished in the New Forest and an attempt to count the toll of trees in Kent gave up at 17,000'. Many believed that the storm was a visitation of the anger of God. After it had blown out, Queen Anne's government announced that the calamity 'loudly calls for the deepest and most solemn humiliation of our people' and proclaimed a national day of fasting on December 16th in recognition of the 'crying sins of this nation'.

Margaret Green of course meantime had never forgotten her treasured, wholesome life and experiences at Vale Royal Abbey, and the intensity of her relationship with Hugh Cholmondeley, 2nd Lord Delamere. She and Hugh regularly corresponded, expressing their fondness for each other and how much they needed each other's company, companionship and support. It did not take Margaret Green too long, with her determined character, to decide and arrange, but not without great personal emotional stress, for her now grown up daughters, plus her other two younger daughters to be

---

[21] One of the worst storms in British history was the "Great Storm of 1703" during the reign of Queen Anne. According to the 'Climatic Research Centre' in the University of East Anglia in Norwich the following facts are provided. "In London alone, approximately 2,000 massive chimney stacks were blown down. The lead roofing was blown off Westminster Abbey and Queen Anne had to shelter in a cellar at St James's Palace to avoid collapsing chimneys and part of the roof."

The Delamere Saga: Part 2

cared for and supervised by helpful family members in Crompton, after Walter had deserted her and the family. She eagerly accepted the Hugh's invitation to return to Vale Royal Abbey and resume her duties as 'housekeeper', which she did in 1875. What neither Hugh nor Margaret fully realized was that this coming together again after her forced departure would now be far more involved, intense and complicated it had been before.

Hugh Cholmondeley's emotional ties and his personal life was far less complicated than those of Margaret, as his second wife Augusta had basically deserted him. She and their two children, Hugh Jnr. and Sybil were never at Vale Royal Abbey and Hugh very rarely ever saw or heard from them. Their upbringing was left entirely in the hands of Augusta with the help of governesses, and it also appears that their father had neither the time or interest in their upbringing. In letters to a friend, Augusta commented that her husband was a "poor father, a weak person and had no strength of character".

Despite her derogatory view of him, Hugh courageously handled the very difficult task of keeping the Vale Royal Abbey intact and fully operational while under great duress from 1855-1887, especially in view of the severe financial problems inherited from his father, the 1st Lord Delamere.

Vale Royal Abbey, England, today now stands as a tribute to the dedication and commitment of Hugh, 2nd Lord Delamere, and his contribution plus his tireless endurance to care for the preservation of the Great House and Great Hall during his lifetime, even under such very difficult personal circumstances. Today, we are pleased to report that Vale Royal Abbey is a Listed Building and National Heritage site, which we can all enjoy, thanks in a large part to Hugh and the support he received from all his hard working downstairs staff, most of them employed from the community of Cheshire.

The year that Margaret resumed her duties as housekeeper at Vale Royal Abbey, in 1875, Hugh very quickly regained his happy, relaxed personality again, being able to spend quality time with his confidant of many years. Margaret had already shared many of his life's difficult experiences, his disappointments and the personal problems he had to cope with over the previous years, especially the death of Lady Sarah and then also the dramatic loss of his much younger, only sister Henrietta Charlotte, and, although Margaret was officially the housekeeper, she very quickly fell into the role of becoming Hugh's lover.

Their relationship was one of a mature, deeply emotional need for each other, not like the common salacious extra-marital affairs reported by many of the neighboring well-off families in the Cheshire and English aristocracy. It was only a matter of time before Margaret became pregnant and although the drastically reduced downstairs staff gossiped, now that it was out in the open, it did not discourage Hugh or Margaret from continuing their intimate relationship, but they both still presented a dignified display of their respective roles to the household during the daytime hours, to prevent even more gossip. Their son was born on the 10 November 1876 and named John William, after the two respective kings of England who had played a vital role in the establishment of this beautiful county of Cheshire in England.

It was a common practice in those days for the aristocracy to have illegitimate children. Even the ruling monarchs at this time, King George IV (1762-1830), and his successor King William IV (1765-1837), had numerous illegitimate children many of them even being given and appointed by royal decree, various honorable titles.

Before long a second son was born to Hugh and Margaret on 23 September 1878, who they named Herbert, after Margaret's late father from the city of Chester.

The ensuing years unfortunately took a heavy toll on Hugh Cholmondeley, as the estate affairs at Vale Royal Abbey were going from bad to worse. Although he had the support, help and guidance of his friend, the experienced architect John Douglas, it soon became very clear to them that the Great House and Great Hall was deteriorating at a faster rate than any maintenance or renovations could be administered, plus the finances of the estate had been so severely reduced by the past extravagance of Hugh's late father, Thomas, 1st Lord Delamere during previous years, and was now reaching a critical level. They were faced with the prospect of Vale Royal Abbey having to be abandoned to become just another ruin like many other once proud, grand Houses and Estates throughout England. Hugh had to defer making any further decisions because of the now dangerous condition of the main structure of the Great House.

Of course, this dreadful possibility ultimately affected his relationship with Margaret Green, and eventually they had to face up to the reality of the situation, so it was mutually decided that she should return to her cottage in Cowlishaw Village, where the rest of her family now lived. It was a truly sorrowful, heart wrenching day when Margaret along with her two illegitimate young sons left Vale Royal Abbey for the last time in 1881.

As he now had no other choice, Hugh struggled on alone as he deliberated what steps he could take to save his treasured family home at the Vale Royal Abbey. But as a result of his now somewhat stressful solitary life, plus, according to family journals and private letters, he also had severe personal health problems to cope with, including probably prostate cancer, plus a very serious skin condition, which today would be described as 'pustule psoriasis' [psoriasis is from the Greek meaning 'itching condition' or 'being itchy' from psora, 'itch' and iasis, 'action, condition'].

Hugh also had at this critical time of his life so many mixed emotions and memories to look back on—some wholesome and up-building—others most depressing and nauseating. As he approached his 76th year in 1886 he began to reflect on his past life as being a futile waste after he lost his first wife Lady Sarah. Then his second wife Augusta, whom he had foolishly and impetuously married, with his two children, Hugh, Jnr. and Sybil no longer a part of his life, became a reality he had to accept. All of this was seriously compounded by his financial plight and the questionable survival of the Vale Royal Abbey.

Hugh had come to realize that Augusta had only married him in 1860 to obtain the title of 'Lady Delamere', and had tried to gain access to some of the rapidly reducing financial assets of the Cholmondeley family and the vast estate at Vale Royal Abbey. He came to resent having made such a foolish decision to marry Augusta in the first place, as he now realized that he had been completely and absolutely manipulated by this woman and her scheming mother. He was also depressed that he was unable to play any meaningful role in the upbringing of his two children, and very rarely saw them or enjoyed their youthful energy and company.

Hugh's most consoling memories however, in contrast, included the pure love he had once enjoyed with Lady Sarah, despite her gentle, delicate personality and poor health, and the permanent testimony of his love for her he had undertaken in the completion of St John the Evangelist Church, which is still standing today.

Of course Hugh also now had the more recent memories of Margaret and for John William and Herbert, both of whom he truly loved despite them not being allowed to bear his name. Reflecting on this period of his life, his memory took him back to the days when he first met Margaret Green, when his father was still alive, the time when she began working at Vale Royal Abbey, as the chambermaid to his sister, Henrietta Charlotte, and how Margaret helped so much in keeping Henrietta sane while prepared for her arranged marriage to the sexual pervert, Lord Berners, and of course also how Margaret had helped Hugh personally to remain calm and stoic as he tried to handle the stressful circumstances of managing the rapidly deteriorating house and estate at Vale Royal Abbey.

One last and significant final event in the life of Hugh Cholmondeley, 2nd Lord Delamere was his heart's desire to see his beloved Margaret and their two sons one more time. Against the advice of his doctor, Hugh departed Vale Royal Abbey in his coach and horses, undertaking the long journey in January 1886, to Cowlishaw, which was a overwhelming journey in the middle of winter for a person in his physical condition, but it was a case of his heart ruling his head.

The verbal account supplied by Herbert Green (1878-1943), often repeated and confirmed by Herbert's two half-sisters, Mary Ann and Elizabeth, who also now lived in Sandy Lane in the nearby town of Royton, Lancashire, was also confirmed by Herbert's older brother, John William, who lived in Alfred Street, Crompton: an elderly, gray haired "well-off" gentleman in a horse drawn carriage came to visit Margaret Green, at her cottage in Cowlishaw Village.

The coach was bearing a "coat of arms displaying the image of three Horizontal Lions and a Pastoral Staff" according to the report passed down by Elizabeth the daughter of Margaret. This was unmistakably the original Coat of Arms of Vale Royal Abbey on the door or the side panel of the coach; therefore this must have been a coach and horses carrying a visitor from Vale Royal Abbey. Margaret was not home at the time, and, according to Elizabeth

The Delamere Saga: Part 2

Green, "she was probably at Shaw and Crompton Market, as it was a Thursday". The "gentleman" told someone in the household, probably the grown up daughters of Margaret Green, that "he would return later in the day", but in fact he never did return. Hugh Cholmondeley, 2nd Lord Delamere, died the following year on 1 August, 1887, aged 76 years, a sad, dejected and a very lonely man, never again to see his "close friend, confidant and intimate lover" Margaret Green and their two sons.

Vale Royal Abbey Coat of Arms

Before we leave this section of our story, one other fascinating account occurred during Hugh's lifetime, connecting Vale Royal Abbey and the grandiose, and now world-famous, Tatton Hall in Cheshire. This is the intriguing story of the Head Cook of Vale Royal Abbey, Mildred Duffy and the Head Butler, namely, William Clarke of Tatton Hall, home of Lord William Tatton Egerton (1806-1883).

Margaret Green, who, approximately 1858, was serving as the housekeeper at Vale Royal Abbey was a very close friend of Mildred Duffy. Margaret, often served as advisor and confidant to Mildred Duffy. This beguiling and amusing but also very sad and poignant story regarding Mildred Duffy and William Clarke was passed down by the letters and notes of Margaret Green and sheds some fascinating light on the 'goings-on' of the downstairs staff of these two stately homes in Cheshire.

Mildred Duffy had first met William Clarke of Tatton Hall, when he and his master paid a visit to Hugh Cholmondeley at Vale Royal Abbey during 1858. It was the usual practice in those days for the Butler to accompany their master on such auspicious visits. It certainly was not love at first sight between Mildred and William, with both of them being very strong, stubborn and forthright characters.

When William Clarke entered the domain of Mildred Duffy, her very well regimented and organized kitchen at Vale Royal Abbey, sparks really flew when William started to instruct the kitchen staff to perform certain duties on behalf of his master Lord Egerton. At this point Mildred stepped forward and immediately retaliated with her usual bombastic and forceful manner, demanding that William vacate her kitchen immediately. This was such an absolute instruction from Mildred that William felt so intimated that he could hardly ignore this forceful command from Mildred, so off he marched out of the kitchen with his dignity truly in tatters.

It is useful to be aware of the very important, respective duties and the roles of a butler and also the head cook in a household of the caliber of Vale Royal Abbey and Tatton Hall in England in the 19th century.

The word 'butler' comes from Anglo-Norman *buteler*, variant form of Old Norman *butelier*, corresponding to Old French *botellier*, "officer in charge of the king's wine bottles", derived of *boteille* "bottle", Modern French *bouteille*, itself from 'Gallo-Romance' *Buticula* "bottle". The role of the butler, for centuries, has been that of the chief steward of a household, the attendant entrusted with the care and serving of wine and other bottled beverages, which, in times gone by, might have represented a considerable portion of the household's assets.

In Britain, the butler was originally a middle-ranking member of the staff of a grand household. In the 17th and 18th centuries, the butler gradually became the senior, usually male, member of a household's staff in the very grandest households. However, there was sometimes a steward who ran the outside estate and financial affairs, rather than just the household, and who was senior to the butler in social status into the 19th century. Butlers used to always be attired in a special uniform, distinct from the livery of junior servants, but today a butler is more likely to wear a business suit or business casual clothing and appear in uniform only on special occasions. Butlers were head of a strict service hierarchy and therein held a position of power and respect. They were more managerial than 'hands on' more so than serving; they officiated in service. For example, although the butler was at the door to greet and announce the arrival of a formal guest, the door was actually opened by a footman, who would receive the guest's hat and coat. Even though the butler helped his employer into his coat, this had been handed to him by a footman. However, even the highest-ranking butler would 'pitch in' when necessary, such as during a staff shortage, to ensure that the household ran smoothly, although some evidence suggests this was so even during normal times.

The typical staff of a household similar to Tatton Hall & Vale Royal Abbey during the 19th century, courtesy of the National Portrait Gallery, Washington, USA. [Notice the dominant role of the Butler and the Head Cook standing at his left side].

The household itself was generally divided into areas of responsibility. The butler was in charge of the dining room, the wine cellar, pantry, and sometimes the entire main floor. Directly under the butler was the first footman (or head footman), although there could also be a deputy butler or under-butler who would fill in as butler during the butler's illness or absence. The footman—there were frequently numerous young men in the role within a household—performed a range of duties including serving meals, attending doors, carrying or moving heavy items, and they often doubled as valets. Valets themselves performed a variety of personal duties for their employer. Butlers engaged and directed all these junior staff and each reported directly to him.

The role of Head Cook in a household of the size of Vale Royal Abbey was also a senior position that deserved and also demanded the respect of all other members of the household staff, including visiting butlers!

What were the basic duties of Head Cooks? They coordinated the work of other cooks in the kitchen, who prepare most of the meals. They also had many duties beyond the kitchen. They designed the menu, review food and beverage purchases, and often train cooks and other food preparation workers. These duties also included the following: planned and wrote nutritious menus for all meals including special dietary needs which comply with household guidelines; directed the preparation of food; prepared and served food; arranged and directed the appropriate storage of food and supplies; maintained safety standards throughout all food preparation and storage areas; monitors and maintained the inventory of food and supplies; estimates daily food preparation amounts; prepared purchase orders and ordered food and supplies in sufficient quantities for weekly meals; determined work schedule assignments for the staff; scheduled approved substitute staff as directed; monitored and assisted in daily clean-up of kitchen, service and dining areas; maintained a variety of records related to meals served, inventory, prepared documentation and completed annual required reports; scheduled maintenance and repairs for kitchen equipment; ordered new kitchen equipment as directed and initiated maintenance contracts; directed and monitored work of other kitchen staff, and substitute staff.

It is little wonder that Mildred Duffy was held in such great esteem at Vale Royal Abbey, and she was very proud of her role in this important position of Head Cook for many years and reflected this in her character and personality. When Mildred met William Clarke that day in 1858, it was like two stubborn goats going head to head, and the on-looking downstairs staff shuddered in fear of any subsequent consequences from this initial clash.

Fortunately in the following few days of this special visit by Lord Egerton to Vale Royal Abbey, accompanied by his butler William and other additional supporting staff, the stiff and uncomfortable atmosphere distinctly softened between Mildred Duffy and William Clarke, and before the week was out they had become firm friends. During the following years Mildred and William often met for social occasions during their time off from their respective duties and a warm, loving relationship gradually developed.

Unfortunately, this came to an abrupt end some years later when William informed Mildred one day that he was leaving his position as Head Butler at Tatton Hall to go and live down in the county of Kent on the South coast of England because of his health problems. The story goes that this departure was prompted and personally managed by Lord Egerton himself!

It appears that the son of William Tatton Egerton (1803-1886) Wilbraham Egerton (1832-1909), while sowing his 'wild oats', had a brief affair with a beautiful maid on the estate at Tatton Hall. When it was discovered she was pregnant, the maid was married off to William Clarke, in a private agreement between Lord Egerton and his butler. There is a record of this 'transaction', as William was given a handsome 'golden handshake' plus a toll road concession in Kent as payment in return for marrying the maid. Of course Mildred Duffy was truly saddened when she learned of this decision made by her now intimate friend, William Clarke, but being a stalwart, solid and determined woman she picked up the threads of her life again and with the support of confidant Margaret Green, she continued with her duties at Vale Royal Abbey until she eventually died a lonely spinster in 1902.

It is appropriate that, with the Lords Egerton having now been introduced into our *Delamere Saga*, and, as they were prominent in the history of the county of Cheshire, and also the scenic country of Kenya in Africa, plus their connections with the Vale Royal Abbey, we therefore include some brief details about their fascinating lives.

Here is a brief overview of the Egerton family of Tatton Park, Cheshire:

Chapter Six: Hugh Cholmondeley, 2nd Lord Delamere

Samuel Egerton was born on 28 December 1711 at the family home, Tatton Park in Cheshire. Samuel was the son of John Egerton, a grandson of John Egerton, 2nd Earl of Bridgewater, and Elizabeth Barbour, daughter of Samuel Barbour. As the second son of the family, and not the heir to the estate, he travelled to Italy, where from 1730 to 1735 he was an apprentice to the art-dealer and connoisseur Joseph Smith in Venice.

In 1738, Samuel Egerton became master of Tatton Park on the early death of his elder brother. In 1752 he became one of the wards of Jane Revell, daughter of a relation by marriage, Thomas Revell of Fetcham Park. She was a minor in possession of a considerable fortune. In 1758 she eloped with and married George Warren, MP for Lancashire. In 1758, Egerton inherited a vast legacy from his uncle, Samuel Hill, and was then able to invest in major improvements to Tatton Park.

Samuel Egerton married Beatrix Copley, daughter of the Rev. John Copley. Their only child was a daughter, Beatrix, who married Daniel Wilson of Dallam Tower. Beatrix Wilson died in childbirth in 1779, without leaving a surviving child. His sister Hester therefore became heiress of the Tatton estates. On 8 May 1780, her name was legally changed to Egerton by Royal License; her son William also adopted the surname of Egerton and was the ancestor of the now famous Barons' Egerton.

Lord [Baron] Egerton of Tatton. The title Baron Egerton was created and acquired in 1859 by William Tatton Egerton (30 December 1806 - 21 February 1883). He became the 1st Lord Egerton. William was also MP for Lymington, Cheshire North, from 1832 to 1858. He married Lady Charlotte Elizabeth Loftus on 18 December 1830, and they had two sons—Wilbraham and Allan. He was educated at Eton College in Windsor. He was returned to Parliament as one of two representatives for Lymington in 1830, a seat he held until 1831, then representing Cheshire North from 1832 to 1858. He was a major landowner in the Manchester area and a benefactor to Chorlton-cum-Hardy.[22]

---

[22] Chorlton probably means Ceolfrith's farm or settlement from the Old English personal name and tūn, an enclosure, farmstead or village. Hardy is derived from a personal name, Hearda, or Anglican for island or dry ground in a well-watered land. It has alternatively been suggested that Hardy may mean 'by the woods', in reference to the ancient forest of Arden

The Delamere Saga: Part 2

> *Wilbraham Egerton* (son of William) was (17 January 1832 - 16 March 1909). Wilbraham became 2nd Lord Egerton on the death of his father in 1883. He was also created Earl Egerton of Tatton and Viscount Salford in 1897, as he was the driving force and Chairman of the world-famous Manchester Ship Canal (1887-1894).[23]
>
> Wilbraham married twice: Lady Mary Sarah Amherst (sometimes recorded as Lady Mary Sarah Amhert) on 15 October 1857, and Alice Anne Montgomery on 8 August 1894. Wilbraham had one daughter by his first wife, called Gertrude Lucia (9 January 1861 - 7 June 1943) and, owing to the fact that Wilbraham had no male heir, the titles Earl Egerton of Tatton and Viscount Salford became extinct on his death; he was the first and last Earl. The other title, Baron Egerton, was passed onto his brother, Allan de Tatton Egerton.

Wilbraham was also the researcher and writer of the famous book *Indian and Oriental Armour* (1896) and the collection and artifacts he had acquired during his research were eventually bequeathed and left to the Manchester Art Gallery in England and are definitely worth viewing.

In the editorial review of *Indian and Oriental Armour*, the following is revealed:

> Long a vital source book of information on the military history of India, this excellently illustrated volume provides factual accounts of events ranging from the earliest invasions of the subcontinent in 200 BC to the First Burmese War in 1824. A shorter section of the book includes detailed information on Arabian and Persian arms and Japanese armor. Illustrations and notes describe helmets, daggers, sabers, maces, blowpipes, and other weapons--all grouped

---

Wood that grew on both sides of the River Mersey in the area. Chorlton was recorded as Chollirton in 1250, Chollerton from 1292 and as Chourton in 1572. The ancient hamlets of Chorlton and Hardy, separated by the Charlton Brook, together with Martledge and Barlow Moor, did not come under the combined name of Chorlton-cum-Hardy (*cum* is Latin for "with") until the 18th century.

[23] The Manchester Ship Canal is a 36-mile-long (58 km) inland waterway in the north-west of England linking Manchester to the Irish Sea. Starting at the Mersey Estuary near Liverpool, it generally follows the original routes of the rivers Mersey and Irwell through the historic counties of Cheshire and Lancashire. Several sets of locks lift vessels about 60 feet (18m) up to Manchester, where the canal's terminus was built. Major landmarks along its route include the Barton Swing Aqueduct, the only swing aqueduct in the world, and Trafford Park, the world's first planned industrial estate and still the largest in Europe.

according to geographical areas. It is a comprehensive reference for enthusiasts of arms, armor, and military history.

The following is also provided, courtesy of the National Trust:

> The Mansion Tatton Hall was completed and furnished in very elegant and fashionable style during the tenure of Wilbraham Egerton (1781-1856), but on a reduced scale to the original plans. Lewis William Wyatt, the nephew of Samuel Wyatt, designed many of the present interiors and Wilbraham was responsible for the purchase of many of the fine paintings and artifacts within the collection including much of the Gillow furniture for which Tatton is now famed.
>
> Further alterations were made to the Mansion in the 19th century. In the 1860s an upper floor was added to the family wing, with the addition of the Family Entrance Hall in 1884, which became an informal access to the Mansion in the time of Wilbraham, Earl Egerton. This was also the year in which Tatton became one of the first houses outside London to benefit from the installation of an electrical system which was powered by a plant on the estate.
>
> During Wilbraham's ownership of Tatton Park, the house received many illustrious visitors, perhaps the most famous of which were their Royal Highnesses the Prince and Princess of Wales in 1887, and the Shah of Persia and Crown Prince of Siam in the 1890s. It was in the late Victorian period that the Egertons of Tatton reached the pinnacle of their social status, with Wilbraham, Earl Egerton, hosting great house parties here at Tatton.

Alan de Tatton Egerton (19 March 1845 - 9 September 1920) brother of Wilbraham, became 3rd Lord Egerton in 1909 upon the death of his brother. Allan later married Anna Louisa Taylor in 1870 and they had three sons: William and Cecil (died in childhood) and Maurice (1874-1958). Alan de Tatton Egerton was a younger son of William Egerton, 1st Baron Egerton, and his wife Lady Charlotte Elizabeth Loftus. Wilbraham Egerton, 1st Earl Egerton, was his elder brother. He was elected to the House of Commons for Cheshire in 1883, a seat he held until 1885, when the constituency was abolished, and then he represented Knutsford from 1885 to 1906. The Honorable Alan de Tatton Egerton MP was commissioned as a Captain in the Paddington Rifles (later 5th Volunteer Battalion, Rifle Brigade) in 1877, and was later Major and Honorary Lieutenant-Colonel in the Cheshire Imperial Yeomanry. He was the first President of the Institute of Refrigeration, formed in 1899 as the Cold Storage and Ice Association. Also he was appointed a Deputy Lieutenant of the County of Chester on 24 December 1901, and Vice-Lieutenant of the county on 11 January 1902.

Maurice Egerton (4 August 1874 - 30 January 1958), youngest and only living and surviving son of Alan de Tatton Egerton, inherited the title Baron Egerton and became Maurice, 4th Baron Egerton in 1920 upon the death of his father, he also inherited the now well established, beautiful Tatton Park in Cheshire. Maurice never married and died without heir in 1958 while living in Kenya, and the title Baron Egerton became extinct. Maurice spent most of his life in Kenya and upon his death he left his estate, consisting mainly of the beautiful Tatton Hall Park to the National Trust of England. It is now listed as a Grade I Listed Building by the Historic Buildings and Monuments Commission for England.

Maurice was known as an aviation and motor car enthusiast, and also a personal friend of the Wright brothers[24] as he spent some time living in the United States of America and also Canada, where he owned a large ranch. He served as a lieutenant in the Royal Naval Volunteer Reserves during the First World War (1914-1918) after which he was granted some land by the British government in Ngata area near Nakuru in Kenya under the Soldier Settlement Scheme. He later purchased a further 21,000 acres in the same area from Hugh Cholmondeley, 3rd Lord Delamere. On this land, he founded a school in 1939 named Egerton Farm School (now the well-established and respected Egerton University of Kenya). The school was originally meant to prepare white European youth for careers in agriculture.

We quote from this enlightening report by Frances Kindon in the *Warrington Guardian* newspaper:

---

[24] The Wright brothers, Orville (1871-1948) and Wilbur (1867-1912), were American aviators, engineers, inventors, and aviation pioneers who are generally credited with inventing, building, and flying the world's first successful airplane. They made the first controlled, sustained flight of a powered, heavier-than-air aircraft on December 17 1903, four miles south of Kitty Hawk, North Carolina, USA.

Chapter Six: Hugh Cholmondeley, 2nd Lord Delamere

Egerton was a man of contradictions. On the one hand Baron Egerton of Tatton was a motor enthusiast and an aviator who travelled the world. But on and around his estate of Tatton Park many saw him as a recluse after enjoying only the briefest of encounters with him.

The family was marred by tragedy when Maurice's eldest brother, William, died in infancy from Scarlet Fever. His other sibling, Cecil, died while away at school aged just 17. An extract from the *Memoir of the Life and Character of the late Maurice Baron Egerton*, written by his cousin's son, the 9th Earl Abermarle shortly after his death, lamented the fact that many did not get to enjoy his true personality. He wrote: 'He was of a kind and generous bent, interested in fellow beings, particularly the young, yet the whole appearance was marred by the desire of keeping himself to himself yet when he was amongst friends he gave many smiles and good fellowship, and was capable of thoroughly enjoying himself'.

'I wouldn't say he shunned company, he just wasn't comfortable with large gatherings,' said Caroline Schofield, who today manages the mansion at Tatton Park in Cheshire. 'We believe he was possibly the way he was because his mother kept him at home or close by to her. The experience of losing her two other sons understandably made her very protective.'

Maurice Egerton spent a great deal of time in Kenya, overseeing the growing of tea, coffee and sisal and the working of his boot and blanket factory, and was remembered as being patriotic, philanthropic and generous to his workers.

Between 1930 and 1940 he built Egerton Castle in Kenya, where he died in 1958 aged 84. Upon his death he bequeathed Tatton Park to the National Trust of UK, who in turn leased the property and its 2,000 acres of parkland to Cheshire County Council in 1960. He had no successors and so the peerage died with him. No one is sure why Lord Egerton never married. "There are lots of theories and stories about him asking a woman and being refused," said Caroline Schofield of Tatton Park. "There are also stories that he didn't like women but no historian has ever been able to prove either of these. I think he probably was a bit lonely."

The Delamere Saga: Part 2

In our extensive research we also have not found any name of a woman associated with this contemplated marriage of Maurice Egerton, so we will let our readers draw their own conclusions.

There are however two existing photos we discovered, taken on a trip to France and there is a lady in them, but whether she was special to him we'll never know. Another of Maurice's passions was aviation. He was friends with Wilbur and Orville Wright and had his own planes and landing strip at Tatton Park. Like most early aviators, he was virtually self-taught through a process of trial and error. In 1910 he was set to fly in competitions but crushed two fingers in the engine gears. He had hardly recovered when he almost lost his left leg in a serious crash. This ruined his competition chances and gave him a limp for the rest of his life. Nonetheless, this did not stop him from reaching the rank of Major in the RAF. He also indulged his love of cars and in 1901 bought a 24hp Darracq car bearing Cheshire's first registration plate—"M1". He had a love of speed and is locally remembered for driving fast cars. Despite being a private and complex man, he is remembered fondly for his achievements and good sense of fun. Maurice also owned a ranch and had investments in other cattle ranches in the Cariboo region of British Columbia, Canada.

Seeing this Castle for the first time, which Maurice had built in the Kenyan bush, was awe inspiring and brings up a very interesting story about Maurice Egerton, 4th Lord Egerton of Tatton Hall, who died there without successor in 1958. Of special interest to me, as a lover of organ music, is the account of Lord Egerton's Pipe Organ and the planned restoration by the The Lancastrian Theatre Organ Trust (supported by the National Trust of UK).

Here is an extract from an article by journalist Benson Riungu, written in June 2004, for the *East African Standard*, Nairobi, regarding Maurice Egerton welcoming his supposed future bride.

> Determining to impress her, Lord Egerton set about building a 'house' on a scale that would surely impress her and make her change her mind. He conceived of a castle that would have no comparison in England or any other country for that matter. Dressed stones and zinc tiles for the roof were shipped from Europe; the builders were from Europe and Asia. The result, in 1938, was a stupendous four-storey edifice fitted with some of the most up-to-date mechanical

Chapter Six: Hugh Cholmondeley, 2ⁿᵈ Lord Delamere

and electrical gadgets at the time, including an escalator and a beautiful pipe organ.

Upon completion, the peer threw what was billed as the biggest party ever seen in pre-colonial Kenya, with guests coming from as far away as Rhodesia, now Zimbabwe and Nyasaland, now Malawi. The cheers and congratulations, it was to turn out, had come too soon. When the woman for whom the castle had been built came back to Kenya and viewed it, she dismissed it as 'a museum' and 'a monument to vanity'. Being thus spurned appears to have changed Lord Egerton in a fundamental way. Thereafter he seemed to live in a fantasy world.

He furnished and ran the castle as if the family he had envisaged actually existed. Nobody but the house servants was ever allowed in. But an even more far-reaching change was in his attitude towards women. He developed such a passionate hatred for them that he banned them from his castle and put up notices warning female trespassers that they risked being shot on sight. Visitors, including friends, were to leave their wives and daughters eight miles away from the castle. And when he planned to visit the quarters where his African staff lived, he would issue a two-week notice so that all women would be vacated.

According to our tour guide, the guests' lobby connects a huge ballroom for high caliber entertainment, meetings, celebrations, and rendezvous. Among the 52 rooms are bathrooms, a dark room for photography (where Maurice developed his personal photography films), guestrooms, a library, a kitchen, a reading room, a laundry room, and other partitions created for specific occasions. Besides, it also had a master bedroom, a children's room, numerous other rooms, alleyways, confinements, barricades, artistic lacunas and cloistered venues. An impressive, magnificent grand pipe organ, made with 411 pipes and a cabinet, takes the height of two floors. In 1951 this imported organ was designed and installed by Jack Davies and Son of Northampton, England. Unfortunately over the years this organ has suffered serious deterioration, but thankfully is now in the process of being restored by the generous gifts and donations collected by the Lancastrian Theatre Organ Trust (supported by the National Trust of the UK).

Lord Egerton was an extremely generous, philanthropic individual and the Egerton University (EU) in Kenya plans to establish the Lord Egerton Foundation in his honor (To which the MTC International Foundation (USA) will also subscribe)

Maurice, 4th Lord Egerton, left a lasting legacy in Kenya, where he is still celebrated and held in great affection today. Lord Egerton played a crucial role in Kenyan education. He founded the Egerton University, which was formerly used to train European settlers. Lord Maurice Egerton lived until 1958 as a loner in the castle. Eventually, he died due to serious chest and breathing issues and lies buried in the town of Nakuru, Kenya. We are however also pleased to report that all of this land previously owned by the generous Maurice Egerton, some of which he had bought with hard cash from Hugh Cholmondeley, 3rd Lord Delamere, has now been returned and handed back to the rightful owners—the indigenous people of Kenya.

Part Three: Life & Chronicles of Hugh Cholmondeley, 3rd Lord Delamere (1870-1931)

Chapter Seven: Hugh Cholmondeley, 3rd Lord Delamere

Upon the death of Hugh Cholmondeley, 2nd Lord Delamere in 1887, his official and only legal son and heir, Hugh Jnr., became the 3rd Lord Delamere at the very young age of 17 years. From existing records we do know that Hugh, 3rd Lord Delamere was a very erratic, emotionally unstable, bad tempered, irresponsible individual and he also had developed a reckless and tempestuous streak having received absolutely no parental guidance whatsoever. He was also totally unprepared for this unseen event of his father's death and suddenly being plunged into his new role in life of becoming a Lord of the Realm and belonging to the Peerage. He was also now qualified to sit in the House of Lords in the British Parliament, and this newly gained autocracy sent him reeling with excitement.

To quote from his official biography,

3rd Lord Delamere by Bassano (1930), courtesy of the Standard Media & Nairobi Wire, Kenya and the National Portrait Gallery, London

The new Lord Delamere had grown up with a quick and violent temper which he had never been taught to restrain. At the age of 17 he found himself with an estate, a title and a hunting stable. He went through a period of extravagance which the income from the estate, by no means a large one and considerably mortgaged, was inadequate to meet.

The Delamere Saga: Part 3

Plus this quote, also from his biography:

> The English property "Vale Royal Abbey" was now squeezed dry. A receiver was appointed to collect the income from the estate on behalf of the mortgagees; and Delamere became totally dependant for his livelihood on the profits from his farms in Africa.

This biography by Elspeth Huxley (1935), was not authorized, and therefore not approved by Hugh Cholmondeley as he had died back in 1931. From our research he definitely would not have sanctioned it, and according to Elspeth Huxley's admission, this biography was authorized by the young widow (second wife of a meager three years) of Hugh, namely Gwladys, "Lady Delamere". To quote from the author's notes,

> Thanks to Gwladys, Lady Delamere who entrusted me with the biography of her late husband, and for placing at my disposal all the material bearing on the late Lord Delamere's life and for giving me consistent help and advice whenever I applied for it. I had to deal with the life of a man who wrote no diaries and very few letters.

Hugh Cholmondeley, 3rd Lord Delamere was born in 1870, and was away at boarding school, firstly to Winchester School for Boys and then to Eton College from a very young age and had very little parental guidance or supervision. He was also giving his father a very difficult time. Not only was it costing his father an enormous amount of money each year in school fees to keep up the appropriate life-style of having a son at Eton, when he could ill afford it, but Hugh Jnr. was also a *"tear away"* and a *"very poor student"* according to family journals, always getting into trouble at Eton College, not just small, insignificant mischievous acts, but immoral, dangerous and somewhat rebellious acts, such as alcohol, drugs, gambling and violence.

From a quote in the *Encyclopedia Britannica*,

> Hugh Cholmondeley, 3rd Baron, Lord Delamere, was born at Vale Royal, Cheshire on 28 April 1870 and died on 13 November 1931 in Loresho, Kenya. He was a leader of the European colonists in British East Africa protectorates (now Kenya) and he was controversial and outspoken. Delamere

become the central figure of the white community in Kenya. He believed that civilization could be brought to Africa only by European settlements and was the constant champion of white supremacy.

To round out a brief summary and overview of his character and personality we also quote from a recent article in the reputable, *Old Africa Magazine*:

> Hugh Cholmondeley, was educated at Eton, inherited the barony of Delamere and the Vale Royal estate in Cheshire when he was only seventeen, in 1887. Still an adolescent, with a violent temper, small and red-haired, he ran wild for a time, spending extravagantly. He left school and his crammer's and took to hunting on his estate. English hunting was somewhat tame, however, compared with the hunting of wild animals in Africa recounted in the tales of 'derring-do' (A noun meaning daring deeds or heroic acts used in reference to swash buckling heroes) so popular at the time.
>
> The young, 3rd Lord Delamere inherited a sizeable estate in the North of England, including land that had been in the Cholmondeley family since 1615, 7,000 acres (28 km^2) and the ancestral seat at Vale Royal in the county of Cheshire.

The young Hugh Cholmondeley made his first trip to Africa in 1891 when he was 21 years to hunt lions in British Somaliland, and returned yearly to resume the hunt. In 1894 he was severely mauled by a lion, and was only saved when his Somali gun bearer, Abdullah Ashur, leaped on the lion, giving Hugh time to retrieve his rifle. As a result of the attack, Hugh Cholmondeley limped for the rest of his life; he also developed a healthy respect for Somalis, and maybe also for lions?

It is believed that on one of these Somaliland hunting trips, Hugh coined the term 'white hunter'—the term that came to describe the professional safari hunter in colonial East Africa. Hugh also employed a professional hunter named Alan Black and a native Somali hunter to lead the safari. As the story goes, to avoid confusion, the Somali was referred to as the 'black hunter', and Black was called the 'white hunter'.

According to Brian Herne, in his excellent book "White Hunters" the name 'white hunter' came about thus:

The Delamere Saga: Part 3

By several reliable accounts it was the chance meeting of hunter Alan Black and a reckless amateur hunter known as 'D', the fiery Lord Delamere, which led to the term, 'white hunter'. Delamere had employed the youthful Alan Black to help out on one of his Somaliland safaris in the late 1890s. When Delamere settled in British East Africa he purchased a very large acreage of ranching country. At the time he employed a Somali hunter to shoot meat for his employees, and he also hired Alan Black as a hunter. To differentiate between the two hunters, as well as on account of Black's surname, the Somali hunter was referred to as the 'black hunter', while Alan Black was always called 'the white hunter', and from this difference, or so the story goes, 'white hunter' came into common usage.

In 1896, Hugh Cholmondeley, with a retinue including a doctor, taxidermist, photographer, and 200 camels, set out to cross the deserts of southern Somaliland, intending to enter British East Africa from the north. In 1897, he arrived in the lush green highlands of what is now central Kenya and fell in love with the place.

Chapter Eight: Hugh Cholmondeley, 3rd Lord Delamere, Moves to Africa

Hugh Cholmondeley, 3rd Lord Delamere, aged 29 years, married Lady Florence Anne Cole of Enniskillen, Ulster, Northern Ireland, who was 21 years old in 1899. Lady Florence Anne eventually died in Africa, a physical, mental and emotional wreck at the age of 36 in 1914.

Lady Florence had first met Hugh while she was on a visit to Vale Royal Abbey with her parents from Ireland, Hugh who was laid flat on his back for several weeks after another riding accident on the Cheshire Estate [It appears from records that he was a very poor horseman]. Hugh claims he fell in love with Lady Florence and the couple married on 11 July 1899. Hugh moved to Kenya in 1901 with his new bride, who had in the meantime given birth to a son named Thomas Pitt Hamilton in 1900. The Vale Royal Abbey was in very serious financial trouble and not providing him with any meaningful income whatsoever. Hugh's attitude toward the estate had changed dramatically, despite the fact that it was steeped in ancient English history, and he was now the current legal and responsible owner. Hugh clearly indicated that he did not care in the least about its upkeep and maintenance or even its continued existence as one of the most beautiful, reputable private estates in the whole of England.

Lady Florence Anne Cole, courtesy *Creative Commons*

Hugh Cholmondeley and his bride also abandoned their only child to the care of nannies back on the estate of Lady Florence's parents in Northern Ireland, no doubt a decision made by the head-

The Delamere Saga: Part 3

strong, dominant and very focused father, and they then settled permanently to reside in British East Africa, the country that was later to be named Kenya.

Kenya, now known as the Republic of Kenya, was a founding member of the East African Community (EAC). Its capital and largest city is Nairobi. Kenya's territory lies on the equator and overlies the East African Rift covering a diverse and expansive terrain that extends roughly from Lake Victoria to Lake Turkana (formerly called Lake Rudolf) and further south-east to the Indian Ocean. It is bordered by Tanzania to the south, Uganda to the west, South Sudan to the north-west, Ethiopia to the north and Somalia to the north-east. Kenya covers 581,309 km (224,445 sq. miles), and had a population of approximately 48 million people in July 2017.

The Republic of Kenya is named after Mount Kenya. The origin of the name Kenya is not clear, but is perhaps linked to the Kikuyu, Embu and Kamba words Kirinyaga, Kirenyaa, and Kiinyaa, which mean 'God's resting place' in all three languages. If so, then the British may not so much have mispronounced it (Keenya), as misspelled it. Prehistoric volcanic eruptions of Mount Kenya [now extinct] may have resulted in its association with divinity and creation among the indigenous Bantu ethnic groups, who are the native inhabitants of the agricultural land surrounding Mount Kenya.

The colonial history of Kenya dates from the establishment of a German protectorate over the Sultan of Zanzibar's coastal possessions in 1885, followed by the arrival of the Imperial British East Africa Company in 1888. Incipient imperial rivalry was forestalled when Germany handed its coastal holdings to Britain in 1890. This was followed by the building of the Kenya-Uganda railway passing through the country. The Uganda Railway faced a great deal of criticism in the British Parliament, as many MPs felt that the railway was a Lunatic Line. In his speech before parliament Henry Labouchère, MP, stated,

> What is the use of it, none can conjecture. What it will carry, there is none can define. And in spite of George Curzon's superior lecture, it is clearly naught but a lunatic line.

The term 'Lunatic Express' was coined by Charles Miller in his 1971 book, *The Lunatic Express: An Entertainment in Imperialism*. Its cost

Chapter Eight: Hugh Cholmondeley, 3rd Lord Delamere, Moves to Africa

has been estimated by one source at £5 million in 1894 money; £690 million in 2018 money. During the railway construction era, there was a significant inflow of Indian people to Kenya, who provided the bulk of the skilled manpower required for construction. They and most of their descendants later remained in Kenya and formed the core of several distinct Indian communities such as the Ismaili Muslim and Sikh communities.

Regarding the history of Kenya and East Africa this useful background information also sheds more light. The 'Age of Discovery' first led to European interaction with the region of present-day Kenya. The coastal regions were seen as a valuable foothold in eastern trade routes, and Mombasa became a key port for ivory. The Portuguese established a presence in the region for 200 years, between the years of 1498–1698, before losing control of the coast to the Sultans of Oman.

European exploration of the interior commenced in 1844 when two German missionaries, Johann Ludwig Krapf and Johannes Rebmann, ventured inland with the aim of spreading Christianity. The region soon sparked the imagination of other adventurers, and gradually their stories began to awaken their governments to the potential value of the area.

The rise of New Imperialism in the late 19th century intensified European interest in the region. The initial driving force lay with pioneering businessmen, such as Carl Peters and William Mackinnon seeking to establish lucrative trade routes in the region. These businessmen would in time compel their respective governments to protect their trading interests, and in 1885 Eastern Africa was carved-up between Britain, Germany and France. The British assumed control of the regions of Kenya and Uganda, and governed them through the Imperial British East Africa Company. In 1895, administration was transferred to the British Foreign Office, and the East Africa Protectorate was established, and by 1920 became officially known as the Colony of Kenya.

This enlightening script and report from a BBC documentary indicates the situation in Kenya at the beginning of the 20th century.

> In 1903 there were just fewer than 400 European settlers in British East Africa; by 1912 about 1000. The British government offered 99-year and 999-year leases to encourage settlement, as well as land tax exemption into the 1930s. The

state also subsidized white farmers' produce so that black smallholders could not compete in open markets. From the beginning, European settlement dispossessed Africans, both through legal and extra-legal means, with a discourse arguing that WaKamba, Gikuyu, and Embu had no title to the land, as they had not improved it or were 'nomadic tribes'. Many were crowded onto 'Native Reserves'; some populations came back to their original homes only to be classified as 'squatters' and often then served as cheap labor on colonists' plantations.

It was into this environment that Hugh Cholmondeley, 3rd Lord Delamere and his subjective, gullible young wife, Lady Florence, settled in British East Africa in 1901, after Hugh had abandoned all interest in his inheritance of the beautiful Vale Royal Abbey and the estate in Cheshire. During the early part of the 20th century, the interior central highlands of Kenya were settled by British and other European farmers, some who became very wealthy by farming coffee and tea, others lost everything and had to return home to Europe penniless. One depiction of this period of change from one colonist's perspective is found in the memoir *Out of Africa* (1937) by Danish author Baroness Karen von Blixen-Finecke [pen name, Isak Dineson]. By the 1930s, approximately 30,000 white settlers lived in the area and had gained a political voice because of their contribution to the market economy.

The central highlands of Kenya was already home to over a million members of the indigenous Kikuyu people at the turn of the century in 1900, most of who had no land claims in European terms and lived as itinerant farmers. To protect their interests, the new white settlers banned their growing of coffee, introduced a hut tax, and the landless were granted less and less land in exchange for their labour. A massive exodus to the cities ensued as their ability to provide a living from the land by the local Africans dwindled.

We refer to an extract from this enlightening survey of the history of Kenya, *Writer on the Edge: Lord Delamere*, by Trish Farrell (2014):

> Before the British invaded East Africa in the late nineteenth century (intent on setting up the Imperial British East Africa Company) and concluded that any land not occupied by people at that point in time was EMPTY and thus FREELY

Chapter Eight: Hugh Cholmondeley, 3rd Lord Delamere, Moves to Africa

AVAILABLE, the Massai ranged over vast tracts of the Rift grassland system. It is believed that their ancestors moved out from the Horn of Africa about four thousand years ago.

This means that the Massai lived a life that suited them and apparently with little cost to the environment for 4,000 years before the British came along and herded them into a reserve where the land is least fertile and watered for human purposes, and otherwise known as the Massai Mara. Europeans then set about destroying the wildlife on a breathtakingly ugly scale. The invaders or their activities also became vectors for deadly disease—rinderpest that decimated native cattle, and smallpox and syphilis that took their toll on the human populations.

Before the British annexed East Africa in the 1890s, and all the (deemed) unoccupied territory became the property of the British Crown, and the locals obliged to stay forever on the land where the British happened to find them, land usage and territorial ownership was a much more fluid affair. For instance, up in the Rift highlands, and going back hundreds of years, the Kikuyu farmers had negotiated the legal acquisition of new land with the indigenous Okiek hunters, whom the Kikuyu judged to be the land's original owners. Over the centuries this process of colonisation caused an occupational creep: as land became exhausted or overcrowded, so clan scions left their fathers' homesteads and sought out fresh territories for their own families to cultivate. It is a similar story over much of the continent as the Bantu agriculturalists sought fresh ground.

Again, to quote from the *Old Africa* magazine:

Hugh Cholmondeley was allocated land at Njoro by the British Crown, and Lady Florence's first home was a grass hut, but after a few months she moved to a wooden hut, with beaten earth floors, without a door or windows. A few pieces of Vale Royal Abbey furniture stood incongruously at angles around the walls. Florence must have been very lonely, but life improved slightly when the Njoro farm failed and Hugh Cholmondeley moved to Soysambu, a farm in the Rift Valley, in 1910. By now Hugh had encouraged two of Florence's brothers, Galbraith and Berkeley Cole, to come to Kenya in 1903. Galbraith farmed next door to

Soysambu, at Kekopey, and Berkeley bought land at Naro Moru. Galbraith said of Soysambu: 'There's something about it that always depresses me and I can't help thinking that my sister must have hated it. There's somehow a sort of barrenness about D's surroundings that I can't explain.'

Here is a quote from a descendant of the family of Lady Florence,

'[She] was unable to stand up to the rigours and harshness of pioneering in Kenya,' Lord Andrew Enniskillen, the 7th Earl of Enniskillen says of his ancestor, 'And it helped none that she was left alone for long periods of time in an almost uninhabited tract of land with no close neighbours while her husband was away trying to 'build the (his) new nation'.

Lady Florence, the young wife of Hugh Cholmondeley, suffered so much while living in East Africa; her life being so miserable and this difficult, wretched experience combined with loneliness and her husband's continuous neglect, led Florence to have a very serious nervous breakdown when she arrived back in England, supposedly for a rest and holiday in 1911 under strict orders from her personal doctor. She unfortunately decided to return to Kenya against the advice of her doctors and her mother during 1913, but she soon found her health deteriorating once again and sad to report, Florence died a broken, destroyed woman, aged only 36 years on the 17 May 1914. This tragic brief announcement about this remarkable young woman appeared in the *New York Times* of 19 May 1914: "Lady Delamere, 36 years, wife of Hugh Cholmondeley, 3rd Lord Delamere, died of heart disease in Nairobi, British East Africa."

One highlight that was reported and became uplifting in the drab life of "Lady Delamere" (Florence Anne Cole), while she was living in Kenya, was the private visit by the world famous Theodore (Teddy) Roosevelt some years after he had served as the 26th President of the United States (1901-1909). Theodore on 7 March, 1911 wrote a very touching private letter to Florence, Lady Delamere, after his return to the United States from Africa, no doubt having personally observed the stressful circumstances surrounding her life in the African bush. In his letter written from his home at Sagamore Hill, Oyster Bay, New York, he comments amongst other

Chapter Eight: Hugh Cholmondeley, 3rd Lord Delamere, Moves to Africa

personal observations, on Lord and Lady Delamere's agricultural success and service in East Africa and their troubled relations with the government of England. Roosevelt discusses his return to the United States and future prospects. He also comments on the public expectations for him personally and expresses his thoughts on future political powers in Africa and also in the USA [this 12 page confidential letter is now held in the Theodore Roosevelt Center at Dickenson State University in the USA].

The following is an extract from the *London Times* of 1931, published a short time after the death of Hugh Cholmondeley and provides a deeper insight to the character of Hugh, 3rd Lord Delamere [underlining is ours].

> Cholmondeley, Hugh, third Baron Delamere 1870-1931, pioneer settler in Kenya, was born in London, 28 April 1870, the only son of Hugh Cholmondeley, second Baron Delamere, by his second wife, Augusta Emily, eldest daughter of Sir George Hamilton Seymour. Educated at Eton, he inherited the title with the estate of Vale Royal Abbey, Cheshire, at the age of seventeen, when his father died in 1887. He served for a time in the 3rd battalion, The Cheshire Regiment, and in the Cheshire Yeomanry. As a young man he organized five expeditions to Somaliland in pursuit of big game; the fifth took him from Berbera into the unsettled desert region through which the Kenya-Abyssinia border now runs. He reached the highlands of what is now Kenya Colony in 1897, the first Englishman to traverse this route.
>
> Delamere could not settle down to the life of a country gentleman at Vale Royal Abbey, which he had inherited when his father died in 1887, and in January 1903 he returned to the East Africa Protectorate and decided to take up land. The highlands were still wild and partly uninhabited, but the newly built Uganda railway connected Lake Victoria with the coast.
>
> The commissioner, Sir Charles Eliot, was then embarking on a policy of attracting white settlers, who was also a personal friend of Hugh Cholmondeley. Delamere received a ninety-nine-years' lease on 100,000 acres in the Njoro district, and immediately set about importing rams from England and

New Zealand in order to improve the native sheep. At this time he was suffering from severe injuries to the spine as a result of several bad falls and arrived at his new estate on a stretcher. When the land proved unsuitable for sheep he turned to cattle and finally, after these too had died, to wheat, on which he inaugurated East African research into the breeding of rust-resistant varieties. Although not the first settler in East Africa, he was the first to experiment on a large scale and to sink considerable capital (mostly borrowed, for he was never well off) in these untried farming lands.

Delamere's fiery and autocratic temper, his quickness in debate, his generosity, and his passionate belief in the civilizing mission of white settlement in Africa fitted him for leadership of the settlers in their frequent tussles with colonial officials and their attacks on bureaucratic restrictions and delays. He was elected the first president of the Farmers' and Planters' Association in 1903 (which became the Colonists' Association in 1904), and was one of two unofficial members nominated to the first legislative council in 1907. During the war of 1914-1918 he was at first employed on intelligence work among the Maasai along the German border. The strenuous life and severe malaria did his heart an injury, which was ultimately to cause his death, and he was forced to give up active service. After six months in England he returned to his ranch, Soysambu, on which he had been able to realize his ambition of breeding, on a large scale, high-grade merino sheep.

After the war the European community was enfranchised and Delamere was elected member for the Rift Valley in 1920. He held this position until his death in 1931 and became, in addition, leader of the elected members, and one of two unofficial members of the governor's executive council. In 1923 he headed a deputation to the Colonial Office to resist proposals to enfranchise Indians on a common roll with Europeans and to allow their unrestricted immigration.

Delamere's guiding faith was his belief in the need for strong and permanent settlements of British families in the highlands of Africa. After the conquest of German East Africa he hoped to see this policy extended to Tanganyika

Chapter Eight: Hugh Cholmondeley, 3rd Lord Delamere, Moves to Africa

Territory, and a chain of European settlements forged from Kenya to the Cape. He envisaged the eventual creation of an <u>East African Dominion</u>, working towards the goal of self-government already reached by the white communities of South Africa and Southern Rhodesia, and he persistently pressed for the grant of an unofficial majority in the Kenya legislative council. In 1925 he organized, at his own expense, an unofficial conference of delegates from Kenya, Tanganyika, Northern Rhodesia, and Nyasaland, held at Tukuyu (southern Tanganyika), to promote the solidification of the white ideal. Two other conferences followed, in Livingstone and Nairobi, in 1926 and 1927. The economic crisis, however, put an end to these and other projects for the strengthening of white settlement in Tanganyika and the Central African territories. In 1929 Delamere was appointed K.C.M.G) (Most Distinguished Order of Saint Michael and Saint George) for his public services.

By now the British government had veered away from a belief that the main object of our policy and legislation should be to found a white colony (1920), to a declaration that primarily, <u>Kenya is an African territory</u>, and the interests of the African natives must be paramount (1923). With this latter statement Delamere could never agree, and in 1930 (the year before he died) he headed his last deputation to London to put forward the colonists' point of view to the labour government of England. By this time he was a very sick man, and on his return to Kenya the strain of reorganizing his heavily indebted farms to meet the catastrophic fall in prices, superimposed on exacting political duties, proved too much for a system which he had never spared. He died of angina at Loresho, near Nairobi, 13 November 1931, and was buried on his estate at Soysambu, near Lake Elmenteita.

Delamere was twice married: first, in 1899 to Florence (died 1914), fourth daughter of Lowry Egerton Cole, fourth Earl of Enniskillen, and had one son; secondly, in 1928 to Gwladys Helen (died 1943), daughter of Rupert Evelyn Beckett, formerly wife of Sir Charles Markham, second baronet. He was succeeded as fourth baron by his only son, Thomas Pitt Hamilton Cholmondeley (born 1900).

There are so many extremely sad stories related to this period of time and the events connected to the 3rd Lord Delamere and the country of Kenya during the early 20th century, apart from what happened to his poor wife, Lady Florence and her untimely premature death in 1914, aged only 36 years. Hugh Cholmondeley had apparently persuaded the two brothers of Lady Florence, namely Galbraith Lowry Egerton Cole and Berkeley Cole to also move to Kenya, they were no doubt influenced by the glamorous stories put across by their brother-in-law, the loquacious and very persuasive Hugh Cholmondeley. Both of these characters also came to a sad end in Kenya.

Despite the claim, "I will prove to you all that this land is a white man's country", made by Hugh Cholmondeley, 3rd Lord Delamere, the experience of many European settlers does not make for happy reading. Life in Kenya proved to be very hard for many of these disillusioned white settlers. For example, we only have to read about the very sad life of Hugh Cholmondeley's own first wife, Lady Florence and her dreadful experiences of living in Africa, leading to her premature death as a destroyed woman in 1914. We can also take a brief glimpse of some of the better-known European characters who moved to Kenya under the false illusion that it was a "white man's" country.

We briefly recount the life of Baroness Blixen (1885-1962) from Denmark, whose experiences and life was extremely hard in East Africa and she had to face the failure of the coffee plantation, as a result of mismanagement, the elevation of the farm, drought and the falling price of coffee caused by the worldwide economic depression, all of which forced Blixen to abandon her beloved farm and estate 'Karen'. Blixen and her husband were quite different in education and temperament, and Bror Blixen was unfaithful to his wife. She was diagnosed with syphilis toward the end of their first year of marriage in 1915. According to her biographer Judith Thurman, she contracted the disease from her husband. She returned to Denmark in June 1915 for treatment, which proved successful. Although Blixen's illness was eventually cured (some uncertainty exists), it created medical anguish for years to come. By 1919, the marriage had run into serious difficulties, causing her husband to request a divorce in 1920. Against her wishes, the couple separated in 1921 and they were officially divorced in 1925. Bror

Chapter Eight: Hugh Cholmondeley, 3rd Lord Delamere, Moves to Africa

Blixen was dismissed as the farm manager by Aage Westenholz, chairman of the Karen Coffee Company, and Karen Blixen took over its management herself in 1921.

The land was not suited for coffee cultivation, being too high in elevation. The couple had hired local workers, predominantly the Kikuyu people who lived on the farmlands at the time of their arrival but there were also Wakamba, Kavirondo, Swahili and Maasai. Initially Bror Blixen-Finecke worked the farm, but it soon became evident that he had little interest in it and preferred to leave running the farm to his wife Baroness Blixen while he went on safari.

The family business later sold the land to a residential developer, and Baroness Blixen returned to Denmark in August 1931 to live with her mother. She remained in Rungstedlund for the rest of her life, a sad disillusioned woman. In her analysis of Blixen's medical history, biographer Donelson points out that Blixen wondered if her pain was 'psychosomatic' and states that during Blixen's lifetime her illnesses were rumored to be fabricated. Her publisher in private indicated that Blixen's syphilis was a myth, but publicly, Blixen blamed syphilis for her chronic health issues. Donelson concluded: "Whatever her belief about her illness, the disease suited the artist's design for creating her own personal legend."

Unable to eat, Baroness Blixen died in 1962 at Rungstedlund, her family's estate in Denmark, at the age of 77, apparently of malnutrition. Others attribute her weight loss and eventual death to anorexia nervosa.

Denys Finch Hatton (1887-1931), 'another square peg in a round hole' so to speak, developed a close friendship with Baroness Blixen and her Swedish husband, Baron Bror von Blixen-Finecke. Denys left Africa in 1920 but returned in 1922, investing in a land development company. Born in Kensington, London, England on 24 April 1887, Denys Finch Hatton was the second son and third child of Henry Finch Hatton, 13th Earl of Winchilsea, who was also known as the 8th Earl of Nottingham, by his wife, the former Anne "Nan" Codrington, daughter of Admiral of the Fleet, Sir Henry Codrington. Finch Hatton was educated at Eton and Brasenose College, Oxford. His father Henry, although he was a member of the English aristocracy, was penniless, and from 1875 until 1887, he was a cattle-farmer and gold miner in Queensland, Australia.

The Delamere Saga: Part 3

By this time, Karen Blixen had separated from her husband, and after their divorce in 1925, Finch Hatton moved into her house and began leading safaris for wealthy sportsmen from overseas who were keen on making their "kill' of the wild life of Africa. Also Finch Hatton, from records and reports, lived a debauched life and he died in 1931 when his small aircraft crashed in the bush of Africa. On the morning of 14 May 1931, Denys Finch Hatton's de Havilland Gypsy Moth aircraft took off from Voi airport in Southern Kenya; circled the airport twice, then plunged to the ground and burst into flames. It is rumored that he was 'blind drunk' and intoxicated when he climbed into the cockpit of his small plane that sad day back in 1931. Other rumors claim that someone who wanted him dead had mixed water with the petrol in his gas tank, thus causing his aircraft to crash to the ground.

Regarding both of these individuals, Baroness Karen Blixen and Denys Finch Hatton, their lives, plus lifestyle, is over glamorized in the book and also in *Out of Africa*. which was directed and produced by Sidney Pollack of Hollywood, personal friend of Robert Redford.

Pollack (1934-2008) who died in Los Angeles aged 73, was producer, director and actor of over 44 films, and is also well-known for his incredible film, also staring his friend Robert Redford, *Jeremiah Jones*, partly filmed on Redford's private estate in Sundance, Utah, which displays the incredible beauty of America's natural resources. Sydney was so restricted in financial support to make this film and was only allowed funds to make it in Southern California. But to make sure it reflected the true image of the beauty and nature of America's mid-west, he re-mortgaged his house in Los Angeles to create sufficient funds to move the production to the beautiful scenery of Utah. This is one of my favourite places to visit, when I spend time at our family home in Salt Lake City, Utah.

Robert Redford had bought this acreage near North Fork Canyon, Utah, and it spans over 5,000 acres on the slopes of Mount Timpanogos in Utah's Wasatch Mountain Range. It was renamed from Timp Haven to Sundance, after the role that Redford played in the film *Butch Cassidy and the Sundance Kid*, and Redford, a dedicated conservationist, used his proceeds from that film made with his friend Paul Newman to purchase this land in 1968. Today it is retained as one of America's outstanding natural resources as

Chapter Eight: Hugh Cholmondeley, 3rd Lord Delamere, Moves to Africa

part of the Uinta National Forest. The name "Sundance" is based on a Native American ceremony. But we are becoming somewhat distracted, so let us leave beautiful Utah behind and get back to the subject at hand, and return to the scenic country of Kenya in Africa.

There are so many additional stories of the hardships and failures of other European settlers in Kenya that do not always make the headlines, but it proves beyond all doubt in most cases that Kenya was NOT and is NOT a 'white man's country'. But, in fact, as my maternal grandfather Herbert Green, a highly intelligent, educated and a well-read man, told me when we discussed Africa and my dreams of living there someday, "Always remember old chap [he always used that expression as a term of endearment even though I was a youngster], *Africa belongs to the Africans.*"

When I was a young boy, my grandfather often used to read to me from the H. Ryder Haggard books, which he regularly borrowed from the Carnegie Royton Library in Lancashire, especially the books about Allan Quartermain (see Appendix 10). Allan Quatermain was the protagonist of the writer, H. Ryder Haggard.

I also remember my grandfather taking me along to the Royton Pavilion Cinema [bioscope], also known locally by its nickname as "The Bug Hut", to watch the films of *Tarzan the Ape Man,* always set in Africa, which seemed to be a regular treat before the days of television. I was always amused when my grandfather told me that the owner of the cinema, Mr. Cheetham, who was a very mercenary character (he and his family also owned a few old neglected filthy cotton mills in the local area), would cut out a large section or slice of the celluloid film before the reel was returned to the owners and distributors in Manchester, and Mr. Cheetham would then cut the section of film into single frames of approximately one square inch (35 millimetres) and then sell these at a penny each to the children who poured out of the cinema after the advertised film ended. It was rumored that he made more tax-free money from the illegal sale of these film cuttings than he did from the attendance money paid by the patrons!

I also vividly remember being mesmerized regarding the adventures of the fictional Allan Quatermain, and I so envied his lifestyle. To quote from the foreword:

The Delamere Saga: Part 3

> Quatermain is an English-born professional big game hunter and occasional trader in southern Africa, who supports colonial efforts to 'spread civilization' in the 'dark continent', though he also favours native Africans having a say in their affairs. An outdoorsman who finds English cities and climate unbearable, he prefers to spend most of his life in Africa, where he grew up under the care of his widower father, a Christian missionary.

No doubt as I listened to these fascinating accounts of Africa and its intriguing history, seeds were sown in my impressionable, young mind, because—a local lad from Royton, Lancashire—later in life I spent over 30 years of my adult life living on this beautiful and awe inspiring continent, enjoying the gorgeous beauty of God's creation and all its stunning, spectacular wildlife.

My grandfather, besides being an avid reader of African news, was also a shrewd observer of African current affairs, especially related to eastern and southern Africa. I also think he personally knew from information passed down from his mother, Margaret Green (1835-1908) former housekeeper at Vale Royal Abbey, and confirmed in her private letters, that his biological half-brother Hugh Cholmondeley Jnr. (1870-1931), lived in Kenya, and he intensely followed his career and exploits. He was also a great believer in quality education and he personally accomplished the almost impossible task of securing a "scholarship" for his only child [my mother Margaret Green] to attend the well-known and highly respected, Hulme Grammar School for Girls, founded in 1691 in the town of Oldham, Greater Manchester, England.

Herbert Green also collected news clippings of articles related to British East Africa and any news that related to his biological half-brother, Hugh Cholmondeley Jnr., whom he never met though they had the same father. Hugh had gone to live in British East Africa in 1901 when he abandoned Vale Royal Abbey, the family estate in Cheshire, that he had inherited in 1887. When my grandfather died in 1943 my mother passed these news clippings onto his only older brother, my great-uncle John William (1876-1945) who lived in Alfred Street, Crompton, and who placed these for safe keeping in a family heirloom, a small ornamental oak box that he had inherited from his mother Margaret Green.

Chapter Eight: Hugh Cholmondeley, 3rd Lord Delamere, Moves to Africa

This precious, solid oak box was about 18 inches in length and about 12 inches in height and width. It was decorated with solid brass corner pieces and a brass lock, and on the lid were carved the initials MG in ornamental letters. I still remember it because, as a young boy, whenever I visited my great uncle's house in Crompton, it was proudly on display on the welsh dresser in the living room. Being the eldest living son of Margaret Green, John William had inherited this oak box and its contents, which included copious hand written notes and private letters of his mother between herself and Hugh Cholmondeley, Snr. of Vale Royal Abbey. Also it contained many news clippings from Cheshire newspapers related to Vale Royal Abbey, as Margaret had been born in Chester and worked at Vale Royal Abbey.

When my great-uncle died in 1945, he had no children, so the contents of his house were to be auctioned off. My mother being one of the next of kin was offered her choice of some ornaments and trinkets that held some sentimental value, but when she enquired about this precious oak box, it had disappeared along with some other small valuable items. My mother always said that she knew of the suspected thief but as she had no proof she was helpless to take any further steps. The sad thing is that whomever stole that box would not be interested in its precious contents as they would be meaningless to anyone apart from our immediate family. They were probably destroyed by this thoughtless thief.

One precious item my mother did obtain was the priceless Green family Bible that John William had inherited from his mother, which contained family records written in the exquisite handwriting of Margaret Green, plus it also contained copies of birth certificates and some old family photographs. I am pleased to say that this very same family Bible is still in the possession of the Hebdon family today and will remain so.

I still vividly remember the very night when my grandfather died in 1943, as he was by circumstances forced to work in the cotton factories of Lancashire, whose greedy, unfeeling owners totally disregarded the need for safety and health protection of the incumbent workers. He was a victim of the Industrial Revolution. He died that night, as he slept in the same bedroom as I did, but not in a bed—slumped upright in a rocking chair, as that was the only way he could breathe due to his industrial disease of Byssinosis.[25] Every night, between his violent coughing attacks, he read from the adventures of Allan Quatermain in Africa until I fell asleep in our cottage in Rochdale Lane, Royton. I was awakened by my mother, who at this time was eight months pregnant carrying my dear, only brother Leslie. This was in the early hours of that winter's morning in February of 1943, and I remember being hurriedly moved to the neigbouring cottage of Mrs. Williams. I was never to see my beloved grandfather alive again or hear his comforting deep voice as he read about Africa. During his last night on Earth he fell into a deep sleep, never to awaken again and see the glorious sunrise each morning over the Pennine Chain hills. I so loved that man!

The wife of Herbert Green, my grandmother Alice (1878-1924), who I never met or knew, died 15 years before I was born of the same dreadful disease Byssinosis at the young age of 46 years as a result of of working in the cotton factories, which appeared to be the only available employment for most of the local people in Lancashire. My grandfather often spoke about her, and with such endearing terms that she came 'alive' in my fertile mind. My grandfather also recounted many private and happy moments they shared in the few short years they had spent together, especially the trips to their favorite place in England, the gorgeous clean air, lakes and mountains of the Lake District of Cumberland (Cumbria, especially Derwentwater), and its association with William Wordsworth and other Lake Poets, also with Beatrix Potter and John Ruskin. According to my mother's recollections, my grandfather never fully recovered from his wife's untimely death and he seemed to retreat within himself for the remainder of his life.

I slowly grew to love my grandmother, even though I had never met her. This was through the nostalgic stories recounted by my grandfather, as he so often spoke about the personality and appearance of this incredible woman and the warm intimate stories of their life spent together. This was truly their love story!

So today, as a result, I now have etched in my mind the vivid

---

[25] Byssinosis, also called "brown lung disease" or "Monday fever", is an occupational lung disease caused by exposure to cotton dust in inadequately ventilated working environments. Byssinosis commonly occurs in workers who are employed in yarn and fabric manufacturing industries. Brown lung can ultimately result in narrowing of the airways, lung scarring and death from infection or respiratory failure.

Chapter Eight: Hugh Cholmondeley, 3rd Lord Delamere, Moves to Africa

vision of this beautiful young 'mystery' woman with her flaming red hair, her emerald green eyes, her aquiline nose, her strong jaw and her sweet unassuming voice and I also grew to love and admire her! My grandfather recounted the times they often sat in the parlour of our family home in Rochdale Lane and the love that his wife had for her black cat called "Sooty". Her cat always sat on her lap every evening in front of the warm crackling fire, as my grandfather read to my grandmother the poems of Byron and Wordsworth. In my crazy imagination, today I even visualize myself sitting with them, an unseen onlooker of this touching scene. I still have in my possession today and regularly use a now priceless book, previously owned by my grandfather, *The Poetical Works of William Wordsworth*.

My fondness for her is based on family photographs of her, along with my grandfather taken shortly after they married back in 1914 and also founded on the nostalgic memories passed on to me by her beloved husband Herbert, plus the heritage and blessings she passed on to our family through her only daughter Margaret, my mother born in 1916. Margaret became our family's matriarch and 'guiding star' until she sadly passed away on 12 March 2003, aged 87 years.

The cottage of my grandfather and grandmother in Rochdale Lane, which had been their family home from the day they married back in 1914 up until his death in 1943, was also my home along with my parents and siblings. In 1947 my parents decided to purchase an old Victorian vicarage in Queen Street, Royton to accommodate their growing family and today I am proud to relate that this same old vicarage, now a beautiful Victorian home, has been lovingly restored with its original Victoriana features. This new home is full with so many happy memories, and of course like most normal families with some sad memories also. It is still in the hands of the next generation of the Hebdon family, over 70 years later.[26]

My grandfather was a very compassionate and gentle soul, no doubt characteristics inherited from his father, Hugh Cholmondeley, 2nd Lord Delamere of Vale Royal Abbey, whereas his mother Margaret Green was very outspoken and tended to be

---

[26] It is of interest to note that the beautiful and impressive floor tiles in the large hallway of our family home in Queen Street, Royton, were from the Accrington Brick and Tile Manufactures. The very same identical floor tiles were also exported to the USA and were used in the construction of the main entrance hallway and photo gallery of the State Capitol Building of California in Sacramento built in 1860.

The Delamere Saga: Part 3

a strong willed woman, according to reports and her private letters. Herbert was also a great lover of poetry, just like his father Hugh Cholmondeley, and his favourite poet was Lord Byron.

At the funeral of his wife Alice, his first and only true love, he read, with tears streaming down his cheeks, from his favourite poet, Lord Byron, whose ancestors had lived in Royton Hall for over 400 years (see Appendix 7). Byron's poem, "A Picture of Death", perfectly describes the pain that my grandfather felt in his heart and the great loss that he was now experiencing, the loss of his lovely, graceful wife Alice, who had died at the age of 46 years in 1924.

A Picture of Death

That first dark day of nothingness,
The last of danger and distress,
Before decay's effacing fingers,
Have swept the lines where beauty lingers,
Hers is the loveliness in death,
That departs not quite with parting breath,
But beauty with that fearful bloom,
That hue, which haunts it to the tomb,
A gilded halo hovering around decay,
The farewell beam of feeling past away;
Spark of that flame, perchance of heavenly birth,
Which gleams, but warms no more its cherished earth!

– Lord Byron, courtesy of the Lord Byron Trust

As mentioned in the Preface, over 80% of the people of Royton, Lancashire worked in the textile industry. Alice Green had worked in the 'carding or card room', which was the filthiest and most polluted area in the factory. We provide a brief overview of that part of English history and what took place in these "dark satanic mills", a description so brilliantly highlighted by William Blake in his well-known, powerful hymn, "Jerusalem".

As to what happened and took place in these mills the following was derived from the *Handbook of Textiles* by Ann Collier (1974). Additional description is provided from my first-hand knowledge of the cotton mills, plus by our team of researchers.

Chapter Eight: Hugh Cholmondeley, 3rd Lord Delamere, Moves to Africa

After the bales of cotton arrived in the factories of England, most having been shipped from the United States through the docks at Liverpool on the English west coast and then transported up the Manchester Ship canal. These bales consisting of raw cotton, grown and picked by the black slaves brought from Africa in the abominable slave ships by ruthless British slave traders and then sold to the wealthy plantation owners in the Southern States of America. A large number of early settlers in America grew cotton. To grow cotton and to pick and then 'gin' (remove seeds from the white fluff) and then bale it took a great deal of work. Therefore large numbers of slaves were purchased from Africa to do this work. The industry was given a boost by the invention of Eli Whitney's Cotton Gin in 1793. With the aid of a horse to turn the gin, a man could clean up to at least fifty times as much more cotton as before. This increased the demand for slaves. For example, in 1803 alone, over 20,000 slaves were being brought into Georgia and South Carolina from Africa to work in the cotton fields.

Now that these bales of cotton had arrived in the cellars of the cotton mills in Lancashire the process of preparing this raw cotton now begins. When the bales of cotton were broken open by the 'bale breakers' on the stone floor of the 'carding room' the bales of raw cotton very often still contained foreign objects such as stalks and seed husks of the cotton bushes. On many occasions they even found dead rats and on one occasion it is reported that in the 'carding room' of the old Shiloh Mill in Royton, that the severed hand of a black slave fell out of the bale onto the stone floor as the cotton bale was opened.

The raw cotton was laid in layers by the 'picking machines' and this was the way the bales were packed when received in the factory. The cotton comes out of the bale in laps, and is then taken to the carding machines. The carders line up the fibres nicely to make them easier to spin. The carding machine consists mainly of one big roller with smaller ones surrounding it. All of the rollers are covered with small teeth, and as the cotton progresses further on the teeth get finer (i.e. closer together). The cotton leaves the carding machine in the form of a sliver; a large rope of fibres.

In a wider sense carding can refer to the four processes of willowing, lapping, carding and drawing. In 'willowing' the fibers are loosened. In 'lapping' the dust is removed to create a flat sheet or lap of fibres; 'Carding' itself is the combing of the tangled lap into a thick rope or sliver of 1/2 inch in diameter, it can then be optionally combed, which is used to remove the shorter fibres, creating a stronger yarn.

The combing machine plays a large part of cleansing the rough cotton. In 'drawing' a drawing frame combines 4 slivers into one. Repeated drawing increases the quality of the sliver allowing for finer counts to be spun. Each sliver will have thin and thick spots, and by combining several slivers together a more consistent size can be reached. Since combining several slivers produces a very thick rope of cotton fibres, directly after being combined the slivers are separated into 'rovings'. These rovings (or slubbings) are then what are used in the spinning process. For machine processing, a roving is about the width of a pencil. The rovings are collected in a drum and proceed to the slubbing frame which adds twist, and winds onto bobbins. Intermediate Frames are used to repeat the slubbing process to produce a finer yarn, and then the roving frames reduces it to a finer thread, gives more twist, makes it more regular and even in thickness, and winds onto a smaller tube, all now ready for the spinning process either on the 'mules' or 'ring' frames.

The spinning mule is a machine used to spin cotton and other fibres. They were used extensively from the late 18th to the early 20th century in the mills of Lancashire and elsewhere. Spinning Mules were worked in pairs by a minder, with the help of two boys: the little piecer and the big or side piecer. From this process we then go to the winding rooms in the factory. Winders are used heavily in textile manufacturing, especially in preparation to weaving where the final product moves on to the weavers and looms in the weaving sheds and the yarn is wound onto a bobbin and then used in a shuttle. Weaving is a method of textile production in which two distinct sets of yarns or threads are interlaced at right angles to form a fabric or cloth. The longitudinal threads are called the warp and the lateral threads are the weft or filling. The final product now known as a "bolt" of cloth or fabric and is now ready for making your new suit, blanket or dress depending on whether the material needs colouring or dyeing.

In those days there was no compensation for the victims of this terrible disease Byssinosis, which plagued the local employees who worked in the cotton mills, it was only in later years that the British government after extensive and numerous court cases and legal actions admitted any liability for the negligence and failure in monitoring these greedy industrialists and their lack of providing health and safety protection to their employees. The Government then started a scheme, subsidized by the British taxpayer, of granting compensation and special pensions to the unwitting and unfortunate victims of the cotton industry in Lancashire. My grandfather and grandmother gained no benefits from this legislation as they had both already prematurely died and were both victims of the greed and neglect of the very wealthy, agregious cotton mill owners.

Byssinosis first became compensatable in Great Britain in May 1941. The claimants were examined by a specially constituted board consisting of chest physicians and medical specialists from the Manchester area. Following the *Industrial Injuries Act of 1946*, which became operative in July 1948, the examinations were taken over by the Manchester Pneumoconiosis Medical Panel. At first only men who had worked for at least 20 years up to and including cotton carding processes could claim. They had to be permanently and totally incapacitated by the disease. Women workers, who made up to at least 65% of the mill employees, were only included much later, and the disablement requirement was reduced from total to 50% in December 1948. As experience with the diagnosis was gained, the law was changed to cover any degree of disablement in 1956, and in 1974 those with Byssinosis Grade II were included.

Lancashire was the ideal location for the booming cotton industry, which was one of the major industries in England for over a century, as Lancashire was known for its climate of being wet and damp and this was perfect for the cotton spinning and weaving industries. This climate was also unfortunately responsible for the chest infection of 'chronic bronchitis' known as the "Englishman's disease", which seemed to affect half of the population of Lancashire in those days.

The Delamere Saga: Part 3

This quote from the report by the Manchester Museum, *Remembering Slavery*, is also very enlightening:

> Of all the goods associated with the transatlantic slave trade, cotton was the most important in the Greater Manchester region. The north-west had a long history of textile production from the 1400's, based mainly on wool and linen.
>
> With the availability of cheap cotton grown by enslaved Africans in the Americas, cotton processing and production soon became the most important local industries and led to the regional development of towns such as Bolton, Oldham and Rochdale. Raw cotton was grown by the enslaved Africans and imported through Liverpool for processing. Lancashire was perfect for making cotton cloth. The damp climate made the cotton fibres less likely to snap during spinning. There were also many engineering works making spinning and weaving machinery and local coal supplied the boilers firing the mill engines. The region's long tradition of small scale textile production meant a ready supply of skilled labour, although growth was so rapid that additional labour, including children, had to be brought in from outside Lancashire.
>
> The importance of the cotton industries continued in the north-west long after the British abolition of slavery. Cotton grown in the southern states of the USA, where slavery was still legal until 1865 was critical to the expansion of the north west of England and its industrial growth.

The following are a series of short comprehensive reports from our research outlining the working conditions of the mill workers back in the 19th century and expose the dreadful, shudder-some conditions in those "dark satanic" mills.

> There were no guards on the large machines in the mills, so many workers could get caught or trapped! Accidents were common because people were unfamiliar with the machines; they had to crawl under them and also were exhausted because they worked such long hours. Sadly, some children were killed or crushed under them. Fencing and the placing of guards over the machinery was not made

Chapter Eight: Hugh Cholmondeley, 3rd Lord Delamere, Moves to Africa

compulsory until 1844.

When I was twelve years I started at 6am in the card room and I lost all my fingers. We used to 'fettle under' (clean and oil, the principal meaning of the verb means to 'gird up', or to 'make ready', and the noun, that the subject is ready and in fine order, as in 'fine fettle') while the machines were still running. I was oiling and cleaning the machine at ten past six in the morning and still half asleep when it happened.

Accidents were accepted as part of life in the mill. In 1833, the Government established the Factory Inspectorate to try to regulate conditions in the mills and reduce accidents. This wasn't very effective though because there weren't enough inspectors for all the factories and the inspectors weren't present all of the time.

The working conditions in many cotton mills were notoriously bad, not to mention dangerous! A few responsible mill owners tried to provide better and safer conditions for their workers. Most others though were not interested in considering the health and welfare of their workers because it might cost them money and reduce their profits. There were many dangers that mill workers were exposed to on a daily basis.

We went to our work at 6 in the morning until 6 at night without anything at all to eat or fire to warm us. For about a year after I went into the mill we never stopped for breakfast. Later the breakfast was brought to the mill in tin cans on large trays. It was milk, porridge and oat cake. They brought them into the work rooms and everyone took a tin and ate his breakfast as he could catch it, working away all the while. We stopped at 12 o'clock and had an hour for dinner (lunch) but also had the cleaning to do during that time. It took some of us half an hour to clean and oil the machinery. We then went to dinner (lunch) in the adjoining canteen, which was potato-pie five days in the week.

The card room was so dusty the workers cannot even see each other unless very close up. The floors of the mill were often covered in machine oil and water. The workers often had to work in their bare feet as this appeared to be the best way to work while being so close to unguarded machines, and to get the best grip with ones feet. [This revealing report is extracted from the papers of the Sadler Committee, convened by Parliament of 1832.]

In addition to these appalling working conditions of the employees in the cotton industry, we must also be reminded of the dreadful air pollution that these cotton mills created. The coal burning boilers of the engines rooms generated filthy black smoke and soot that belched out into the atmosphere from tall chimney stacks and created such atrocious pollution that affected all the inhabitants of the local towns. Royton, for example, with a population of approximately 16,000 inhabitants, had more than 40 factories disgorging filthy black, sooty smoke, so you can easily imagine why chest ailments, bronchitis and chest infections were rampant in these areas. Larger towns like Oldham, Rochdale and Bolton had even a larger number of factories creating the same pollution. Oldham in Lancashire became the most productive cotton-spinning town in the world and at one time had 360 textile mills, which operated day and night, creating the same filth and smoke over the local areas (see the photo of Royton (1905) in the Preface).

To motivate and inspire our readers who still love England and especially Cheshire, Yorkshire, Lancashire and the Lake District, that "green and pleasant land", we provide the words of this poem written in 1808 by William Blake, which was later set to music by Sir Hubert Parry in 1916. You will also find very inspiring the background behind this moving poem, if you so decide to investigate further.

Jerusalem

And did those feet in ancient time,
Walk upon England's mountains green:
And was the holy Lamb of God,
On England's pleasant pastures seen!

And did the Countenance Divine,
Shine forth upon our clouded hills?
And was Jerusalem builded here,
Among these dark Satanic Mills?

Chapter Eight: Hugh Cholmondeley, 3rd Lord Delamere, Moves to Africa

Bring me my Bow of burning gold;
Bring me my Arrows of desire:
Bring me my Spear: O clouds unfold!
Bring me my Chariot of fire!

I will not cease from Mental Fight,
Nor shall my Sword sleep in my hand:
Till we have built Jerusalem,
In England's green & pleasant Land.

– William Blake, courtesy of the Rylands Library & William Blake Archives

Through these examples of hard work, dedication and sincere Christian living we live and prosper today, and to their memory and example we dedicate our future.

But enough of this part of English history and my personal memories, as Forrest Gump said, "That's about all I got to say bout that." The remainder of my research will be covered in my next project, which is a book based on the personal history of the Greenwood family of Lancashire and the cotton trade; from the 'black' slaves of America to the 'white' slaves who worked in the mills of Yorkshire and Lancashire, entitled "The Birth, Life & Death of King Cotton".

Now we reluctantly travel back to Kenya and to underscore the dangers and consequences of 'whites' living in Africa, the newspapers still continuously report; even today, the savage murders and killings of Europeans. Many of these murders remain unsolved to this day, but in remembrance of some of these outstanding Europeans that sincerely made a personal contribution to Kenya and whom the world sadly lost while living in this incredible country of Kenya, we 'memorialize' the following individuals:

- Julie Ward (1988) wildlife photographer.
- Gabriella Maina (2017) Australian schoolteacher.
- Tristan Voorspuy (2017) retired British Army Officer.
- Kuki Gallamn (2017) environmental activist, and conservationist, plus of *I Dreamed of Africa* fame.
- George Adamson (1989) of the book and film *Born Free* fame.
- Josslyn Victor Hay (1941) 22nd Earl of Erroll a British peer,

famed for the unsolved case surrounding his murder and the film *White Mischief*.

- Joan Root (2006) the world famous conservationist.
- Lois Anderson and her daughter Zelda White (2007)—missionaries and hospital volunteers
- Placidus Timmons (1997) Irish Catholic Missionary
- Campbell Bridges (2009) famous gemologist
- John Anthony Kaiser (2000) Roman Catholic Priest
- Ted Loden (2013) retired British Army Officer
- Alexander Monson (2012) son of the British aristocrat, 12th Baron Nicolas Monson
- Bruce McKenzie (1978) Minister of Agriculture, Kenya
- Hulda Stumpf (1930) Christian Missionary
- Brian Thorpe (2008) Roman Catholic Missionary
- Esmond Bradley Martin (2018) world leader in conservation

The list goes on and on. These victims are in addition to the countless number of other British settlers, murdered and slaughtered during the atrocities of the Mau Mau Uprising of 1952-1960.

We must not forget of course the unknown number of local Africans who were also murdered and killed during those distressing years of turmoil in Kenya during the 20th century, plus the atrocities committed by the British troops, especially in the prisons and camps established by the British Colonial Government. The book *Britain's Gulag in Kenya* by Caroline Elkins chronicles how the British had battled this anti-colonial uprising by "confining some 1.5 million Kenyans to a network of detention camps and heavily patrolled villages." It was a tale of systematic violence and high-level cover-ups.

Regarding Galbraith Cole, the brother of Lady Florence Delamere, the newspaper *The Standard Digital Media* of Nairobi provides a fascinating review of this generous gift of local land by Hugh Cholmondeley (which he did not rightfully own) to Galbraith Cole:

> A 30,000-acre piece of land Lord Delamere was gifted to his brother-in-law, the Honorable Galbraith Lowry Egerton Cole (1881-1929). The Lake Elementeita area became

a white settlement when Lord Delamere (1870-1931) established Soysambu, now a 48,000-acre (190 square km) ranch that covers two thirds of the shoreline on the western side of the lake. To the East of the lake stands Kekopey Ranch, the 30,000-acre piece of land that Delamere gifted to his brother-in-law. A brick farmhouse, the main building of Kekopey Ranch, was built in 1917 and is today preserved as the Lake Elementaita Lodge. From the house, a panoramic view opens up; that of the Soysambu conservancy framed by a series of hills, among them the 'sleeping warrior' or the 'nose of Delamere', a kopje so named by the Maasai.

At the foot of the hills is the lake that is located between Lake Naivasha and Lake Nakuru. Elementaita is derived from the Masaai word 'muteita', meaning 'dust place', a reference to the parched appearance of the land between January and March. It is in Kekopey that part of the blockbuster films, *Tomb Raider* and *Out of Africa* was shot.

The Lake Nakuru/Lake Elementaita basin is home to over 400 bird species and it attracts visiting flamingoes, both the Greater and Lesser varieties. Tilapia, brought in from Lake Magadi in 1962, attract many fish-eating birds that also feed upon the flamingo eggs and chicks. Over a million birds that formerly bred at Elementaita are now said to have sought refuge at Lake Natron in Tanzania. Lake Elementaita has been a Ramsar.[27] site since 2005, an internationally recognised wetland. This year of 2005 it was, as were Lakes Nakuru and Bogoria, declared a UNESCO World Heritage Site for the birdlife around them.

But the tragic story of Galbraith Cole, a man as temperamental as he was adventurous, is revealing today. Wikipedia eulogises him thus:

> Galbraith was a pioneer settler and farmer of the East Africa Protectorate since 1905. He entered the 10th Royal Hussars as a lieutenant in 1900, at age 19, and went to South Africa for the Second Boer War. After being injured in the war, he made his way to Kenya where his sister Florence had married the prominent British settler Lord Delamere.

---

[27] The Convention on Wetlands, called the Ramsar Convention (so named after the Iranian city of Ramsar), is an intergovernmental treaty that provides the framework for national action and international cooperation for the conservation and wise use of wetlands and their resources.

The Delamere Saga: Part 3

> When he received the piece of land from Hugh Cholmondeley, he named it 'Kekopey Ranch', a name derived from a Masaai word meaning 'place where green turns white'. This is in reference to the soda and diatomite around the hot springs at the southern end of the lake. Very popular for bathing, the local Maasai claim that it has therapeutic powers. The reed beds nearby are fishing grounds for night herons and pelicans. In 1917, Galbraith married Lady Eleanor Balfour, niece of former British Prime Minister Lord Balfour. Cole was deported to the German East African Protectorate after he shot dead a farm labourer for stealing one of his favorite Marino rams, imported from New Zealand. It was not until he returned secretly to Kekopey dressed as a Somali and his mother the Countess of Enniskillen, pleaded his case with the British Government that he was allowed to return. But dogged by misery, the arthritic Galbraith became blind in one eye and was wheelchair-bound due to the excruciating pain. He finally shot himself through the head in 1929 at the age of 48, and was buried at his favourite spot, the viewpoint where his memorial now stands.

Regarding his younger brother, Berkeley Cole (1882-1925), who was also the brother of the late, Lady Florence, wife of Hugh Cholmondeley, 3rd Lord Delamere, these comments were also made in the Kenyan Press.

> The founder of the Muthaiga Club on the outskirts of Nairobi was Berkeley Cole (1882-1925), an Anglo-Irish aristocrat, the brother of Lady Florence and Galbraith Lowry Egerton Cole, as he wanted a place where a bell would summon a drink on a "spotless tray". According to his friend Karen Blixen, his daily consumption kicked off with a bottle of champagne at 11am – resulting in a fatal heart attack in 1925 at the age of 43. The Muthaiga Club's first president was Hugh Cholmondeley, third Baron Delamere, who shaped Kenya in this and many other ways after falling in love with the country in 1901. Blixen's close friend, Denys Finch Hatton, played by Robert Redford in *Out of Africa*, was a familiar figure, slouched on bougainvillea-shaded terraces, throughout the Twenties. A colourful description of Berkley is found in the British expatriate improvising a charmed life among the colony's well-to-do. Reginald Berkeley Cole

Chapter Eight: Hugh Cholmondeley, 3rd Lord Delamere, Moves to Africa

Flamingos on Lake Nakuru in the Rift Valley of Kenya, courtesy of *Creative Commons*

(1882-1925), an Anglo-Irish aristocrat from Ulster (being a son of the 4th Earl of Enniskillen), was a veteran of the Boer War, a possessor of a sly wit who affected a dandy's persona in the Kenya colony.

According to the newspaper report in the *London Daily Telegraph* of 13 April 2014 this comment was also made regarding the Muthaiga Club.

> In his mansion on the 20-acre Karen estate, Lord Delamere's stepson, Michael Cunningham-Reid (who died in February 2014), shared vivid memories of New Year's celebrations at the Muthaiga Club. 'We jumped horses over the tables and shot guns in the air, but it seems a long time ago,' he said with undisguised regret. 'Best of all was the night a famous socialite danced naked in the men-only bar.' He chortled lasciviously, as only an octogenarian can in today's judgmental world.

In *Out of Africa*, the character Berkley Cole is brilliantly portrayed by Michael Kitchen, best remembered for his portrayal in the TV series, *Foyle's War*, a British detective drama series set during (and shortly after) World War II.

Caroline Elkins (2005), in *Imperial Reckoning: The Untold Story of Britain's Gulag in Kenya*, describes the Muthaiga Club as having had a reputation during colonial times as "the Moulin Rouge of Africa", where the elite "drank champagne and pink gin for breakfast, played cards, danced through the night, and generally woke up with someone else's spouse in the morning."

From another recent report in the Kenyan press regarding the 'Happy Valley' crowd:

> Basically, with much of the world at war, a number of bored British aristocrats lived dissolute and hedonistic lives committing immorality and drugging themselves to oblivion to pass the time. The so called happy valley set was a group of ultra-privileged white hedonists who settled in the Wanjohi Valley region and became infamous for engaging in weapon grade hedonism with a carefree curriculum of sex, drugs, adventure and booze. But then culturally prevalent sexual inhibition that they engaged in with the most gusto, wild orgies and wife-swapping were virtually a prerequisite for any who wished to be embraced in the Wanjohi valley social scene, which had the Muthaiga Country club in Nairobi as its focal point. Evenings that began with tasty gazelle chops and champagne with classical, jazz or folk music from gramophones would degenerate into levels of substance addled debauchery that made Sodom and Gomorrah seem like priggish puritanical folklore. One post-dinner parlour game involved male attendees lining up behind a sheet and then poking their aroused genitalia through holes cut in it, so that the ladies present could cast their votes on their favourite!

This additional more serious report from the Jewish Virtual Library about the Whites settling in Kenya also provides an interesting insight as to what was envisaged by the British Government in the early 20th century:

> Ironically, one of the first ideas the British government considered as a settlement option was to make the fertile Kenya highlands—known later as the 'white highlands'—available to the Zionist movement as a Jewish homeland under British protection. The plan, presented by the British colonial secretary to Zionist leaders in 1903 (and often nicknamed the 'Uganda Scheme' because the territory was then governed out of a headquarters in Kampala, Uganda) was considered but rejected.

Chapter Eight: Hugh Cholmondeley, 3rd Lord Delamere, Moves to Africa

It wasn't for another two years that the British offer was finally refused. And as a result a breakaway group, the Jewish Territorial Organisation (led by 'the Jewish Dickens' Israel Zangwill), set about trying to find a homeland in such places as Libya, Australia and Angola. On the hundredth anniversary of Chamberlain's offer, this programme looks at a forgotten moment that reveals much about both Zionist and British colonial history.

For Britain, the offer of land in what's now Kenya was intended to kill two birds with one stone. It would take the pressure off Jewish immigration into London's East End, which was the 'asylum seekers' issue of the day: and it would provide white settlers for a bit of the Empire that few British people wanted to go to. But the small community of British settlers in East Africa, led by Lord Delamere, orchestrated a vicious campaign against the offer of land to 'pauper aliens'.

Several people played key roles in the settlement plan. Hugh Cholmondeley, better known as Lord Delamere, is best remembered as one of the first white men to enter Kenya by land (1899) and the subject of the Elspeth Huxley biographical classic, *White Man's Country*. In 1903, the nobleman acquired from the British colonial authorities 100,000 acres in the fertile rift valley, which he developed as the Equator Ranch. One historical record of East Africa, written in the late colonial years, describes Lord Delamere as a symbolic 'father' to white settlers in Kenya who used his considerable influence until his death in 1931 toward a 'single ambition of making Kenya a white settler's paradise'.

We also quote from the book *History of Kenya* by Robert Hallett (1970), which also sheds even more light on Kenya during the days when Hugh Cholmondeley settled there.

One of the most famous settlers in those early days was Hugh Cholmondeley, third baron of Delamere, better known as Lord Delamere (1870-1931). Model of English aristocracy, bon vivant and adventurer, Delamere liked travelling to Somalia for lion hunting. In one of those expeditions he reached the Kenyan Highlands and had a crush on them, deciding to settle there. He bought a farm near Nakuru in 1903 and devoted himself to livestock and to the culture of European species, in which he was initially unsuccessful,

The Delamere Saga: Part 3

spending in his Kenyan estate all the returns generated by his properties in England. As years passed by, Delamere purchased more lands, reaching a profitable situation. His passionate spirit gave him the leadership of settlers, whose association he presided from 1904 and whom he represented since the constitution of the first Legislative Council of British East Africa in 1907. Delamere left an important heritage, adapted several crops to the local conditions and boosted agricultural development in the Highlands in a decisive way. But he was also a convinced racist, an admirer of Cecil Rhodes and of the Apartheid system. As Elspeth Huxley narrated, his dream was to make of Kenya, Africa 'a white man's country', and a place similar to South Africa. Today, his name still survives at the Norfolk Hotel's bar, in Kenyatta Ave, Nairobi.

In 1905, the British East Africa Protectorate acquired the status of a Colony. England attempted to set up a system of local administration controlled by the colonial government, but the settlers, headed by Hugh, 3rd Lord Delamere, flatly refused. The first governor had to move through swampy grounds, brutally repressing the uprisings of the natives whose lands had been invaded, but simultaneously also calming down the settlers' land hunger, since the number of farmers increased steadily as Lord Delamere's success spread among European circles. Nairobi was very much like the old 'Wild West' cities of the United States at this same time in history, wild, free and promiscuous, being a place where life was risked everyday.This interesting quote from the book *The Long African Day* by Norman Myers (1972) also reflects on Kenya's development.

> Ten years after Kenya's independence, the main bar of Nairobi's venerable Norfolk Hotel is still called the Delamere Room, after Kenya's legendary settler, and is decorated with the mounted heads of His Lordship's trophies. An eager hunter thrice mauled by lions, Lord Delamere used to ride through the streets of Nairobi shooting out the lights of streetlamps with a pistol. He once bought a hotel for the sole purpose of staging window-smashing contests in it, using oranges as ammunition. What a good sport, his fellow settlers said, he bought the hotel first.

Chapter Eight: Hugh Cholmondeley, 3rd Lord Delamere, Moves to Africa

On a more serious note, from W. R. Lester's *Unemployment and the Land* (1936):

> So the white settlers have set about 'civilizing' these people by destroying their tribal land system. They are taking the lands from the natives and wherever they have done so, the result has been an abundant supply of 'labour on the market' with wages kept down by the competition of landless men, just as they are at home (England). This is confirmed by evidence given before the Native Labour Commission (Kenya) in 1912-13. Settler after settler came before the commission and demanded in the most precise terms that the natives should be forced out of "Reserves" to work for wages by cutting down their land so that they should have less than they could live on. Lord Delamere, himself owner of 150,000 acres, said: 'If this policy is to be continued that every native is to be a landholder of a sufficient area on which to establish himself, then the question of obtaining a satisfactory labour supply (for the whites settlers) will never be settled.' The process of reducing men to unemployment and poverty is here stated in all its nakedness and simplicity.... In refusing Land an "adequate" supply of labour on the market would be guaranteed.

At the political level, the indigenous populations were marginalized from power 'en masse' through the policy of racism. The cultures, institutions and values of the Africans were corrupted by the institutions and values of imposed British culture. Within such a social environment of disequilibrium, corruption broke loose. However, it rarely became a "public" concern because it was basically confined within the European population with its victims being Africans. Also, because of the widespread illiteracy among the African people, and because the colonial regime was an autocracy, avenues to express concern about the existence of such a social menace were discouraged. For example, the British colonial regime handed over to Lord Delamere, 100,000 acres of the best Kenya land at the cost of a penny per acre. Also, at a give-away price, Lord Francis Scott and the East African Estates, Ltd. got 350,000 acres at the same price. If this is not corruption, then one should not quibble over the prevailing practice of the KANU [Kenya's ruling party today, Kenya African Democratic Union] regime of giving "government" land and property at a throw-away price to its supporters.

To quote once more from the *Old Africa Magazine* [details and facts as confirmed in the biography of Hugh Cholmondeley, 3rd Lord Delamere, *White Man's Country & The Making of Kenya* by Elspeth Huxley (1935)]:

> When the first white settlers started farming in Kenya in the early twentieth century, their enterprise was far from successful. Potatoes were tried, but they died of blight. At his first farm at Njoro Lord Delamere decided to raise sheep. He ordered Ryeland rams from England; and from New Zealand, Leicester, Lincoln and Romney March rams. The English batch arrived early in 1904 under the care of a shepherd, Sammy McCall. They were joined later that year by 500 pure-bred merino ewes from New Zealand, as well as Hereford cattle from England. The cost of all this was borne by Delamere mortgaging his English estate.
>
> Soon the sheep began to sicken and die. Why? The local name for the land Delamere had bought was 'angata natai emmin', Maasai for 'the plain of the female rhino without any milk'. The Maasai had never grazed their flocks in the area Delamere occupied. His merinos got footrot, his Ryelands lung disease and all his sheep had worms and harboured a grub which hatched in sinews. Four-fifths of the merinos died, as well as many of the others.
>
> It was not until 1925 that the disease suffered by his livestock was identified, by the Rowett Institute in Aberdeen. It was named 'Nakuruitis', and was found to be caused by the land being deficient in minerals, mostly cobalt. Not until then was the disease conquered by giving animals mineral supplements. Meanwhile, at Njoro Delamere turned to cattle. He imported more Herefords, crossing them with native cattle. Unfortunately the native cattle gave the imported ones pleuro-pneumonia, while Redwater fever felled his imported Shorthorns. But some survived and gradually a grade herd was built up. This, too, was a failure because East Coast fever struck, for Njoro was infested with the ticks carrying the disease.
>
> Delamere quickly decided that the land was to blame and, facing the inevitable, he looked for another area where he

Chapter Eight: Hugh Cholmondeley, 3rd Lord Delamere, Moves to Africa

could buy land. He was allocated land near Elementaita, which he called Soysambu. It is an area still farmed by his descendants. At Soysambu Delamere turned to wheat farming. He made a furrow three miles long, ploughed by an old steam engine originally used in constructing the railway. The engine proved to be impractical, so he used a thousand bullocks instead. But who could drive the bullocks? The Boers (of South Africa) beginning to come to the Eldoret area were skilled managers of bullocks and could be employed on piece work. Consequently 1,200 acres of wheat were sown, and binders and threshers were imported at great expense. Again, there was disappointment, for the wheat was infected with rust and destroyed. Delamere did not give up. Employing a scientist, he established a laboratory at Njoro and began to breed rust-resistant varieties of wheat, importing different strains from all over the world. Within three years he had harvested two trainloads of wheat. But he was £40,000 in the red and he had lost most of his lands in England. When he died in 1931 he was £500,000 in debt to the bank – an enormous sum in those days. His experiments, and those of other early white farmers, nonetheless established modern agriculture in Kenya.

Extract from the Parliamentary Records of 1936 [courtesy of the Parliament Trust] indicating the ongoing issue of white settlers in Kenya spearheaded by Hugh Cholmondeley, 3rd Lord Delamere up until his eventual death in 1931 and beyond:

SETTLERS IN KENYA (LORD FRANCIS SCOTT'S VISIT TO LONDON IN 1936)

HC Deb. 20 May 1936 vol 312 cc1183-4 1183 38.

Major Milner asked the Secretary of State for the Colonies in what capacity Lord Francis Scott is coming to England to lay the grievances of the 1184 Kenya settlers before him; and why representations as to those grievances are not being made in the usual way through the Governor?

Mr. J. H. THOMAS: As I stated in reply to the Hon. Member for Wentworth (Mr. Paling) on 26th February, I do not wish to encourage the idea that anybody can appeal to London without recognising the Governor. At the same time, Lord

The Delamere Saga: Part 3

Francis Scott occupies a position as an Elected Member of the Legislative Council in Kenya, and if he wishes to discuss matters informally I think it would be a mistake for me not to take advantage of his presence in England to do so. I may add that other members of the Kenya Legislative Council who have visited London (including Lord Delamere) have from time to time availed themselves of the opportunity of seeing me.

Major MILNER: Can the right hon. Gentleman say in what capacity Lord Francis Scott is coming? Is it on his own behalf or, if not, on whose behalf?

Mr. THOMAS: In precisely the same capacity as at least three members of the Legislative Council, representing different interests, on a visit to London, thought it necessary to seek an interview with the Secretary of State. I have always taken the view, without compromising or interfering with the Governor's position, that it would be a mistake not to allow an elected member to present his views, but they need not necessarily influence the judgment of the Secretary of State.

Major MILNER: Will the Right Hon. Gentleman be willing to see representatives of the natives in the same informal way?

Mr. THOMAS: One of the representatives of the natives was in London three or four weeks ago, and he sought an interview and I very readily granted it, and I had a very interesting talk with him.

Brigadier-General Sir HENRY CROFT: Is the Right Hon. Gentleman aware that Lord Francis Scott has the confidence of an overwhelming number of British citizens in Kenya?

Mr. SPEAKER: That question does not arise.

Hugh Cholmondeley, 3rd Lord Delamere, meantime appeared totally unaffected and untouched by the earlier death in 1914 of his poor, emotionally impoverished young wife, Lady Florence from Northern Ireland and he continued, unabated in his lifetime goal of setting up his 'private white empire' in Kenya. In order to accomplish his wild and crazy ambition and to raise more money to support his grandiose plans, Hugh placed numerous and quite

Chapter Eight: Hugh Cholmondeley, 3rd Lord Delamere, Moves to Africa

valuable works of art belonging to the Cholmondeley family estate back at Vale Royal Abbey that included one of the most valuable, precious collection of books, manuscripts and documents ever held by a private individual in the whole of England, all of these items, the largest ever to be sold at public auction are listed in a "private catalogue" of Sotheby's and also some items later in the auction house of Christie's, London, in 1905. [These sales include some examples and typical items, both paintings and antiques that were sold by the 3rd Lord Delamere from 1893-1905 to realize more funds for the support and promotion of his grandiose exploits in East Africa.]

Painting of Christie's auction room in 1808 by Thomas Rowlandson (1756–1827), courtesy of the British Museum

We list some typical examples revealed in our research, directly related to this erratic decision of Hugh, 3rd Lord Delamere, in disposing of valuable works of art inherited from the Cholmondeley family estate to acquire more private funds to be sent from England to Africa to support his ludicrous plans as a 'megalomaniac' for the building of his new 'white empire', of course with him personally claiming to be the 'King' or 'Emperor' in Kenya.

Example 1. Portrait of Catherine Howard, by Hans Holbein the Younger. This painting came from Overleigh Hall, near Chester.

Portrait of Catherine Howard the 5th wife of King Henry VIII, courtesy of the National Portrait Gallery, London

It passed into the collection of Thomas Cowper who gained possession of the estate, in part through descent and in part through purchase, in about 1660. It then descended through the family to Thomas Cholmondeley. The label on the reverse of the portrait, which reads T.C., probably refers to him. In 1816 the Overleigh pictures and portraits were removed to Condover Hall. The portrait was then sold in the Cholmondeley of Vale Royal Abbey sale at Christie's in 1897, as 'a Lady, in a black dress'. It was purchased by the National Portrait Gallery in 1898 as "Catherine Howard" for a nominal fee and today is now priceless.

Catherine Howard (c. 1523 - 13 February 1542) was Queen of England from 1540 until 1541, as the fifth wife of King Henry VIII. She (then aged 16 or 17) married him (then aged 49) on 28 July 1540, at Oatlands Palace, in Surrey, almost immediately after the annulment of his marriage to Anne of Cleves had been arranged.

Anne of Cleves was a young German girl who was Queen of England from 6 January to 9 July 1540 as the fourth wife of King Henry VIII. The marriage was declared unconsummated and, as a result, she was not crowned Queen Consort. The couple's first night as husband and wife was not a successful one according to our records. Henry confided to Cromwell that he had not consummated the marriage, saying, "I liked her before not well, but now I like her much worse." Anne was commanded to leave the Court on 24 June, and on 6 July she was informed of her husband's decision to reconsider the marriage. Witness statements were taken from a number of courtiers and two physicians which register the king's disappointment at her appearance. Henry had also commented to Thomas Heneage and Anthony Denny (grooms of Henry, VIII),

Chapter Eight: Hugh Cholmondeley, 3rd Lord Delamere, Moves to Africa

that he could not believe she was a virgin. Anne was asked for her consent to an annulment, to which she readily agreed [probably to avoid the 'axe']. She later died of cancer at Chelsea Old Manor on 16 July 1557 aged 41 years.

Catherine Howard was also stripped of her title as Queen of England within 16 months in November 1541. She was beheaded three months later, aged 19 on the grounds of treason because, it was claimed; although unproved, for committing adultery while married to Henry.

Portrait of The Cholmondeley Ladies, courtesy of the Tate Gallery, London

Example 2. Portrait of The Cholmondeley Ladies, by an unknown English artist (1610). The painting is of two young women sitting on a bed and holding, we may assume, their babies wrapped in red christening robes. The painting is named after Thomas Cholmondeley, to whose collection this portrait originally belonged. The women may be his daughters or nieces, or sisters who married into the Cholmondeley family. This valuable painting was presented to the Tate Gallery in London by an anonymous donor in 1955.

Example 3. Cholmondeley Bowl. An extremely rare and large 18th century punch bowl, known as the "Cholmondeley Bowl", now on display at the Grosvenor Museum in Chester, courtesy of a long-term loan by the Chester based 'Tyrer Charitable Trust'. The

The Delamere Saga: Part 3

Cholmondeley punch bowl, courtesy of the Grosvenor Museum, Chester

huge porcelain punch bowl, one of a small number of such bowls made in the Chinese city of Canton, now known as Guangzhou, is decorated with the arms of the Cholmondeley family of Vale Royal Abbey and the monogram of Thomas Cholmondeley.

Report from the *Cheshire News* regarding the Cholmondeley bowl:

> Thomas Cholmondeley (1767-1855), second cousin to William Pitt the Younger, continued a long family tradition of participating in political life when he was elected as Member of Parliament for Cheshire in 1796, having also served as High Sheriff for the county in 1792.
>
> Although it is uncertain who commissioned this piece to commemorate his election, they certainly wished Thomas Cholmondeley and his family well, for the mottoes Prosperity to the County of Cheshire and Success to the Plough and the Sail to the sides, as well as the Chinese symbolism of the pagoda landscape to the interior, were very pertinent to the landowning family at that time.
>
> Measuring an impressive 21in (53cm) diameter, and surviving in excellent condition, the bowl belongs to a small group of bowls of unusually large size marked in script to the base Canton Syngchong (this example also dated Fecit 1797). Although little appears to be known about Syngchong, in his journals Major Samuel Shaw, the first American consul to Canton in 1786, refers to him as "the principal porcelain merchant of Canton".

Chapter Eight: Hugh Cholmondeley, 3rd Lord Delamere, Moves to Africa

Antique Silver Drum Teapot, courtesy of Birmingham Museum of Art

Example 4. Antique Silver Drum Teapot. This is a beautiful antique teapot by the celebrated silver smith, Hester Bateman (1708-1794), which is made in sterling silver and there is no mistaking its unique quality and design. It bears the hallmark for London, 1775, with the maker's mark, plus has a beautiful engraved coat of arms and crest of the Cholmondeley family.

Example 5. Portrait of Hugh Cholmondeley, 2nd Lord Delamere. Hugh Jnr., his son and heir callously tried to sell in 1904, this now priceless, impressive oil painting, a portrait of his very own dignified father, Hugh, 2nd Lord Delamere. The original print is now owned by the National Portrait Gallery in London, England, but an unknown local Cheshire artist reproduced a fine oil painting of this print, approximately 48 inches by 24 inches, and was displayed for many years in the main library at Vale Royal Abbey up until 1904. The location of this reproduced portrait in oil is now unknown and could well be stored away, unnoticed, somewhere cloistered in the attic

Copy of a print of Hugh Cholmondeley, 2nd Lord Delamere (1860), courtesy of the National Portrait Gallery, London.

or basement cellar of one of the old world cottages in beautiful Cheshire, and if so, it is now worth a fortune. According to records from the local "downstairs staff", this beautiful oil painting of Hugh Cholmondeley was admired by all the staff at Vale Royal Abbey. But based on the report from one of the servants, she reported that one day it simply disappeared, possibly taken by one of the staff, anticipating the eventual demise and closure of the Great House and Estate at Vale Royal Abbey in the near future, so it was removed and stored away in an unknown location for future security.

Example 6. Winsford properties: Delamere Street: Nos. 16, 24, 26, 28, 30, 32, 47, 48, 49, 51, 53, 55, 92, 94, 140, 142, 144, 146, 148, 150, 152, 154, 279, 281, 283; Grange Lane: Nos. 5, 7, 23, 33, 35, 37, 39; Swanlow Lane: Nos. 54, 56, 58.

The two beautiful cottages at 92 and 94 Delamere Street were also sold by the 3rd Lord Delamere, as part of a large disposal sale in 1912 along with numerous other properties along Delamere Street in Over, Cheshire. The sale catalogue described these properties as a valuable grocers and bakers shop with adjoining house with outbuildings of three stall stables, a shippon (a pigsty) for five, root house, hen pen, store house and two pig cotes, good garden and orchard. The market hall on the other side of the cross was built in 1840 for £500 after the previous market had ceased in 1800. Hugh, 2nd Lord Delamere had bought it in 1850 for £800 and he granted it to the Vicars of Over to use as a national school on a permanent basis.

The George and Dragon public house opposite, which was also once the property of Lord Delamere, is first mentioned in documents dating back to the year 1810. The records also state that the well-respected Mayor of Over's duties included the task of 'walking the fair', where the mayor and his entourage would walk in a procession around the village and along Delamere Street in Over, Cheshire.

Fortunately some valuable estate items had already previously survived this 'clearance sale' of the Vale Royal Estate possessions and treasures, the sale as personally instructed by the 3rd Lord Delamere around 1904, and they thankfully now remain today in Cheshire as permanent records of the prosperous days of Vale

Chapter Eight: Hugh Cholmondeley, 3rd Lord Delamere, Moves to Africa

Royal Abbey. For example in the records of Winsford Council offices, another reference is made to Hugh Cholmondeley, 2nd Lord Delamere (1811-1887), mentioning that he donated a priceless 17th century ornamental mace[28] to the "Over Borough Council", which was always carried in the Mayor procession. When the Borough of Over and the Borough of Wharton became the Winsford Urban District Council, the mayoral procession always carried two maces, one donated by Hugh Cholmondeley, 2nd Lord Delamere, the other by Sir John Branner MP. In 1974 Winsford UDC became part of the Vale Royal Borough Council, but Winsford still kept its role as a Parish Council and still has the two maces even today. The original silver mace was taken to Kenya by Hugh Cholmondeley, 3rd Lord Delamere in 1912. It was rightfully his property and he had previously personally approved each mayor by presenting the mace. But he resisted the giving and donation of the mace and title to the newly formed Winsford Urban District Council [possibly because he wanted to sell them on the open market for much needed cash for his projects in Kenya]. In 1946 his son and heir Thomas Pitt Hamilton, who had also settled in Kenya, thankfully returned the old mace to Winsford Parish Council as a gift, when he finally disposed of the remaining few family land holdings, possessions and last remnants of the family estate in Cheshire.

17th century ornamental mace, courtesy of Winsford Parish Council

---

[28] A ceremonial mace is a highly ornamented staff of metal or wood, carried before a sovereign or other high official in civic ceremonies by a mace-bearer, intended to represent the official's authority.

What we should remember is that the personality of Hugh Cholmondeley, 3rd Lord Delamere was molded; strongly influenced and probably based on his distorted view of his father, Hugh, 2nd Lord Delamere and the so-called irrefutable private lifestyle and rumors of his father's immoral conduct with his housekeeper. This information was no doubt passed on to him by his mother Augusta, including his reaction to and personal repulsion toward his father, probably when he learned of his father now having two other 'illegitimate' sons. He was also probably being influenced by his inherited genes and characteristics passed down from his authoritative, strong willed, temperamental grandfather, 1st Lord Delamere, who ran the Vale Royal Abbey with an 'iron rod' during his lifetime.

Hugh, 3rd Lord Delamere, personally had also by this time in his life now concluded that Vale Royal Abbey and the Estate in Cheshire was a 'millstone around his neck'. He also now had his own private life carefully, intricately and fully planned out, plus his strong driving ambition and desire was laid out in his distorted mind to become the appointed 'White King of Kenya in Africa'. In addition his dream also included creating an 'African Dominion' under 'white' authority to control Africa from Cairo to the Cape, no doubt visualizing himself as its 'supreme' ruler?

Thus the mentally unbalanced Cholmondeley broke up, disposed of and sold off one of the most valuable collection of books in England, a massive collection and also a priceless, prestigious library that had been built up and preserved over many years at Vale Royal Abbey by his father, grandfather, and previous ancestors of the Cholmondeley family, especially Charles and Essex Cholmondeley back in the 1700s. He did so without any consideration for the future of classical literature in England, which reflects his attitude toward education and culture. He was only interested in his own personal ambitions in Africa and his crazy attempt to promote a white European controlled empire of Kenya [similar to the repulsive system in South Africa under Apartheid rule]. In fact many Afrikaners [Boers] from Northern Transvaal in South Africa were encouraged by Delamere to relocate to Kenya to share in developing this 'white empire', which is confirmed by reporter Andrew Nightingale in *Reel Africa* magazine:

Chapter Eight: Hugh Cholmondeley, 3rd Lord Delamere, Moves to Africa

In order to get white people to come to British East Africa (Kenya) and settle here, they now needed to spin the bullshit and to market this place," says Andrew Nightingale, director of *Reel Africa* and also a friend of the family. "While the 3rd Baron Delamere used his influential status to convince his friends of the merits of investing in the new nation, a brochure published in 1911 [believe it or not, by the British Government itself] touting Kenya as a worry-free place, crowned with beautiful highlands now available for white settlers to live in, did just as much to drive colonial goals.

Making such an extremely grave decision of abandoning the beautiful Vale Royal Abbey in Cheshire for a new life in a then almost unknown country, namely, Kenya would simply be in line with Cholmondeley's character and personality.

We have all heard of this well-known saying by Aesop, "A man is known by the company he keeps". Reports from "Documents of Winston Churchill" and confirmed in the records of *Het Buitenlandsche Boek, 1935 [The Foreign Book, 1935]* plus *The Cambridge History of the British Empire* (1929-1961), indicate that Hugh Cholmondeley, while he was a member of the House of Lords in the British Parliament, became a personal friend of Basil Zaharoff, (1849-1936), a little known Greek arms dealer and industrialist. We could not discover any logical or justifiable reasons why this secret friendship was developed in the first place, so we can only speculate that it was probably related to financial matters and perhaps monetary loans to help Cholmondely with his business interests and exploits in Kenya. One of the richest men in the world during his lifetime, Zaharoff was described as a "merchant of death" and "mystery man of Europe". His success was forged through his cunning, often aggressive and sharp business tactics. These included the sale of arms to opposing sides in conflicts, sometimes delivering fake or faulty machinery and weaponry. He often used his friendships and connections with the aristocracy in Europe, including Hugh Cholmondeley, to advance his wicked schemes. This relationship only lasted a few years as Zaharoff disliked Africa intensely. He also personally believed that the "black races" were a cursed people, in fulfillment of the Bible text at Genesis, Chapter Nine in which it records that Noah cursed Canaan the son of Ham and said "Let him become the lowest of slaves to his brothers" and Noah thus condemned his descendants through Cush the son of Ham, grandson of Noah, to become slaves for perpetuity.[29] When Hugh moved permanently to live in Kenya and abandoned the prestigious Vale Royal Abbey, this friendship no longer suited the ambitions of Basil Zaharoff and he informed Hugh, 3rd Lord Delamere accordingly.

In addition, Hugh Cholmondeley was also now showing the clear signs of megalomania.[30] This observation is based accordingly on numerous additional reports we have researched. One of Hugh's adversaries sarcastically referred to him as the presumptive "White King of East Africa" and this actually thrilled Hugh Cholmondeley in a similar way that it did his future daughter-in-law, five times married, Diane Caldwell-Motion-Broughton-Colville-Cholmondeley, former model and barmaid [who eventually became Lady Delamere, 1913-1987) and who was dubbed, the "White Queen of Africa"]. This was because Diane had accumulated so much land in East Africa through her marriages, primarily when she married wealthy, reclusive, homosexual landowner Gilbert Colville in 1943, who was one of the wealthiest and most powerful landowners in Kenya. Upon his death in 1955 she inherited most of his fortune.

Diane later married Thomas Pitt Hamilton Cholmondeley, 4th Lord Delamere [heir of Hugh] in 1955, she now becoming his third wife and further increasing her holdings as part of the Cholmondeley family in Kenya. According to this article in the gossip blog, *Cocktails with Elvira*:

> In 1937, pregnant again, she married Vernon Motion. According to Leda Farrant the child was not his. The marriage lasted about a fortnight and the pregnancy was terminated. Diana was already involved with Sir Jock Delves Broughton and left with him for Africa in 1940. The couple married in Durban, South Africa. Vernon Motion (1904-1980) is usually listed as a musician, a second pianist in Carroll Gibbon's orchestra.

---

[29] Quoting from the book *Black History in the Bible*, "As the sons of Ham began to spread out from "the land of Ham", it is Cush (which means black) that settles the area currently known as Sudan and Ethiopia. It is here that Cush begins to have sons that also eventually spread out to all other areas in Africa." The fact that Cushites were black or dark skinned is also alluded to in the Bible text at *Jeremiah 13* v 23, "Can the Cushite change his skin?" In his book *Antiquities of the Jews*, which contains an account of history of the Jewish people, written in Greek for Josephus' gentile patrons, the historian Flavius Josephus also corroborates the association between Ethiopians and the Cushites.

[30] A mental illness marked by delusions of greatness, wealth, etc. plus an obsession with doing extravagant or grand things, also related to the narcissistic personality disorder.

Chapter Eight: Hugh Cholmondeley, 3rd Lord Delamere, Moves to Africa

It is also reported that as "White Queen of Africa", Diane, the new Lady Delamere, then lived in a lesbian ménage with Lady Patricia Fairweather, who was a permanent house guest in the 1960s and 1970s up until the death of Lady Patricia, her lesbian lover in 1981. Diane, Lady Delamere later died in London in 1987 of heart failure, aged 74 years, her fifth husband, Thomas Pitt Hamilton Cholmondeley having died earlier in Kenya in 1979.

Research also revealed:

> Once the British had staked their claim in British East Africa, the Bantu farming communities that inhabited the higher hillside zones of Kenya were also enclosed in Reserves (Similar to the South African "locations" or "Kraals", i.e. Gugulethu and Langa in Cape Town, plus Soweto in the Transvaal. The occupants could only leave their location or kraal to work for Europeans if they could display their "pass card". The fictitious justification for creating reserves with designated boundaries (and they were quite large areas) was to protect tribal land holdings from the incoming white settlers.

Kraal is an Afrikaans and Dutch word (also used in South African English) for an enclosure located within an African settlement or village surrounded by a fence of thorn-bush branches, a palisade, mud wall, or other fencing, roughly circular in form. These locations also usually had only one or two entrance and exit roads, which enabled the controlling powers an easy way to block or restrict and contain the movement of the occupants. The 3rd Lord Delamere was anti-Semitic and also pro-fascist according to many records; this is based on extracts from news articles of the day. In addition, this extract from the *African Review* (p. 350) published by the Royal African Society, reveals a comprehensive analysis of the character of the 3rd Lord Delamere:

> A man with a very marked inferior complex—heir to an impoverished estate—self-willed—mentally unstable—anti Semitic, etc., etc.

Hugh Cholmondeley, 3rd Lord Delamere had originally applied for a land grant from the British Crown in May 1903, but was ultimately denied because the Governor of the Protectorate, Sir

The Delamere Saga: Part 3

Charles Eliot, thought the land area was too far from any population centre. His next request for 100,000 acres (400 km^2), near what is now Naivasha, was denied because the government felt that settlement by a colonising farmer might ignite conflicts with the Maasai tribesman who lived on the land. Lord Delamere's third attempt at land acquisition was successful. He received a 99-year lease on 100,000 acres (400 km^2) of land that would be named 'Equator Ranch', requiring him to pay a £200 annual rent and to spend £5,000 on the land over the first five years of occupancy; his ludicrous cost was "one old penny per acre". In 1906, he also acquired a large farm in Gilgil division, which would eventually include more than 50,000 acres (210 km^2), located between Elementeita Railway Station, Elmenteita Badlands and Mbaruk Railway Station. This ranch he named Soysambu. Together, these vast possessions made Lord Delamere one of Kenya's largemen— the local name for the handful of colonists with the greatest land holdings.

Lord Delamere also embodied the many contradictions of the committed East African settler. He was personally fond of many Africans, and particularly enjoyed the company of the Maasai (even gently tolerating their habit of pilfering his cattle for their own herds), but he fought fiercely to maintain British supremacy in the colony: "The extension of European civilization was in itself a desirable thing," he wrote in 1927. "The British race... was superior to heterogeneous African races only now emerging from centuries of relative barbarism... the opening up of new areas by means of genuine colonisation was to the advantage of the whole world."

Colonel Richard Meinertzhagen, CBE, DSO (1878-1967), himself a complex figure of Africa's colonial days, was a British soldier, intelligence officer and ornithologist. He was also a prolific diarist and published four books based on these diaries. He quoted Lord Delamere as proclaiming to his audience, "I am going to prove to you all that this is a white man's country." There have been at least three biographies written about this controversial character, Meinertzhagen. Some lionized him as a master of military strategy and espionage, plus an expert in African history, while later works such as *The Meinertzhagen Mystery* by Brian Garfield (2007) presented him as a fraud for fabricating stories of his feats and speculated he was also a murderer. For our fellow students of African history,

Chapter Eight: Hugh Cholmondeley, 3rd Lord Delamere, Moves to Africa

these biographies, still in print, are all worth reading.

These various opinions regarding Hugh Cholmondeley held great sway amongst the settlers in Kenya because Lord Delamere was their undisputed, if unofficial leader and, in some measure, their spokesman for 30 years. He was a member of the Legislative Council, the Executive Council, and in 1907, became President of the Colonists' Association. In 1921 he established the political Reform Party. Errol Trzebinski, author of a number of books on Kenya's colonial elite, wrote of him: "Delamere was the 'Cecil Rhodes' of Kenya and the settlers followed him both politically and spiritually." Another contemporary and former colonist said more or less the same: "[His] ascendancy over the settlers of Kenya has been enjoyed long enough for him to expect all men—and women—to do his bidding, and do it promptly. He is their Moses. For 25 years he has been their guide."

Dane Kennedy, in *Islands of White* (1987), offers a novel perspective on the social dynamics of white settler colonies in imperialist Africa. Kennedy convincingly illustrates how these white societies were able to create a distinct and unified culture. Presenting a new interpretation of white settler society, Kennedy analytically demonstrates how the social identity of white colonists was radically recast to accommodate their special circumstances. Kennedy's study is of lasting importance to the field of African history because it reveals the powerful dynamics of solidarity within colonial societies, which consequently enabled them to create and maintain a system of domination over the indigenous and poor, also illiterate African population.

One of our researchers, who holds a Masters Degree in Psychology, and who has delved deeply into the life of Hugh Cholmondeley, 3rd Lord Delamere, expressed the following.

> Hugh would never have approved of the writing of this biography, *White Man's Country – Lord Delamere and the Making of Kenya* by Elspeth Huxley, published in 1935, and in my opinion it was solely the brain-child of his young, headstrong and opinionated widow Gwladys (wife of only three years), who now proudly displaying the title, Lady Delamere and later as the Mayor of Nairobi. Hugh would only have authorized a biography that must be full of praise and adulation, outlining the grandiose things, plus what

The Delamere Saga: Part 3

notable steps forward on behalf of the British Empire that he claimed that he had personally accomplished in Africa. But this would only have gone to print <u>after</u> he had finally achieved his life ambition of becoming, the 'king', 'emperor' or 'president' of a 'white man's country' of East Africa or more likely his dream of completely ruling the 'Dominion of Africa' from Cairo to the Cape.

His young widow, Gwladys, Lady Delamere, no doubt also used her powerful influence in 1932, as being on the exclusive "white only" City Council of Nairobi and later the first female Mayor of the council, a decision was made to rename Nairobi's prominent Sixth Avenue to *Delamere Avenue* in a surreptitious effort to commemorate her late husband Hugh's 'permanent' place in the development of the colony, and also financed by city funds to erect an eight-foot bronze statue at the street's head, across from the recently built, new five-star Stanley Hotel [so named after Sir Henry Morton Stanley, a Welsh explorer best known for his explorations of central Africa and his successful search for missionary and explorer David Livingstone]. This dominating statue of Hugh Cholmondeley was designed by the Lady Kennet, Kathleen Scott, wife of Robert Falcon Scott, the Antarctic explorer who died in 1912 on the Ross Ice Shelf at the South Pole.

The term 'whites only' will no doubt create shudders down the spine of many of our readers, who have perhaps visited or lived in South Africa during the Apartheid era. It was during this period of 'separate development' known as Apartheid [Afrikaans word for Apartness or Separateness], when the majority of the whites by their 'deafening' silence and passive acceptance of this abominable practice, legally enforced by the whites-only government of separating the races by means of the colour of their skin. This lack of action or protest was nothing more than actually condoning or being complicit with this practice of Apartheid, and all the obscene rules and regulations laid down by the then existing white government. Many of my personal friends and associates were actually deported and exiled from the country because they raised their voices in protest. The definition of Apartheid is eloquently expressed in *Wikipedia*:

Chapter Eight: Hugh Cholmondeley, 3rd Lord Delamere, Moves to Africa

This was a system of institutionalised racial segregation and discrimination that existed in South Africa from 1948 until the early 1990s. Apartheid was characterised by an authoritarian political culture based on white supremacy, which encouraged state repression of Black African, Coloured, and Asian South Africans for the benefit of the nation's minority white population.

My personal memory while living in South Africa goes back to this time period when the magnificent, but also very expensive, opulent Nico Malan Opera House [named after the politician and Administrator of the Cape of Good Hope Province of South Africa but now known as the Artscape Theatre Center] built on the reclaimed land of the Foreshore in Cape Town, South Africa, and was surreptitiously built for 'whites only'. When this beautiful entertainment complex, built with money from all tax payers in South Africa, was opened in 1971 it was declared to be for 'whites' only. Many local 'white' citizens of Cape Town boycotted this centre as a 'silent' protest that this Government building was not open to all citizens of South Africa regardless of race.

Other examples come to mind. The public toilets [rest rooms] on the beach front of Sea Point, a major tourist focal point, displayed the sign, 'whites only' [where the non-whites went to relieve themselves you can only imagine] and the Post Office had two doorways, one for 'whites only' the other displaying the sign 'non-whites only'. What made the practice of separate development even sillier is that both of these doors opened into the same lobby and public counter, where standing behind the secure wire screen was a white person, as they were the only ones approved and supposedly qualified for most government official employment. Also prominently displayed on the counter of many post offices was a handgun to remind all patrons who entered that this was a "secure" location to protect the citizens of South Africa.

The most glaring example of Apartheid was the way that the government-owned South African Railways classified their passenger coaches. The coaches were classified in two categories, 'first class' for whites only, and 'third class' for the non-whites. Because of embarrassment and to avoid possible world criticism, there was no classification as "second class" coaches for obvious reasons. To see first hand the dreadful result of this practice, one only needs to read the enlightening book *Life of Mahatma Gandhi* by Louis Fischer (1950), which was the basis for the brilliant film *Gandhi* by the late Sir Richard Attenborough. The majority of personnel employed by the railways were white Afrikaners, many whom had a poor education could not speak English, but were nevertheless guaranteed employment by the white government plus subsidized housing, with the clear understanding that they would always vote in every general election to keep the white National Party (1948-1994) in power. Remember, in those dark days, only whites were allowed to vote in any general election and all non-whites were disenfranchised. Apartheid not only meant separate and inferior public services, benches and building entrances for non-whites. It also stripped South African blacks and non-whites of their citizenship (placing them into tribally-based *Bantustans* instead) and abolished all non-white political representation.

Freedom of the press was severely curtailed in South Africa during those years and many international news organizations were banned. Television was only introduced to South Africans in 1976, as it was viewed by the government and the Dutch Reformed Church as an instrument of the Devil. Prime Minister Hendrik Verwoerd compared television with atomic bombs and poison gas, claiming that "they are modern things, but that does not mean they are desirable. The government has to watch for any dangers to the people, both spiritual and physical."

Dr. Albert Hertzog, Minister for Posts and Telegraphs at the time, said that TV would come to South Africa "over [his] dead body," denouncing it as "only a miniature bioscope which is being carried into the house and over which parents have no control." He also argued that "South Africa would have to import films showing races mixing; and advertising would make black Africans dissatisfied with their lot." This new medium was then regarded as the "devil's own box", for disseminating communism and immorality.

Even after the introduction of TV in 1976, with only one single channel of 3 hours per day viewing, split between the English and Afrikaans languages (the blacks were completely ignored at this time mainly because they not even have the basic facility of electricity) and it was under the direct control of the SABC (South African Broadcast Corporation) that in turn was owned and controlled by the Apartheid government. Many programmes from overseas were

Chapter Eight: Hugh Cholmondeley, 3rd Lord Delamere, Moves to Africa

banned, especially if they showed or portrayed love scenes between whites and blacks, or if they displayed blacks as being successful in life.

As I sit today in my son's comfortable home in multiracial, sunny California and look back on my past days of living on our gorgeous private property in an exclusive white suburb of Cape Town, I nostalgically visualize and see my three young children sitting on the rug in our luxurious lounge eagerly awaiting and staring at the 'test card' (test pattern) on our new TV set, imported from Japan, until the children's programmes started at 5pm. This TV viewing was as a reward after completing their homework from the exclusive all white schools they attended. The programme was probably the cartoon character, "Little Heidi" a programme in German but was always dubbed into Afrikaans; of course my young children had a smattering of the Afrikaans language, as it was a compulsory subject in all white schools.

I always struggled with this government policy, as Afrikaans, which is a corrupted language based on Old Dutch and Flemish languages, developed and used by the original Dutch settlers and was previously referred to as "Cape Dutch" (a term also used to refer collectively to the early Cape settlers) or "Kitchen Dutch" a derogatory term used to refer to Afrikaans in its earlier days. My view, as a 'citizen of the world' is that Afrikaans is a useless language for international purposes, as South Africa is the only country in the world where this language is used extensively and only by an ever-reducing minority group: Afrikaners. Although it is still one of the 11 official languages it is also a shrinking, dying language due primarily to population trends and the demographics of South Africa. The rapidly expanding, burgeoning black population very rarely use or even recognize this language as it represents to them the symbol of the past oppressor and Apartheid rules of the now extinct white supremacist government.

There were so many other silly and ridiculous situations that existed under Apartheid. For example, how did the white Afrikaans government of the day decide that the Chinese were classified 'black' but the Japanese were classified 'honorary whites'?

Much more about the abominable practice of this Apartheid system in South Africa will be covered in my next book, "Zero Hour of the Apartheid Regime of Zuid Afrika", to be published in 2020.

The Delamere Saga: Part 3

This book will also cover the rise of the African National Congress (ANC) and the eventual introduction and now ultimate failure of the Black Economic Empowerment (BEE). Affirmative Action or Black Empowerment is a racially selective programme launched by the new South African government (ANC) to try and redress the inequalities of Apartheid by giving the Black, Coloured and <u>Indian</u> South African citizens, economic privileges not available to Whites. Many argued that Black Economic Empowerment only serves a few elite black individuals who have made massive fortunes by having inside knowledge of government contracts and tenders plus using corruption and bribery to an unbelievable level while still leaving millions of poor blacks in 'dehumanising poverty'.

Although South Africa is subject to various types of corruption, like many other countries, two prevalent forms are tender rigging and BEE fronting. Recent scandals involving many South African black politicians and the notorious Gupta family from India [who all became South African citizens under very suspicious circumstances] have brought both types of corruption into the public spotlight. The Gupta family in particular, being non-white, very quickly entered into the corrupt racket that involved bidding for, and winning lucrative government contract, along with junior members of President Zuma's family all under the guise of the BEE. Petty corruption is another relevant issue affecting public services and day-to-day life in South Africa. Today the respected organisation of 'Transparency International' lists South Africa along with Kenya as two of the most corrupt countries in the world.[31]

Meanwhile, back in Kenya, we have now come to realize from recorded history that Hugh, 3rd Lord Delamere never achieved his grandious ambition, this 'dream' of being the 'supreme head' of a 'white man's country', which unfortunately was the vision of a person with a 'narcissistic personality disorder' (NPD) [this term might be more familiar with our American readers as they struggle to understand and handle the current (2019) presidential and White House politics in Washington].

---

[31] For an amusing and compelling personal account of a young mixed race boy and his personal account of growing up in the Apartheid system of South Africa, we recommend reading the excellent bestseller book, *Born a Crime* by Trevor Noah, host of the popular *The Daily Show*, an American satirical TV news program.

Chapter Eight: Hugh Cholmondeley, 3rd Lord Delamere, Moves to Africa

Narcissistic Personality Disorder (NPD) is characterized by exaggerated feelings of self-importance, an excessive need for admiration, and a lack of loyalty or empathy. Those affected often spend a lot of time thinking about achieving power or success and also on their physical appearance. They often take advantage of the people around them and blatantly, repeatedly exaggerating and lying without any conscience. This behavior typically begins by early adulthood and may develop from an impaired attachment to their primary caregivers, usually their parents [remember that Hugh Cholmondeley had absolutely no parental guidance whatsoever and was in boarding school from four years of age][32] and occurs across a variety of social situations and the person expects and usually demands to be treated as superior, regardless of their actual status or achievements. This is also because they are very deeply and profoundly 'wounded' and emotionally immature individuals. They know themselves to be 'nothing' and are highly shameful of themselves and guilt-ridden. This is because during childhood they suffered a moment, or moments, of shame or humiliation so devastating to their psyche that they could not recover. They spend their lives trying to deny this 'truth' about themselves. To achieve this, they destroy everyone around them.

Additional characteristics displayed by a person with **NPD** are reported in the medical newsletter *Narcissistic Personality Disorder – Symptoms & Causes* (Mayo Clinic, 2017) and are listed amongst other things as, grandiosity with expectations of superior treatment from other people; fixation on fantasies of power, success, intelligence and attractiveness; self-perception of being unique, superior; needing continual admiration from others; pompous and arrogant demeanor, and being drunk with power. The word 'narcissistic' is based on the name of a character in Greek mythology named Narcissus.[33] When asked by one of our research team what is the fate of a narcissist, I replied:

---

[32] According to the diaries of Sybil (1871-1911), the sister of Hugh Cholmondeley (1870-1931), 3rd Lord Delamere, what deeply and emotionally affected her brother more than anything else, was when they both found out that their father Hugh Cholmondeley, Senior, 2nd Lord Delamere (1811-1887) had two illegitimate sons born in 1876 and 1878 by means of his housekeeper, Margaret Green, who worked at Vale Royal Abbey during that time. Hugh Junior was born in 1870 and was only six years when he learned of this very negative and humiliating news, which no doubt contributed to his mental condition of "narcissistic personality disorder".

[33] In Greek mythology, Narcissus was a hunter who was known for his physical beauty. He was very proud, in that he disdained those who loved him. Others noticed this behavior and also what attracted Narcissus to a pool, where he saw his own reflection and fell in love with it, not realizing it was merely an image. Narcissus is the origin of the term narcissism, a fixation with oneself and one's physical appearance or public perception.

That is very simple, its loneliness, which I truly believe they are the most terrified of, but not in the sense that they don't want to feel lonely, because I believe they are incapable of such emotions. I believe they don't want to be left alone to their own thoughts; to discover that they aren't as great as they thought they were.

Psychologist Stephen Johnson wrote in *Psychology Today* that the narcissist is someone who has

> buried his true self-expression in response to early injuries and replaced it with a highly developed, compensatory false self. This alternate persona to the real self often comes across as grandiose, 'above others', self-absorbed, and highly conceited. Narcissism is often interpreted in popular culture as a person who's in love with him or herself. It is more accurate to characterize the pathological narcissist as someone who's in love with an idealized self-image, which they project in order to avoid feeling (and being seen as) the real, disenfranchised, wounded self. Deep down, most pathological narcissists feel like the 'ugly duckling' even if they painfully don't want to admit it. Many narcissists enjoy spreading and arousing negative emotions to gain attention, to feel powerful, and keep you insecure and off-balance. They are easily upset at any real or perceived slights or inattentiveness. They may throw a tantrum if you disagree with their views, or fail to meet their expectations. They are extremely sensitive to criticism, and typically respond with heated argument (fight) or cold detachment (flight). On the other hand, narcissists are often quick to judge, criticize, ridicule, and blame you. Some narcissists are emotionally abusive. By making you feel inferior; they boost their fragile ego, and feel better about themselves they also come to understand that the most terrifying thing to a narcissist is loss of control.

Another well-known and respected analyst says:

> As the narcissist gets older their reservoir of resentment is deeper, the narcissist feels entitled and views themselves as the victim, never having received ALL that they 'should' have had or entitled to and the extent of the behavior and actions that they commit and that they have never paid any

consequence for, only serves to entrench the bad behavior."

The analyst added:

> Narcissistic individuals often end up alone because they have chased away those they seemingly cared for or people have simply packed up and left. Alone because they often have an inability to be dependent on others and in essence are used to being alone either emotionally and/or physically. Alone because they tire out relationships and cannot keep most close to them because of being so difficult to be around. In their older years they may find a caregiver to help and support them, but it's likely most other people will have left; family and friends included. At their very core, they believe and 'know' that they are 'nothing'. As a response to this, subconsciously they construct a facade of grandiosity and perfection around themselves which they will protect and defend at all cost to themselves and others. So, they destroy anything or anyone that gets close. Thus, anytime you disappoint them, anytime you show them empathy or love, anytime you 'call them out' they will fight back. They are so dangerous because, while they are emotionally toddlers, they have all the intentionality, strength, intelligence, and capabilities that come along with being an adult. They do not have they capacity for healthy, constructive anger; they experience pure rage and 'act out'. They will, with purpose, verbally or physically, many times both, assault you.

The analyist also pointed out,

> In my exposure and fully vetted experience with a narcissist, I think there are two primary things that frighten a narcissist. (a) Not being in control or losing control, and (b) Being exposed for what they truly are.

> Those two things are what frighten a narcissist or anyone with absolutely no conscience. The Narcissist or the unconscionable types want and need to think they are in control and will only persist in relationships where they can maintain that control. If they don't think they can continue to use manipulation and deception tactics to exploit you and benefit from you any longer, which means a point has come where they recognize that they are losing or have lost control, then they don't just get frightened—they get filled

with often silent rage, resentment, and will resort to overt or covert retaliation to make you want to leave them—which is what they want at the point where they know they have lost control. Their final act is often trying to make you want to leave them to, once again, control things all the way to the very end. And, if you put up a strong enough of a fight, they will sacrifice that final act of trying to control how the relationship ends and leave you first because the more you push them back down with the facts, truth, indefensible evidence, etc., the closer you are to exposing them and slapping that mask off their face. And they fear and hate being exposed even more than losing control. They spend a lot of mental effort and energy on protecting and isolating themselves from exposure well in advance of any potential exposure they might face later on down the road. I wouldn't waste your time trying to expose them and here's why. By the time you get to the point of even knowing there is something to expose, they were already way ahead of you and they usually plan well in advance on how to deal with you and any situation where you might try and expose them.

We have come to understand that the most terrifying thing to a narcissist is loss of control. Sometimes the tables are turned and the victim becomes the victimizer. After all, what goes around usually comes around. Narcissists are paranoid and do not give their victims opportunities to become abusers. They are terrifying to be around when they become vindictive and insulted. Humiliation at the hands of a weak opponent is intolerable to a narcissist. People with Narcissistic Personality Disorder are extremely self-centered. Even when they regret their behavior, it is usually because they are experiencing negative consequences—not because they feel bad that they hurt someone else.

As expressed by psychologist Elinor Greenberg:

Most of the Narcissists that I know—when their grandiose defenses are intact—live by some simple rules:

- I am right.
- If you disagree with me, you are wrong.
- If I was mean, it is your fault. You provoked me. You deserved it.
- Someone else is to blame.

Chapter Eight: Hugh Cholmondeley, 3rd Lord Delamere, Moves to Africa

- Did that happen? I don't remember. Let's move on. No point dwelling in the past.
- People with narcissistic personality disorder are pathological liars.

Most people with Narcissistic Personality Disorder do not reflect on their behavior. When they do, they use the above firmly held beliefs to rationalize their behavior.

A further interesting analysis was also submitted to our research team:

> Before a narcissist ever opens his mouth, he can always be counted on to telegraph his narcissistic reality, which is characterized by bifurcated polarized extremes. In other words, the narcissist is an either/or, black/white, and all or nothing individual in regard to every aspect of his life. Therefore...

- If the narcissist tries to appear confident, in actuality, he is feeling vulnerable.
- If the narcissist tries to be perceived as being relaxed, he is in reality feeling very anxious.
- If the narcissist tries to present as calm, cool, and collected, he is likely to be 'shaking in his boots'.

> Internally the narcissist often feels scared, and uncertain. On the other hand, externally he has a smug smirk on his face, and his shoulders are pulled way back and his chest is bowed far out which makes him appear to be a parody of himself. When a person begins to observe the narcissist's cartoonish exaggerated external presentation, it seems to be the antithetical representation of the how the narcissist feels internally. I believe this pronounced and prominent dichotomy to be the number one sign that you are dealing with a narcissist. Narcissistic people also usually rage excessively when challenged. When done by a pathological person, this is what is known as narcissistic rage. This occurs when a person feels slighted or when they feel their sense of superiority is negated in any way. Raging at the perceived offender allows the toxic person to reclaim some measure of control and reaffirms their sense of superiority. Narcissistic people are destroyed by their own paths of destruction, which they create out of their own inner fears of abandonment, rejection and neglect.

An additional opinion was expressed:

> A narcissist's biggest problem is that he cannot see what the problem is. When things don't go well for a narcissist and this occurs very often, he is blind to the cause of the problem, which means he cannot fix it. He cannot see that he is causing his own problems. To him, it looks like everyone else is the problem, so he lashes out at what he thinks is causing the problem and makes his problem worse. He cannot even see what the problem is. It is pretty hard to take down a narcissist without taking down yourself in the process as they play very dirty and there is no way to compete with them unless you are willing to do so as well. I would not advise trying to destroy them though because this is what they specialize in, this is their game, this is their world, and unless you have the same type of deranged self-aggrandizing win at all costs mentality it's going to be pretty hard to go beyond the pale in order to get the upper hand permanently with someone like this. They view life in terms of winning and losing and to them losing is much worse than not living at all, so be prepared for them to take it to this extreme if it comes to that. In other words they are willing to resort to very violent and dangerous tactics just to wrestle control away from those who they view as threats.

This observation was also submitted:

> A narcissist is a normal person; they work, have friends, feelings, they want to love and be loved. They are usually outgoing, many people look up to them, want to be around them. They usually are of some status, or hang with others of high status. It is what they look for, want, need. They have a gift of knowing what others want, and how to make others feel important, special. This is what pulls their victims in. It is what they do after they have caught the prey that makes them who they are. What they also have is a distorted reality and lack of empathy.

These observations by Phyllis Antebi, a PhD in Clinical Psychology, makes very interesting reading:

> Many things upset narcissists. They are self-centered and egocentric by nature. This mindset provides the narcissist

a hunting ground for all sorts of attacks. Attacks on your appearance, your friends, your personal preferences and any obstacle to the narcissist's sphere of influence. However, the effort you may make to confront a narcissist on his abusive attitudes will result in a hyperbolic effort to shift the cause of your complaint back onto the complainer. You, are the one who is selfish, greedy, demanding, unhinged, unfriendly, unattractive and grossly stupid. He will tell you that others find you repulsive, untrustworthy, illiterate and boring to be around.

To round out our research into this important personality flaw of narcissism, especially as observed in individuals who think they are prominent, all-powerful world leaders or dignitaries, whether imaginary or not, I am pleased to report that from my many years experience as a researcher, writer and observer of human behavior, in my humble opinion I personally believe that very few humans display this flaw of character and are usually only noticed when they are prominent or highlighted in the news media. Most humans are basically good and honest regarding themselves and their behaviour; their daily remarks and personal limitations and their daily example reflects this and they are willing to admit their mistakes when necessary and as god-fearing individuals try to live their lives based on the principles of the Bible, especially the book of Proverbs. Also we are reminded of the words in the Bible at Romans 12: 3, "You are not to think more of oneself than it is necessary to think." According to the *Complete Jewish Bible* (*CJB*): "Don't cherish exaggerated ideas of yourself or importance." Plus the translation in the J. B. Phillip's *New Testament*: "As your spiritual teacher I give this piece of advice to each one of you. Don't cherish exaggerated ideas of yourself or your importance, but try to have a sane estimate of your capabilities."

We are reminded that Hugh Cholmondeley, 3rd Lord Delamere, who is noted from actual records as being a narcissist, had inherited and was entitled to the very large estate of Vale Royal Abbey but lost it through poor financial management and overspending created and inherited from his extravagant grandfather, the 1st Lord Delamere, Thomas Cholmondeley (1767-1855). The father of 3rd Lord Delamere, the 2nd Lord Delamere (1811-1887), had simply accepted the fate of the slow deterioration of Vale Royal Abbey as his father was a gentler, more resigned and accepting individual. He was philosophic about the once opulent estate in Cheshire and knew that its deterioration and lack of essential funds for its upkeep and maintenance were outside and beyond his control, as we have learned in Chapter 6. But the 3rd Lord Delamere, who moved to Kenya in 1901 with his new wife abandoning the Vale Royal Abbey, also after abandoning their only child to the care of nannies and family back in County Fermanagh, Northern Ireland, and as reflected in his personal letters and private records, he felt he had been cheated and resented the fact that he was left with an estate that was now almost bankrupt and felt deep resentment that he had been denied what he was rightfully entitled to as legal heir. Also, for most of his life Hugh Cholmondeley, 3rd Lord Delamere, lived as a self-centered bachelor since his young wife of 15 years, Lady Florence, had died aged only 36 years back in 1914 as a direct result of trying to live in an African country she was not suited for. He only married his second wife, Gwladys Helen Beckett, many years later in 1928—she was 30 years younger than he. It was also a marriage of convenience, so as to have a care giver for the final three years of his pathetic life.

Hugh Cholmondeley and other settlers became known as the so-called 'Happy Valley' set, which was largely a group of hedonistic British and Anglo-Irish aristocrats and adventurers who settled in the "Happy Valley" region of the Wanjohi Valley near the Aberdare mountain range, in colonial Kenya and Uganda between the 1920s and the 1940s. In the 1930s, the group became infamous for its decadent lifestyles and exploits, following reports of excessive drug use and sexual promiscuity.

This enlightening, somewhat amusing quote from the *Christian Science Monitor* states:

> The Muthaiga (Nairobi) club's past includes figures such as Hugh Cholmondeley, the third Baron of Delamere, who, with his upcountry settler friends, would amuse themselves with activities such as shooting live rounds into the stuffed lion displayed in the hallway, throwing gramophones out of ballroom windows, or setting dinner chairs in a row and then pushing them around the club, chugging and hooting like a train.

Chapter Eight: Hugh Cholmondeley, 3rd Lord Delamere, Moves to Africa

This article from *The New York Times* also sheds some light on the Happy Valley Crowd:

> Hugh Cholmondeley, 3rd Baron Delamere, was the first aristocratic settler to colonise the Kenyan White Highlands after the country was made a British protectorate in 1895. His second wife, Lady Gwladys Delamere, was mayor of Nairobi and one of the prime suspects in a murder case that made the 'Happy Valley' set 'shorthand' for decadence, depravity and glamour.

Some notable members of the Happy Valley Set in 1926. 3rd Lord Delamere is on the far right, courtesy of the *Kenya Standard*

Of course the lifestyle of this exclusive, dominant white race group of people, mainly consisting of European settlers in Kenya ultimately had to come to an end and the grandiose ambitions and dreams of Hugh Cholmondeley, 3rd Lord Delamere were ultimately shattered. And indeed the European dominance did tragically end with the Mau Mau Uprising (1952-1960), also called the Mau Mau

The Delamere Saga: Part 3

Rebellion, the Kenya Emergency, and the Mau Mau Revolt, which became a full scale war in British Kenya (see Appendix 11).

Land alienation, forced labor, and African participation in higher education, bureaucratic institutions, and the First World War (1914-1918) all helped spark a substantive Kenyan nationalist movement in the 1920s. Leaders such as Jomo Kenyatta and Henry Thuku highlighted a view of an unjust political and social situation for the vast majority of Kenyans. Following World War II, (1939-1945) some Kenyans began a violent anti-colonial campaign centered largely on the Kikuyu, later known as the Mau Mau Uprising.

During 1928, the Prince of Wales [later to become King Edward VIII and then, after his abdication, the Duke of Windsor] arrived in Mombasa, Kenya, aboard the *SS Malda*, accompanied by his brother Henry, the Duke of Gloucester. Also on board was Gwladys Helen Beckett on her way back from England to marry the widower Hugh Cholmondeley, 3rd Lord Delamere in December of 1928, who was almost 30 years older than her. In *Letters from Africa* (1984), Isak Dinesen commented about the social behavior of Gwladys: "Lady Delamere behaved scandalously at supper, I thought; she bombarded the Prince of Wales with big pieces of bread ... and finished up by rushing at him, overturning his chair and rolling him around on the floor." Friends of Hugh Cholmondeley and Gwladys Beckett commented in letters that this was indeed a bizarre marriage, not only because of the age difference, but also because their personalities were so different; it was a wonder that they could live together under the same roof. But Hugh was very weak and quite ill by this time, and he died of heart disease in 1931 within three years of his marriage to Gwladys. After his death, Lady Gwladys Delamere became the Mayor of Nairobi (1938-1940. In *Taking Land, Breaking Land: Women Colonizing the American West and Kenya* by Glenda Riley (2003), we read:

> In 1934, Gladys Delamere gained election to the council where she did such an outstanding job that four years later she became mayor, an office she held for three terms. As mayor she especially initiated anti-poverty programmes in Nairobi's ghettos and helped Europeans left financially stranded by the depression. Because Gladys helped both blacks and whites, some people criticised her unmercifully.

Chapter Eight: Hugh Cholmondeley, 3rd Lord Delamere, Moves to Africa

Gwladys Helen Cholmondeley (nee Beckett), Lady Delamere, died childless on 22 February, 1943, of undisclosed serious health problems at 46 years.

Lady Delamere, Gwladys Helen Cholmondeley (nee Beckett), courtesy of the *London Times*

In *The Ghosts of Happy Valley: Searching for the Lost World of Africa's Infamous Aristocrats*, Juliet Barnes (2013) writes that Gwladys was sometimes portrayed as "a bossy, bitchy and emotionally unbalanced woman, endlessly carousing at the Muthaiga Club with Happy Valleyites" but also "how she selflessly looked after Delamere in his twilight years." By 1931, Hugh Cholmondeley could hardly walk, was incontinent and confined to a wheelchair, requiring two full-time nurses to assist him during his last few years on his farm in Kenya.

With regard to the vision of Kenya becoming a 'white man's' country, this dream had now all but evaporated. To quote from an article in *The Guardian*:

> By the early 1960s, Britain's political willingness to maintain Kenya as a colony was in decline and in 1962 the Lancaster House agreement set a date for Kenya's independence. Realising that a unilateral declaration of independence course like Rhodesia's was not possible after the Mau-Mau uprising, the majority of the 60,000 white settlers considered emigration. Along with Kenyan Asians, Europeans and their descendants were given the choice of retaining their British passports and suffering a diminution in rights, or acquiring new Kenyan passports. Very few chose to acquire citizenship, and most white Kenyans departed the country. The World Bank led a willing-buyer-willing-seller scheme, known as the 'million acre' scheme that was largely financed by secret British subsidies (the actual cost being passed on to the gullible British tax payer). The scheme saw the redistribution of swathes of white-owned farmland to the now newly prosperous Kikuyu black elite.

The Delamere Saga: Part 3

Photo montage of Nairobi, Kenya. Clockwise from top: Central business district, Nairobi National Park, Parliament of Kenya, Nairobi City Hall and the Kenyatta International Conference Center, courtesy of Clara Sanchez, Jorge Lascar, Ting Chen and Demosh

Chapter Eight: Hugh Cholmondeley, 3rd Lord Delamere, Moves to Africa

Did the 'One Million Acre Scheme' actually work out for the benefit of the majority of the citizens of Kenya? This is a matter of opinion, as the well connected elite black families in Kenya managed to gain control of many of the farms being hurriedly disposed of by the numerous Europeans leaving Kenya and returning to their home countries. It was truly a buyers market! Also these same now wealthy Africans very soon took control of the newly created political situation in the country and these very same few wealthy families still dominate the political scene even today. Meanwhile, the majority of the Kenyan population is living in abject poverty today and listed as living below the 'poverty line'. According to the United Nations records, Kenya is one of the most unequal countries in the sub-region of Africa. Forty-two percent of the population of 44 million people still lives below the poverty line. A visit to the Kibera slums of the city of Nairobi will quickly confirm this to the casual visitor and these slums expand every single day. Most of Kibera slum residents live in extreme poverty, earning less than $1.00 per day. This poverty is compounded by the influx of refugees; and Kenya continues to face humanitarian challenges, particularly the presence of over one million refugees from Somalia and 30,000 new arrivals from South Sudan every single month.

Aerial view of the Kibera slums in Nairobi, courtesy of Schreibkraft photography

We also quote from "Focus of the Land in Africa" (FOLA), a document issued by the World Resources Institute (WRI) of Washington, DC, to confirm the consequences of the One Million Acre Scheme.

> In the early 1960s, on the eve of independence, a program of settlement schemes, including the 'One Million Acre Scheme' was established to defuse tensions, but also to ensure that the (white) colonial land-holding structure dominated by large farms could be preserved without a radical redistribution. Most of the schemes negotiated by the departing colonizers were designed for relatively small numbers of carefully selected (nameless) Kenyan 'farmers'. In contrast, the 1962 'One Million Acre Scheme' was designed to accommodate 35,000 land-poor and landless African families. The colonial administration negotiated terms for the purchase of approximately 1.2 million acres of land from white settlers at a cost of 25 million British pounds. Many white settlers sold their farms and left Kenya either before or shortly after independence.

The only redeeming factor regarding the contribution that Hugh Cholmondeley, 3rd Lord Delamere, made to planet Earth was the development of the local agriculture in East Africa. Hugh eventually created a wheat laboratory on his farm, employing scientists to manufacture hardy wheat varieties for the Kenyan highlands. To supplement his income, he even tried raising ostriches for their feathers, importing incubators from Europe; this venture also failed with the advent of the motorcar and the decline in fashion of feathered hats. Hugh, Lord Delamere was the first European to start a maize farm, Florida Farm, in the Rongai Valley, and established the first flourmill in Kenya. At his death, he left Kenya's agricultural economy healthy enough to develop into one of the most stable economies in Africa.

Before we leave our account regarding this incredibly beautiful country, an update is appropriate. The massive tracts in East Africa were open land that the British Government claimed in the early 20th century. It was expropriated on behalf of the "British Crown" according to Government records, as it was "empty unused land". This was even in view of the fact that the Kikuyu, Maasai and other ethnic, nomadic tribes wandered back and forth with their

Chapter Eight: Hugh Cholmondeley, 3rd Lord Delamere, Moves to Africa

herds of cattle. Later, this very same land and the rights to the occupation thereof was sold for "one old penny per acre" to 'white settlers', including Hugh Cholmondeley, 3rd Lord Delamere, who in 1906 named his newly acquired farm, "Soysambu" [the place of striated rock]. Today, you will be pleased to learn that this very land has now effectively and rightfully been returned to the people of Kenya. In 2007 the expansive Soysambu Ranch in Nakuru, property of the few last remaining members of the Cholmondeley family living in Kenya, passed down to them from the 3rd Lord Delamere of Vale Royal Abbey, has been converted into a wildlife conservancy, a move that is set to boost tourism to the overall benefit of Kenya and its people.

Ms. Kat Combes, who skillfully runs the conservancy today along with her son Guy, said that the 48,000 acre ranch has been converted into an animal sanctuary to protect the wildlife: "The conversion, which started in April 2007, was done to help protect over 15, 000 wildlife on the ranch, as well as attract tourists." She also emphasized:

> Soysambu Conservancy, is a non-profit organisation, and works to conserve the Soysambu Estate as a traditional wildlife area, which supports the integrity of the greater Rift Valley eco-system, while promoting sustainable coexistence of wildlife with livestock and at the same time being relevant to and part of modern-day Kenya.

Soysambu Conservancy today, courtesy of Kathryn Combes and the Management of the Conservancy

Soysambu Conservancy is also now home to more than 450 bird species [28% of the world's population of the Lesser Flamingo] and 10,000 mammals of over 50 species including 90+ Rothschild's Giraffe [10% of the world's population of this endangered species]. Kat Combes and her late husband Simon were the masterminds behind this major accomplishment. Simon Combes was the well-known and respected wildlife painter and conservationist who was gored to death by a water buffalo on 12 December 2004, while out on a quiet peaceful evening walk on his farm. This terrible accident underscores the dangers of living in Africa and the awareness, plus respect, we must show toward its wildlife.

In addition to the establishment of the Soysambu Conservancy area, over the past years many additional wildlife sanctuaries and conservation areas have been established in Africa by farsighted, committed individuals and organisations. They have also seen the urgent need for these wild life sanctuaries to protect the actual survival of many of the wildlife species and that face extinction, beautiful creatures that are being threatened in Africa by trophy hunters and poachers who have no regard for life, as they slaughter these beautiful creatures for their tusks, horns or skins and then export these to the world markets that seem to have an insatiable appetite for these items.

The need for these wildlife sanctuaries was recently emphasised and clearly outlined by, HRH, Duke of Cambridge, Prince William, also the President of the United for Wildlife (UFW), a Royal Foundation, when he said,

> We are increasing attention on the most pressing conservation issues of our time, from the rapid escalation of illegal wildlife trade to the challenges of demand reduction. These issues are having a devastating effect on wild populations of some of the largest and most iconic species like elephants, rhinos and tigers, as well as lesser-known species such as the pangolin. United for Wildlife is on their side, are you. I believe passionately that we have a duty to prevent critically endangered species from being wiped out. If we get together, everywhere, we can preserve these animals so that they share our world with future generations. That's what United for Wildlife is all about, and why I'm proud to be involved.

There are now over 200 existing wildlife sanctuaries in Kenya, plus most of them supported by the many outstanding citizens of the world, who also made major contributions to the preservation of the wildlife in Africa. Today sanctuaries and conservancies have formed a 'governing body' to maintain and supervise the outstanding work that is now taking place. The "modus operandi" of the Kenya Wildlife Conservation Association is:

> Kenya has lost nearly 70% of its wildlife during the past thirty years. Loss of space and connectivity is threatening Kenya's wildlife heritage, its multi-billion dollar tourism industry and the livelihoods for rural communities. This is exacerbated by the increasing development pressures and impacts of climate change. Wildlife conservancies offer hope. Today, conservancies in Kenya cover more than 6.3 million hectares, directly impact the lives of more than 700,000 people and securie the 65% of the country's wildlife that is found outside national parks and reserves.

Before we say farewell to Kenya, we are again reminded what a beautiful and exciting location on our planet it is to see the glories of creation. According to one travelogue:

> Key geographical attractions include the Great Rift Valley, which features extinct volcanoes and hot springs, and Kenya's coastline, complete with reefs and magnificent beaches. Combine all this with a well-developed tourist infrastructure of hotels, lodges, campsites and a variety of activities, and it's no wonder Kenya is a popular tourist destination attracting millions of visitors each year.

Farewell Kenya (God's resting place), until we meet again! (Asante tutaonana siku moja).

The Delamere Saga: Part 3

Eight-foot bronze statue of Hugh Cholmondeley on Delamere Ave, Nairobi, before it was ceremoniously removed and dumped in 1963 and the street renamed Kenyetta Ave, courtesy of Rob Bullock

Chapter Nine: Sybil Burnaby (1871-1911)

Sybil Burnaby (nee Cholmondeley) was born at Vale Royal Abbey, Cheshire in 1871, being the only daughter of Hugh Cholmondeley, 2nd Lord Delamere and his second wife, Augusta Emily Cholmondeley. Sybil saw very little of her father as she was away from Vale Royal Abbey for lengthy periods of time with her mother on extended visits to London and also Bournemouth on the south coast of England, as Augusta spent most of her private life with very wealthy friends who related to her social class and background. Sybil also had little contact with her only brother, Hugh, who became the 3rd Lord Delamere in 1887, and who was one year older than Sybil and away at boarding school from the age of four years.

Sybil confessed in a letter to her mother that, although Hugh was her older and only brother, he was like a "total stranger", as they had both lived separate lives from the age of four or five years of age, away from Vale Royal Abbey, and Hugh had made almost no contact with her during their lifetime, except through the family attorneys.

After spending most of her young life under the dominant, influence and manipulation of her mother Augusta, Lady Delamere, Sybil at 24 years in 1896 married Lieutenant Algernon Edwyn Burnaby, a wild philanderer, and who was by the way, also a very close friend of her mother's family, the Seymours. But Sybil fortunately, after discovering his immoral and salacious life style, divorced him in 1902 after her husband ran off with the misguided Lady Sophie Scott, wife of the famous English politician Sir Samuel Scott, MP.

Sybil Cholmondeley in 1893, aged 21 years, courtesy of the National Portrait Gallery, London

The Delamere Saga: Part 3

Portrait of Algernon Edwyn Burnaby (1928), courtesy of the National Archives, London

To quote from a newspaper report and private letters held in the Parliamentary archives at Westminster, London, which expand on this scandalous affair between Algernon Edwyn Burnaby and Lady Sophie Scott:

> The couple, Lady Sophie and Sir Samuel Scott, married in June 1896, were a society match made in heaven; Lady Sophie, the pretty, indulged youngest daughter of one of the richest men in the land—George, the 5th Earl Cadogan—and Sir Samuel, the wealthy, solid landowner with estates in Scotland, Dorset and Kent.
>
> Three years down the line, however, cracks were beginning to show in the marriage. Sir Samuel, writing later to Sophie's father, admitted candidly 'we were in bad times'.
>
> The Scotts then visit the Burnaby family in 1899, but no one knows for sure where they stayed in Leicestershire. They might have rented a house for themselves and their entourage of servants, or perhaps they stayed with Sir Samuel's friend Algernon Burnaby, his wife Sybil and their young son Hugh at Algy's stately pile, Baggrave Hall, near Market Harborough.

Chapter Nine: Sybil Burnaby

Though chalk and cheese in character, the two men were close—the steady, respectable Sir Samuel regarded witty, suave Burnaby as "a man I thought a friend of the oldest standing". What is certain is that during their three-month stay in the county of Leicestershire, Sir Samuel's bored and disillusioned young wife Lady Sophie started to tease her husband by flirting openly with his friend. Worse still, Burnaby flirted back. A rumored womanizer, no-one doubted his magnetic effect on the opposite sex.

A detailed account by the well-respected news reporter Sarah Staples [late sister-in-law of HRH, Anne, Princess Royal] also appeared in the *Leicester Mercury* some years ago [which we acknowledge also provided helpful support] regarding this divorce and the illicit relationship of Algernon Edwyn Burnaby, husband of Sybil, the sister of 3rd Lord Delamere, with the Lady Sophie Scott, and was sent in by our research team based in Cambridge, England.

After Sybil divorced her immoral and now truly despised, adulterous husband Algernon Burnaby because of this notorious public affair with the young vulnerable Lady Sophie Scott, plus no doubt also based on other known recorded incidents of his immoral, indecent life style, Sybil in a private letter later stated that "she wished she could obliterate this horrible person from her memory." After the divorce, Algernon Edwyn Burnaby and the young Lady Sophie Scott never did marry but they created one of the biggest scandals of the day. An extract from *The Times* of London (12 January 1902) regarding this widely publicized divorce records: "After the examination of several witnesses, Mr. Justice Barnes directed the Jury, who immediately found that the respondent [Algernon Edwyn Burnaby] had been guilty both of adultery and desertion."

Lady Sophie Scott, fortunately, it seems soon came to her senses after being seduced, humiliated and corrupted by the 'Leicester Scoundrel' Algernon Burnaby, and she became reconciled again with her estranged, but also her now very forgiving, admirable husband, Sir Samuel Scott MP. Lady Sophie eventually died in 1937, aged 63 years. She was honored to be invested as a Commander, Order of the British Empire (C.B.E.) in 1918 for her humanitarian services during World War 1, 1914-1918.

The Delamere Saga: Part 3

The spirit of Lady Sophie Scott lives on today in Scotland, at Amhuinnsuidhe Castle Estate, Isle of Harris, Outer Hebrides, according to this report:

> Rumor has it that the Castle is home to the ghost of Lady Sophie Scott who was also a resident of the Castle in Edwardian times. Lady Sophie was a keen sportswoman and reputedly an excellent shot. She and her husband, Sir Samuel Scott were renowned for their hospitality and hosted many shooting parties at the Castle. Although she was very fond of children, she was unable to have any of her own. She was also involved in the breeding of the Scottish Cairn terrier, as she loved animals, especially dogs, very much. She died in 1937 at the age of 63 years. Her remains and those of her husband are buried in the cairn on the hill behind the castle.

Amhuinnsuidhe Castle Estate, Isle of Harris, Outer Hebrides, Scotland, courtesy of the North Harris Trust

Algernon Edwyn Burnaby died on the 13 November 1938, aged 70 years, at his family home and estate at Baggrave Hall, Leicestershire. He died, according to his son, a forlorn lonely figure, both disillusioned and guilt-ridden. After his sordid, scandalous affair with Lady Sophie Scott ended in 1902, he re-married once again in 1908 to the notorious 'many times married and divorced' Mrs. Minna Field Gibson from Chicago, a member of the very wealthy Marshall Field Stores American family.

After the death of Burnaby in 1938, his house and estate at Baggrave Hall soon deteriorated and eventually it was approaching a total ruin until bought and partially renovated by Sir George Earle and his family who in turn eventually sold the property to a Turkish criminal, Asil Nardar, the mastermind behind the scandalous, notorious 'Polly Peck' fraud case.

It is of interest to note that the wealth of the Earle family, who owned Baggrave Hall for a few years, had been built on the notorious slave trade. Sir George Earle, a brusque Yorkshireman, died aged 75 years at Baggrave Hall in 1965. He had donated to the Merseyside Maritime Museum in Liverpool, 17 of the metal boxes containing his family archives, including the captain's log of an Atlantic voyage made by the vessel *Unity*, a slave ship owned by one of his ancestors William Earle during 1769 and 1770. According to *The Guardian*:

> The voyage was notably brutal: on June 27, 1770, the log records, 'The Slaves attempted to force up a grating in the night with a design to murder the whites or drown themselves but were prevented by the watch.' The log concludes: 'In the morning the Slaves confessed their intentions ... Their obstinacy put me under the necessity of shooting the ring leader.'

Baggrave Hall in Leicestershire, England, is a two and three-storey Palladian-style building constructed during the 1750s in Ashlar [finely dressed (cut, worked) masonry, either an individual stone that has been worked until squared or the masonry built of such stone] with a Swithland slate hipped roof and brick ridge chimney stacks. An additional wing in red brick can be dated to 1776. The current grounds of the hall cover 220 acres; the hall was listed as a Grade II Historic Building in 1951, but suffered very serious damage in 1988-90. Later in the 17th century, the hall belonged to John Edwyn, whose grandson—also named John—rebuilt it, but incorporated some parts of the 16th-century manor house. In 1770, his daughter Anna Edwyn married Andrew Burnaby, archdeacon

The Delamere Saga: Part 3

of Leicester, and so ownership of the estate passed to the Burnaby family. Later owners included Edwyn Burnaby, High Sheriff of Leicestershire and Edwyn Sherard Burnaby. Baggrave Hall was the childhood-home of Louisa Cavendish-Bentinck (née Burnaby) who became great-grandmother of our beloved Queen Elizabeth II.

To quote from the National Archives of London:

> The Burnaby connection with Baggrave began with the marriage of Andrew Burnaby, later Archdeacon of Leicester, to Anna Edwyn, whose ancestor purchased the estate in the 1680s. Although the earliest document in this collection is the grant of the manor of Baggrave to the Cave family in 1543, the bulk of the records are from the nineteenth and twentieth centuries. There are letters and personal papers of Algernon Edwyn Burnaby and Mrs Minna Burnaby as well as a wealth of material relating to the family's involvement with the Quorn Hunt. This includes the hunting diaries of Minna Burnaby, photograph albums and kennel cards.

Baggrave Hall, courtesy of the *Leicestershire Mercury*

The fabric of the structure and main building at Baggrave Hall was unfortunately severely damaged in 1988-1990 whilst in the ownership of an overseas company controlled by the notorious Turkish criminal Asil Nadir, who had bought the estate with stolen money for £3 million. Stonework was removed, walls undermined, and interior walls, floors and ceilings ruined. The current owner, who bought it from the now bankrupt Asil Nadir, who had been imprisoned for fraud, has undertaken to rectify all of this damage as far as possible. According to legend, the hall was named "Baggrave" after an incident involving a maidservant. She is said to have let a beggar woman take refuge at the hall, but later noticed by the boots that this was a man in disguise. Fearing he was a robber, she murdered him and wrapped his body in a potato bag, in which he was buried.

An account about the life and family of Minna Field Gibson, who had married Algernon Burnaby in 1908, is a book written by her mother entitled *Florence Lathrop Page: A Biography*. Chapter Two, "Family and Values", pps. 47-73, provides an interesting insight to the life of Minna Field Gibson from the USA and her first meeting in England with Algernon (Algy) Burnaby in 1906 and how the circumstances of this new marriage quickly deteriorated and was plagued with financial difficulties from day one. For example, "You have not the habit of living within your income" (p. 72); "The Burnabys had a large yearly income but they lived a life style costing them double that amount" (p. 69); "Minna and Algy were living beyond their income and should rent out Baggrave" (p. 71); and "Somehow Minna and Algy (Algernon) managed to hold onto Baggrave Hall, where they lived until his death in 1938" (p. 73).

After she divorced her husband, Sybil Burnaby's private life was seriously affected by her failed marriage. Also, her deteriorating financial circumstances were being acutely influenced by the wild, reckless conduct and actions of her brother Hugh Cholmondeley. Hugh, 3rd Lord Delamere, who was now living in Kenya, and who wanted nothing to do with his only sister Sybil, or her problems. Hugh, who had squandered much of the remaining family wealth, was now also selling off large portions of the family estate and properties in Cheshire, consisting of a vast number of farms and houses, plus the very impressive family art collection and valuable library at Vale Royal Abbey, and had allowed the once elegant estate to become a dilapidated, neglected shambles.

Note about the sale of portions of the Cholmondeley (Vale Royal Abbey) Estate Listed in Sotheby's Public Catalog of 1910:

> Sale by Hugh Cholmondeley, 3rd Lord Delamere, included 1048 acres of land of the family estate, including, Knights Grange Farm, Westholme Farm, Salterswall Farm, Marton Hall, Marton Bank Farm, Spring Bank Farm, Chester Lane Farm, Poolhead Farm, Little Lane Farm, Lane End Farm, School Farm, Peartree House and many other properties in Delamere Street, Grange Lane, and Swanlow Lane, Winsford, Cheshire."

See also this extract from Sotheby's catalogue of 1926:

> Delamere Collection. London, Sotheby & Co. Catalogue of a Valuable Collection of Old Engravings, from the Collection of the First Lord Delamere (1787-1855), the Property of a Gentleman, Comprising an Important Series of Engravings & Paintings by Old Masters of the Dutch and German Schools.... April 13, 1926.

Of serious concern to Sybil (expressed in letters to her mother) was that the small annual stipend that Sybil received from the Cholmondeley family estate (a fund established by her late father, Hugh, 2nd Lord Delamere), was also now being seriously jeopardized, as the now reduced funds in the family estate were quickly being exhausted, which would find her extremely short of money to cover her basic family expenses and commitments for herself and her young son Hugh Edwyn. Or maybe she envisaged that she would eventually become totally destitute and penniless; considered a total disgrace for a woman of her standing and caliber in the early 1900s.

In a letter from a close friend of Sybil, who had intervened and appealed to Hugh Cholmondeley directly on her behalf, Hugh had clearly indicated that he was not interested in the least in Sybil's problems since he was focused on his life and his own ambition "To make East Africa a 'White Empire', to the exaltation and benefit of the 'Illustrious and Glorious British Empire'."

Sybil probably foresaw that she would not be able to maintain her well positioned property at the prestigious location of Wilton Place in Westminster-Belgravia, London [not far away from Buckingham Palace], a large town house bought for her by her late mother. Also as her ex-husband, who was well-off financially, had also refused to pay any financial support for her and her

Chapter Nine: Sybil Burnaby

young son, even though this had been authorized by the courts in their divorce settlement. After the divorce was finalized in 1902, Sybil certainly could not move back to Vale Royal Abbey with her young son, Hugh Edwyn Burnaby, because the legal owner of the estate, Hugh Cholmondeley, was still "officially" living in the house until 1907 as his English residence, although he was in fact actually living in Kenya most of the time. His attitude was to bleed the once prestigious estate dry [And let it go the b****y Devil, as he mentioned in one of his letters to a friend in London] so he could finance his own projects in Kenya.

It is very likely that the combination of these numerous personal, financial and family problems that Sybil had to endure, plus the extremely depressing incidents and events surrounding her private life, made her future prospects look very bleak indeed and eventually drove her to take her own life at 39 years of age.

Though records in the archives of Scotland Yard do not establish beyond all reasonable doubt that the death of Sybil Burnaby (nee Cholmondeley) in 1911 was in fact suicide, in written recorded interviews with the servants, at least two members of the household staff, as witnesses, related their attempts to prevent Sybil from "throwing" herself out of the 3rd floor window of her house in Wilton Place. A brief extract from a national newspaper of 13 May 1911 reports: "Witnesses reported to the police that servants appeared to be making an effort to keep Mrs. Burnaby away from the window before they saw her drop to the ground." This same newspaper announced her death two weeks later on 26 May 1911: "Mrs. Sybil Burnaby, a sister of Lord Delamere, who was injured in a fall from a third storey window of her house in Wilton Place, London, two weeks ago, died today."

An additional conflicting report was submitted to Scotland Yard and is retained in the official archives, recording the following.

> Mrs. Sybil Burnaby had been kneeling at an open window on a settle (settee) which ran upon castors and wishing to know the time of the day, which was approximately about 7.00 am in the morning, she stood on the settle and reached forward in order to see the clock of St. Paul's Church in the far distance. The foliage of the trees outside the window obstructed her view, and the account is that as she leaned further forward the settle ran from under her, and she fell

The Delamere Saga: Part 3

out of the window. A nurse, named as Katherine Cleghorn, who had been standing a yard or two away, managed to seize her dress as she fell through the open window and Mrs. Burnaby turned and grasped the wooden window frame. The nurse, retaining a frenzied hold of the dress with both hands, screamed for aid. Mrs. Burnaby's maid then rushed in; she also reached through the window and caught onto her dress, her mistress imploring them, "Don't let me go!" For a moment or two they both held her so, when suddenly the thin silk material of the dress ripped and tore from their hands. Mrs. Burnaby's fingers were wrenched from the windowsill, and she fell from the third floor bedroom window to the pavement area beneath. Suffering from terrible fractures, she was still conscious when admitted to the local St. George's hospital.

At the inquest related to the death of Sybil, the coroner asked the two eye witnesses, the nurse and the maid, why Mrs. Burnaby would undertake this risky and reckless act of leaning out of her third storey bedroom window to check the time of day by means of the clock at St. Paul's Church somewhere in the far distance, when there was already a good, reliable and accurate clock on the mantelpiece over the fireplace in her bedroom. Plus according to the police report there were also numerous other timepieces and clocks in the adjoining rooms and in the passage immediately outside her bedroom, all accurately working and displaying the correct time. No answer from the two witnesses was forthcoming; just an embarrassing silence.

The coroner also established that the butler, who claimed he was a third witness, had only later entered the third floor bedroom from which Sybil had plunged, and this was only in urgent response to the loud screams of the nurse and maid that he had heard while he was in the first floor breakfast room and that in fact he was not a direct eye witness of the tragic incident, except for seeing and viewing Sybil's crumpled, crushed body on the pavement below. The coroner therefore discounted his evidence as merely "hearsay".

Other so-called facts produced by additional witnesses at the inquest also created more confusion in the mind of the coroner. For example, the cousin of Sybil, a Captain Edward Seymour, who was also the executor of the estate of the late Mrs. Burnaby testified that Sybil had been bright, cheerful and very positive in recent

Chapter Nine: Sybil Burnaby

weeks, and had easily recovered from her late mother's death 3 months earlier, and had shown no signs of depression or suicidal thoughts. The coroner further asked the witness Captain Seymour, that if Mrs. Burnaby was emotionally handling without much difficulty her failed marriage and traumatic divorce and also the recent death of her mother and as she was a comparatively young woman, "Why was she in need of a full time nurse if everything appeared to be going so well in her daily life?" The witness replied that this full-time nurse being assigned to care for her was based on the recommendation of Mrs. Burnaby's physician as a precaution. "As a precaution against what?" asked the coroner. The witness simply replied that he had no further comments to add and that this question should be directed at Mrs. Burnaby's doctor.

In contradiction to this evidence presented by Sybil's cousin, the personal physician of Sybil Burnaby and being from Harley Street in London, whose name has been removed from the records for professional reasons, testified that his private patient Sybil had recently shown clear signs of extreme depression and he had prescribed very strong medication to help her sleep at nights. Plus the doctor had also noted that Sybil had recently started drinking alcohol heavily, even during daytime hours, which had been giving him some concern. However he also added that Sybil had never shown signs of being suicidal or even mentioning taking the drastic step of killing herself.

We must remember that the above report and statement regarding Sybil Burnaby, which was also surreptitiously leaked to the press by an unidentified source, was submitted to Scotland Yard by the butler employed at the residence of Sybil in Wilton Place, who was still in the employ of the 'estate' of the recently deceased mother of Sybil. This report by the butler is highly suspicious as he was not even a personal eye witness of this tragic incident and his report, as the 'senior' member of the household staff, is suspect. He was probably the instigator of a hurried, secret consultation with the maid and the nurse, who also were in the employ of the "estate", and this was probably an attempt to cover over this "suicide" and make it appear like an "accident" to help and protect the reputation of Augusta Cholmondeley, as well as the family name and reputation. The result was that the coroner, after considering all available evidence presented at this inquest, gave the official ruling and eventual final verdict on the death of Sybil as "accidental death". The coroner very likely struggled with the conflicting and contradictory evidence presented by the various witnesses at the inquest.

The coroner's final verdict was also based no doubt on the fact that Sybil was the sister of Hugh Cholmondeley, 3rd Lord Delamere, who was also a member of the House of Lords, although he never attended any regular sessions or debates. The coroner also knew that the stigma of having a family member commit suicide, especially a family of the caliber of the Cholmondeleys of Vale Royal Abbey, could reflect on the family's good name and reputation. Sybil never recovered sufficiently to be interviewed by the police at Scotland Yard during the 13 days she lay in a coma in the St. George's Hospital in London. Had she recovered she would have perhaps been able to reveal the truth of this tragic event, but alas she did not, eventually passing away on 26 May 1911.

Chapter Ten: The Vicissitudes of Vale Royal Abbey from 1907 to the Present

In 1907, Vale Royal Abbey was rented out by Hugh Cholmondeley, 3rd Lord Delamere, through the lawyers handling the defaulting and bankrupt estate. It was leased to a Robert Dempster, a wealthy industrialist, owner of the Gas Plant Works and a very successful businessman from Manchester, England. Robert Dempster died while on vacation at the Mount Nelson Hotel in Cape Town, South Africa in 1925, and his daughter Edith Pretty (nee Dempster) took over the lease. Edith had married Frank Pretty in 1926 and taken over the lease from her father until the end of the year 1926 when she vacated Vale Royal Abbey. Vale Royal Abbey was eventually taken over by the British Government and the lawyers handling the defaulting estate of Vale Royal Abbey because of the still increasing and numerous incumbent debts.

A news report in the *Yorkshire Post* on Edith Pretty relates:

> Edith Pretty was born at Elland, Yorkshire, on 1 August 1883, the younger of two daughters of Robert and Elizabeth Dempster. The Dempsters were very wealthy industrialists who amassed their fortune from the manufacture of equipment related to the gas industry. Robert Dempster's Father, Robert Dempster, had founded the company at Elland in Yorkshire in 1855, and this became R & J Dempster & Sons in 1883, which Robert founded with his brother, John. On their deaths the Dempster brothers between them left over a million pounds, an enormous sum in the first quarter of the Twentieth Century. Edith's family embarked on many foreign tours, including one 'round the world', and Robert Dempster took a lease on the huge country house of Vale Royal Abbey, Cheshire, the family seat of Lord Delamere, from 1907-1925. It was here that Edith grew up in palatial style with an indoor staff of twenty five and eighteen gardeners.

To quote from her biography:

> Edith was educated at Roedean School, finishing her education with a six-month spell in Paris. After school, she became involved in good works, including the Red Cross, with whom she served during the First World War in the United Kingdom and France. In 1907 her parents moved to Vale Royal Abbey, which they rented from the 3rd Lord Delamere and soon after moving in, her father, who was intensely interested in archaeology, was given permission to excavate and expose the plan of the Cistercian Abbey church adjoining the house. While watching the work there, Edith acquired a further interest in archaeology and some understanding of excavation methods.
>
> While living at Vale Royal Abbey she did much public and charitable work, both there and in Salford and Manchester. Immediately after the outbreak of war in 1914 she became Quartermaster of the local Red Cross military hospital and at the same time was running a house as a home for a number of Belgian refugees. In 1917 she served with the French Red Cross at Vitry le Francois and Le Bourget. She was one of the first women magistrates in England.

A booklet is available from the Cheshire offices of the Northwich and District Heritage Society called *Life at Vale Royal Great House 1907-1925, the Memoirs of Mary Hopkirk*. The young Mary Dempster's grandfather had leased Vale Royal Great House from Hugh Cholmondeley, 3rd Lord Delamere for 18 years while he was living in Kenya, and this is her vivid account of the grand, country house life in Edwardian England. She takes readers for a conducted tour of the historic house with its opulent furnishings and its acres of glorious gardens. The photographs of the interior rooms plus some portions of the glorious gardens are truly outstanding.

In 1926, Edith Dempster married her long term suitor, Frank Pretty, an Ipswich man who had been a Major in the Territorial Army's Suffolk Regiment during the First World War and who continued to serve the Suffolk Regiment after the First World War, also working in the local family business of clothing manufacture. After their marriage, the Prettys looked for a home near Ipswich. Edith also gave up the lease on Vale Royal Abbey and bought Sutton Hoo House near Woodbridge, Suffolk. Also in 1926 she donated the

Chapter Ten: The Vicissitudes of Vale Royal Abbey from 1907 to the Present

Dempster Challenge Cup to Winsford UDC, Cheshire, which has been awarded annually to a plot-holder on the town's allotments.

In 1938, Edith enlisted the help of a Suffolk archaeologist, Basil Brown, to dig into ancient mounds on her land. Some promising finds were made, and Brown returned in the summer of 1939 to make further excavations. He soon unearthed the remains of an enormous burial mound, later identified as a 7th century Saxon ship and probably the last resting-place of King Rædwald of East Anglia.

In September 1939, a treasure trove inquest determined that the fabulous grave goods unearthed from the ship were Pretty's property to do with as she chose. Within days, she made the greatest donation to the nation made in a donor's lifetime, giving the treasure to the British Museum. In recognition, Prime Minister, Winston Churchill later offered Pretty the honor of a CBE, but she declined.

This amazing discovery at Sutton Hoo deserves mention and edification for our readers. We are also grateful to the British Museum for the following:

> Sutton Hoo, near Woodbridge, East Anglia, is the site of two 6th and early 7th century cemeteries. One contained an undisturbed ship burial, including a wealth of Anglo-Saxon artifacts of outstanding art-historical and archaeological significance, most of which are now in the British Museum in London. The site is now in the care of the National Trust.

Sutton Hoo House, Suffolk, England, courtesy of Michèle Abson

The Delamere Saga: Part 3

Sutton Hoo is of primary importance to early medieval historians because it sheds light on a period of English history that is on the margin between myth, legend, and historical documentation. Use of the site culminated at a time when Rædwald, the ruler of the East Angles, held senior power among the English people and played a dynamic, if ambiguous part in the establishment of Christian rulership in England; it is generally thought most likely that he is the person buried in the ship. The site has been vital in understanding the Anglo-Saxon Kingdom of East Anglia and the whole early Anglo-Saxon period.

The ship-burial, probably dating from the early 7th century and excavated in 1939, is one of the most magnificent archaeological finds in England for its size and completeness, far-reaching connections, the quality and beauty of its contents, and the profound interest of the burial ritual itself. The initial excavation was privately sponsored by the landowner. When the significance of the find became apparent, national experts took over. Subsequent archaeological campaigns, particularly in the late 1960s and late 1980s, have explored the wider site and many other individual burials. The most significant artifacts from the ship-burial, displayed in the British Museum, are those found in the burial chamber, including a suite of metalwork dress fittings in gold and gems, a ceremonial helmet, shield and sword, a lyre, and many pieces of silver plate from Byzantium. The ship-burial has from the time of its discovery prompted comparisons with the world described in the heroic Old English poem Beowulf, which is set in southern Sweden. It is in that region, especially at Vendel, that close archaeological parallels to the ship burial are found, both in its general form and in details of the military equipment contained in the burial.

Although it is the ship-burial that commands the greatest attention from tourists, two separate cemeteries also have rich historical meaning because of their position in relation to the Deben estuary and the North Sea, and their relation to other sites in the immediate neighborhood. Of the two grave fields found at Sutton Hoo, one (the "Sutton Hoo cemetery") had long been known to exist because it consists of a group of approximately 20 earthen burial mounds that

Chapter Ten: The Vicissitudes of Vale Royal Abbey from 1907 to the Present

rise slightly above the horizon of the hill-spur when viewed from the opposite bank. The other, called here the "new" burial ground, is situated on a second hill-spur close to the present Exhibition Hall, about 500 metres upstream of the first. It was discovered and partially explored in the year 2000 during preliminary work for the construction of the hall. This also had burials under mounds, but was not known because these mounds had long since been flattened by agricultural activity. The site has a visitor centre, with many original and replica artifacts and a reconstruction of the ship burial chamber, and the burial field can be toured today in the summer months and at weekends and school holidays year-round.

A replica of the Sutton Hoo helmet produced for the British Museum, courtesy of the British Museum

An interesting personal report in a Cheshire newspaper was submitted from a maid who had once worked at Vale Royal Abbey while it was occupied by the Dempsters recalls the memories of her mother, who also worked in the Vale Royal Great House:

> Joan Henry's mother used to cycle to work, where she was taken on as a laundry maid, earning £2 a month." Joan also said: "My mother talked with great reverence of Mr. and Miss. Dempster, father and daughter, her employers, but would see very little of them apart from the annual servants ball, as she would be below stairs and involved with the washing and ironing for her employers and for the 17 servants.

> Apparently the servants' food was inadequate and they were often hungry. My granny would bake cakes for my mother to take back after her weekends off—one a month.
>
> She met my father at the house when she was 16.
>
> My father came from the Belvoir Castle Estate, Leicestershire, where his father had been butler to the Duke of Rutland and joined the other servants at Vale Royal Great House as a footman. He was 19.
>
> After her father died in 1925, Miss Dempster gave up the tenancy and married Colonel Frank Pretty moving to Sutton Hoo in Suffolk.
>
> My parents married in 1928 and my grandparents and parents decided to stay in Cheshire as it was such a beautiful county.

Meanwhile, Vale Royal Abbey from 1926 onward entered into an extremely severe decline. The estate was unable to pay its liabilities and very little maintenance or repairs were being undertaken by the administrators of the now defunct estate of the Cholmondeley family, supposedly under the direct control of Hugh Cholomondeley, 3rd Lord Delamere and his lawyer friends and associates. The property, now under the control of the British Government and the lawyers acting for the mortgagees, was eventually leased out and used by the local salt industry in Cheshire as a storage facility and offices for the ICI Chemical firm. This was the situation that existed on the occasion that I visited and saw Vale Royal Abbey for the first time when I was six years old in 1946.

Various ideas had been presented to utilize the property for a more constructive purpose but none came to realization until the property was eventually sold to the current owners, a private golf club, and, as a result, with great expense on their behalf, Vale Royal Abbey has been restored to its former glory.

These comments by the current owners, the Vale Royal Abbey Golf Club, explain the most recent history of this historic Abbey and Mansion:

> The development of the Vale Royal Abbey has been many years in the planning. Following the acquisition of the Abbey in 1987, the owners, in partnership with English

Chapter Ten: The Vicissitudes of Vale Royal Abbey from 1907 to the Present

Heritage and the Vale Royal Local Authority, formulated an overall development plan which included a top quality golf course, and the conversion of the Great House into a stunning clubhouse with separate apartment wing. The development plan saw the restoration of the Great House and the creation of the golf course as the cornerstone of the project with its long-term future secured by the addition of a prestige development of luxurious private houses within the estate. This stunning Grade II listed building and adjoining site of the ancient monument provide an extraordinary setting when compared with conventional golf clubhouses. This important and historic building undoubtedly ranks alongside the best of the few great period buildings in this use in the United Kingdom and a place that members will be proud to bring their guests.

Created from the former Royal Parkland and magnificent Grade II listed Great House, Vale Royal Abbey Golf Club is set within one of the County's most important historic estates. The superb 18-hole golf course opened in October 1998 and is built to top international standards. It is a rarity among modern courses in that it is laid out on fine natural golfing terrain and rolling sandy soil, which surrounds the awe inspiring converted Mansion. Bounded by the River Weaver, and enjoying stunning views through mature woodland, lakes and meadows, the course is already remarkably mature for its age. No-one who visits Vale Royal Abbey can fail to be impressed by its clubhouse, possibly the oldest in the world, what was formerly the home of Lord Delamere now provides members and guests with an outstanding environment for casual and corporate entertainment. The Great House provides clubhouse facilities of unparalleled grandeur creating the underlying atmosphere of opulence, security and quality that is the cornerstone of the Club. Access to the course and facilities at Cheshire's most prestigious private club is restricted to members only and their guests.

We must also reflect on one of the many fascinating historical events related to Vale Royal Abbey, for example the Abbey even has its own legend. This report from the *Cheshire Magazine* quoted below, relates this interesting account. This version is also confirmed and recorded in the book *Prophecy, Politics & People of Early Modern*

England by Timothy Thornton (see also *Cheshire Notes & Queries, Vol. 7*, p. 174 (1887)).

The Cheshire Prophet, Robert Nixon—truth or legend?

For centuries the prophecies of Robert Nixon have stirred the imagination of Cheshire folk. Supposedly born in 1467, on a small farm held by his father under the Abbey of Vale Royal, Nixon has become to Cheshire what Mother Shipton[34] is to Yorkshire.

Robert Nixon was known as the 'Cheshire Ploughboy Prophet', said from his earliest years to be remarkable only for his stupidity, indeed so much so that it was with great difficulty that he was taught to drive a team of oxen, or to look after his father's cattle.

Yet he apparently became so famous that he was commanded to foretell the future for a king!

The story goes that whilst working in the fields, Nixon made many predictions, notably concerning the Abbey of Vale Royal which stood near to the River Weaver a few miles from the old town of Over. Vale Royal, founded by King Edward I in 1277, was in its heyday the largest Cistercian abbey in England.

Nixon told one abbot who annoyed him: 'When you the harrow come on high, Soon a raven's nest will be'. This prophecy is supposed to have come true at the Reformation when the last abbot, whose name was Harrow, was called before Sir Thomas Holcroft and put to death for refusing to acknowledge that King Henry VIII was the supreme head of the Church. Henry had given the monastery and all its lands to Sir Thomas whose crest was a raven!

Sir Thomas Holcroft demolished the abbey and built in its place the great house of Vale Royal, which has recently partially been converted into apartments and also serves as the clubhouse for the newly-created Vale Royal Abbey Golf

---

[34] Ursula Southeil (c. 1488-1561) better known as Mother Shipton, is said to have been an English soothsayer and prophetess and she was born in Knaresborough, Yorkshire, in a cave now known today as Mother Shipton's Cave. This historic site still exists and is well worth visiting.

Chapter Ten: The Vicissitudes of Vale Royal Abbey from 1907 to the Present

Club. Can there be a more historic 19th hole anywhere in the world?

Nixon is also said to have foretold the outcome of the Battle of Bosworth Field[35], Whilst ploughing in Whitegate, the simpleton stopped his team and with his whip, pointed from one hand to the other, crying 'Now Richard! Now Harry!' several times over, until at last he said, 'Now Harry, get over that ditch and you gain the day'. The plough-holder related what had passed and the truth of the prediction was verified by special messenger sent to announce the proclamation of Henry, King of England, at Bosworth Field. Legend has it that Nixon was duly sent for by the king, but upon receiving the royal command, he ran like a madman around the town of Over, declaring that at court he would be starved to death.

On his arrival and by way of a test, the king hid a valuable diamond ring and asked the ploughboy to help him find it, whereupon Nixon said: 'He who hideth can find'. From then on, the king ordered that whatever Nixon said should be written down. The upshot of the tale was that Nixon, exactly as he had predicted, became locked in a closet and died of starvation.

Other accounts of Nixon state that he was born during the reign of James I (1603-1625) and that he was for some time in the service of Thomas Cholmondeley, when master of Vale Royal after 1625.

'When an eagle shall sit on top of the house, then an heir shall be born to the Cholmondeley family' was another of Nixon's revelations. And so it came to pass that when an heir was most needed a large eagle perched on the edge of a great bay window and refused to be driven away until a son was born.

---

[35] The Battle of Bosworth Field (or Battle of Bosworth) was the last significant battle of the Wars of the Roses, the civil war between the Houses of Lancaster and York that extended across in the latter half of the 15th Century. Fought on 22 August 1485, the battle was won by the Lancastrians. Their leader Henry Tudor, Earl of Richmond, by his victory became the first English monarch of the Tudor dynasty. His opponent, Richard III, the last king of the House of York, was killed in the battle. Historians consider Bosworth Field to mark the end of the Plantagenet dynasty, making it a defining moment of English and Welsh history. The actual tomb of Richard III has been a subject of great controversy in recent years and the eventual outcome is that his tomb now reburied from Greyfriars Church in Leicester to the Leicester Cathedral has now been established and recognized as the genuine resting place of King Richard III.

The Delamere Saga: Part 3

That important and significant heir proved to be Charles Cholmondeley (1684-1756) the great-grandson of Thomas Cholmondeley (1594-1652) who had inherited Vale Royal Abbey from his mother, Lady Mary Cholmondeley (nee Holford) in 1625 [see Chapters 1 and 3].

Quoting once again from *The Good Gentlewoman*:

Robert Nixon was a plough boy, driveller and dullard. A sometimes violent character, strange looking and with a prodigious appetite, Nixon was well-known in the Vale Royal area where he worked for local farmers until he wore out his welcome. He was also in the habit of falling into a trance like state behind the plough, standing there for up to an hour. Sometimes he would recover and carry on as if nothing had happened, sometimes he would speak in incomprehensible words and sometimes he would come out with something quite extraordinary.

A cartoon, possibly of Robert Nixon, depicting a "drooling idiot" from an 18th century chapbook dated in the 18th century, artist unknown

One account of the history of Robert Nixon states that he was born during the reign of James I (1603–1625) [James I founded the Stuart line of English monarchs. He was already James IV of Scotland and he succeeded Queen Elizabeth I in 1603, as the son of Mary Queen of Scots, a descendant of King Henry VII]. This account also states that Nixon was for some time in the service of Thomas Cholmondeley, master of Vale Royal Abbey approximately 1625, the year when he inherited the property. There are also two claimed homes for Robert Nixon: one says he was an illiterate boy who was born in Bark House on a hill between Over and Whitegate. Another source claims Robert Nixon lived at Bridge House near the Forest of Delamere.

Published in 1838, and held in the archive section of the British Library, *Nixon's Original Cheshire Prophecy* describes him as a 17th-century prophet, followed by Nixon's prophecy itself, written in verse, and with an interpretive text:

> The figure of Robert Nixon, was supposedly born in the 15th century, and was a compilation of several characters, including the legendary Thomas the Rhymer. By the late 17th century the Nixon prophecies, largely sourced from The Whole Prophecies of Scotland, England & France ..., published in Edinburgh in 1603 and running into several editions, was being read as a pro-Jacobite text. The kernel of the prophecy was in the last stanza:
>
> Then rise up Richard, son of Richard,
> And bless the happy reign,
> Thrice happy he who sees this to come,
> When England shall know rest and peace again.
>
> This was read as an allegory of the call for the return of the Stuart dynasty. John Oldmixon, was a Whig supporter of the new Hanoverian monarch in 1714, and noted on the title page as editor.

Whether fact or fiction; Robert Nixon's name and his prophecies live on to this very day, as does indeed the Vale Royal Abbey, to enrich the history and folklore of Cheshire. Also the beautiful treasure of our Vale Royal Abbey, England, lives on to enrich our lives today, proudly standing in the Cheshire countryside, and still holding the many secrets and unforgettable memories of the numerous characters who visited, lived, and died there over the centuries, plus their many exploits and intrigues during the colourful history of this incredible place. So we also once again raise our glass and declare, "Long Live Vale Royal Abbey"

Painting of Vale Royal Abbey, artist unknown, c. 1876, courtesy of the Chester Museum of Art

Postscript

This book is also dedicated to the memory of my late dear mother, Margaret Hebdon (nee Green) (1916-2003) who was the inspiration and driving force behind this 'labour of love'. Much of this information was passed down to Margaret from her father Herbert and also her much loved uncle, John William, older brother of her father. Margaret was the only child and daughter of Herbert Green (1878-1943), who was in turn the illegitimate son of Margaret Green (1835-1908), who served at Vale Royal Abbey initially as a chambermaid to Henrietta Charlotte Cholmondeley (1823-1874), the only daughter of Thomas Cholmondeley, 1st Lord Delamere (1767-1855) and also later served as housekeeper during the days of Hugh Cholmondeley, 2nd Lord Delamere (1811-1887).

This book is also in memory of Margaret Green (1835-1908), who figures so prominently in *The Delamere Saga*. Margaret was also the source of important material recorded and listed in her beautiful, exquisite handwriting in the Green family Bible and the numerous letters and records she filed away for her family's posterity.

Photograph of my Great-Grandmother Margaret Green, aged 71, holding the Green family Bible [still in our possession today]

Appendix 1: English Civil Wars

The English Civil War (1642-1651) was a series of armed conflicts and political machinations between Parliamentarians ("Roundheads") and Royalists ("Cavaliers") over, principally, the manner of England's government. The first (1642-1646) and second (1648-1649) wars pitted the supporters of King Charles I against the supporters of the Long Parliament, while the third (1649-1651) saw fighting between supporters of King Charles II and supporters of the Rump Parliament. The war officially ended with the Parliamentarian victory at the Battle of Worcester on 3 September 1651, but many skirmishes took place for a few years following this date, right up until the crowning of Charles II in 1660. The outcome of the war was threefold: the trial and execution of Charles I (1649); the exile of his son, Charles II (1651); and the replacement of English monarchy with, at first, the Commonwealth of England (1649-1653) and then the Protectorate under the rule of Oliver Cromwell (1653-1658) and subsequently his son Richard (1658-1659).

Appendix 2: King Henry II

Henry II (1133-1189), also known as Henry Curtmantle [French: Court-manteau], Henry FitzEmpress or Henry Plantagenet, ruled as Count of Anjou, Count of Maine, Duke of Normandy, Duke of Aquitaine, Count of Nantes, King of England and Lord of Ireland. At various times, he also controlled Wales, Scotland and Brittany. Henry was the son of Geoffrey of Anjou and Matilda, daughter of Henry I of England. He became actively involved by the age of 14 in his mother's efforts to claim the throne of England, then occupied by Stephen of Blois, and was made Duke of Normandy at 17. He inherited Anjou in 1151 and shortly afterwards married Eleanor of Aquitaine, whose marriage to Louis VII of France had recently been annulled. Stephen agreed to a peace treaty after Henry's military expedition to England in 1153, and Henry inherited the kingdom on Stephen's death a year later. *The Lion in Winter* (1968) is a magnificent film about Henry II and Eleanor of Aquitaine:

> It's Christmas, 1183, and King Henry II (Peter O'Toole) is planning to announce his successor to the throne. The jockeying for the crown, though, is complex. Henry has three sons and wants his boy Prince John (Nigel Terry) to take over. Henry's wife, Queen Eleanor (Katharine Hepburn), has other ideas. She believes their son Prince Richard (Anthony Hopkins) should be king. As the family and various schemers gather for the holiday, each tries to make the indecisive king choose their option.

Henry II: Medieval Soldier of War by John Hesler (2007) was reviewed on Amazon.com:

> This book is a monograph on a little known subject: the military career and campaigns of Henry II, from the time (1147) when he was—at age fifteen—yet a contender for the throne of England and the Duchy of Normandy, both of which were held by King Stephen, until his defeat and death in 1189.

The book concentrates essentially on the military aspects of the founder of what has at times been called "The Angevin Empire." Its main merit is to show that Henry, although eclipsed by his much more flamboyant son Richard I ("the Lionheart"), was no mean warlord and a very successful that should rank at par with his son and successor.

From the author's own introduction:

This study concerns itself with Henry's military career between 1147 and 1189, the year of his death. My goal in the book is to provide a comprehensive, though not exhaustive, examination of the different facets of Henry II's military experiences. The first chapter, inspired by C. Warren Hollister's fine precedent in his posthumous biography Henry I (*Yale English Monarchs Series*), surveys the medieval evidence in detail. Chapter Two sketches a short narrative of his military and political exploits and problems. Chapters Three, Four and Five examine the structure of his armies and the nature of his various military operations, while Chapter Six concentrates upon the military aspect of the Great Revolt of 1173 and 1174. The concluding chapter then seeks to construct from these fresh analyses a fuller legacy of Henry, not only as a general but as a soldier of war. I like to think that Henry's record speaks for itself, so I have tried to provide extensive documentation at every step. Whether or not his name stands along those of the greatest medieval generals is immaterial—I believe that in the final analysis he can be viewed as a sound and versatile commander who enjoyed massive success and suffered few setbacks. In any case, whatever our individual opinions, I think all can agree that his warfare is more than worthy of an extended inquiry.

Appendix 3: South Sea Bubble

The South Sea Company [officially, The Governor and Company of the merchants of Great Britain, trading to the South Seas and other parts of America, and for the encouragement of fishing] was a British joint-stock company founded in 1711, created as a public-private partnership to consolidate and reduce the cost of British national debt. There was no realistic prospect that trade would ever take place and the company never realised any significant profit from its monopoly. Company stock rose greatly in value as it expanded its operations dealing in government debt, peaking in 1720 before collapsing to little above its original flotation price. The economic outcome became known as the 'South Sea Bubble'. The South Sea Company had no problem attracting investors when, with an IOU to the British government worth £10,000,000.00 (ten million), the company (crazy as it seems) purchased the "rights" to all trade in the South Seas.

In January of 1720, South Sea Company stock was trading at a modest £128. In an effort to stir up popular interest in the company's stock, the directors circulated false claims of success and fanciful tales of South Sea riches. By the end of June, its share price had spiked to a peak of £1050. Investor confidence began to wane, however. The sell-off began by early July and the collapse occurred very quickly. By the end of August stock was valued at less than £800. By September the share price had plummeted to £175, devastating institutions, the Bank of England and individuals alike. In 1721, formal investigations exposed a web of deceit, corruption, and bribery that led to the prosecution of many of the major players in the crisis, including both company and government officials. In reflection this was probably the original 'pyramid scheme' and what is even more disgusting is that this scheme was started and promulgated by the British Government itself. The stench of corruption reeked through the Halls of Westminster for many years to come.

Many individuals and banks lost all of their investment and faced total ruin. Even Charles Cholmondeley of Vale Royal Abbey

Appendices

was duped by this 'scam', as, according to private family records, he personally lost over £200,000 in this stupid investment. Prime Minister Walpole promised to seek out all those responsible for the scandal, but, in the end, no doubt because of vested interests, he sacrificed only some of those involved in order to preserve the reputation of his friends amongst the government's leaders. The enquiry showed that at least three ministers in Walpole's government had accepted bribes and they were forced to resign, but many other MPs and government officials who were marginally involved and had personal knowledge of this scam but narrowly escaped the 'axe' resulting from this enquiry, without any action being taken against them for their corrupt dealings. The term "south sea bubble" is still used today related to the many investment scams still taking place throughout the world.

Appendix 4: Osborn Collection

The Osborn Collection consists of English literary and historical manuscripts from the Anglo-Saxon period to the twentieth century, with particular emphasis on the seventeenth and eighteenth centuries, plus also on English poetry. Letters and papers of scholars and antiquaries, such as Edmond Malone, Charles Burney, and many lesser-known individuals, are supplemented by historical manuscripts and state papers.

The 'James Marshall and Marie-Louise Osborn Collection' traces its beginnings to the mid 1930s when James Osborn studied at Oxford University in England. Inspired by the example of the eighteenth-century scholar and collector Edmond Malone, Mr. Osborn began to acquire the manuscripts that comprise the core of the collection now housed in the Beinecke Library. This library is one of the world's largest devoted entirely to rare books and manuscripts and is Yale's University principal repository for literary archives, early manuscripts and rare books.

As with Edward Malone, whose collection of books and manuscripts is preserved in the Bodleian Library at Oxford in England, Mr. Osborn sought documents for their value as literary and historical evidence, and like Malone, he intended that his collection would become part of a great library, available for the use of future generations of scholars. Of significant note is that amongst the travel manuscripts of the nineteenth century, the correspondence of Howe Peter Browne, Second Marquis of Sligo, during his travels to the Levant, deserves particular mention. A friend of Lord Byron's from Cambridge University, Sligo toured the Levant in 1810 with a considerable entourage, collecting archaeological fragments, before he was joined by Lord Byron for a tour of the Morea the Peninsula in southern Greece in 1814.

James Osborn's own papers, which amount to 76 boxes containing carbon copies of outgoing letters filed with incoming correspondence, including private and very personal letters from the Cholmondeley family of Cheshire, are also being consulted by researchers. This wide correspondence in itself constitutes a chronicle of the progress of English literary and historical studies in the mid-twentieth century.

Appendix 5: Newstead Abbey

Newstead Abbey, in Nottinghamshire, England, was formerly an Augustinian priory. Converted to a domestic home following the Dissolution of the Monasteries, it is now best known as the ancestral home of Lord Byron.

The priory of St. Mary of Newstead, a house of Augustinian Canons, was founded by King Henry II of England in about 1170 as one of many penances he paid following the murder of Thomas Becket. Contrary to its current name, Newstead was never an abbey—it was a priory.

Sir John Byron of Colwick in Nottinghamshire was granted Newstead Abbey by Henry VIII of England on 26 May 1540 and started its conversion into a country house. He was succeeded by his son Sir John Byron of Clayton Hall. Many additions were made to the original building. The 13th century ecclesiastical buildings were largely ruined during the dissolution of the monasteries. It then passed to John Byron, an MP and Royalist commander, who was created a baron in 1643. He died childless in France and ownership transferred to his brother Richard Byron. Richard's son William was a minor poet and was succeeded in 1695 by his son William Byron, 4th Baron Byron of Rochdale.

Early in the 18th century, the 4th Lord Byron landscaped the gardens extensively, to which William Byron, 5th Baron Byron, added Gothic follies. It became a stately and glamorous estate. The 5th Baron, also known as "the Wicked Lord", was eccentric and violent; he also ruined the estate. Lord Byron's son and heir (also named William) eloped with his cousin Juliana Byron, the daughter of William's brother John Byron. Lord Byron felt that intermarrying would produce children plagued with madness and strongly opposed the union. He also needed his son to marry well to escape the debt that had been incurred in the Byron name. When defied by his son, he became enraged and committed himself to ruining his inheritance so that, in the event of his death, his son would receive nothing but debt and worthless property. He laid waste to Newstead Abbey, allowing the house to fall into disrepair, cutting down the great stands of timber surrounding it, and killing over 2,000 deer on the estate.

His vicious plan, however, was thwarted when his son died in 1776. William also outlived his grandson, a young man who, at the age of 22, was killed by cannon fire in 1794 while fighting in Corsica, a mountainous Mediterranean island. The 5th Lord Byron of Rochdale died on 21 May 1798, at the age of 79 and, on his death, it is said, great numbers of crickets he kept at Newstead Abbey left the estate in swarms. His title and Newstead Abbey was left to his great-nephew, George Gordon Byron, the world-famous poet, who became the 6th Baron Byron of Rochdale, "Lord Byron".

Photograph of Newstead Abbey today

Appendix 6: Rochdale & Rochdale Town Hall

Rochdale is a town in Lancashire, England, at the foothills of the South Pennines on the River Roch, being approximately three miles from Royton Hall, the home of the main branch of the Byron family for 12 generations. It is from the name of this town 'Rochdale' that Lord Byron inherited the title, 6th Baron Byron of Rochdale. But also of special interest to our readers, includes the fascinating history of Rochdale Town Hall and the connection of this impressive, magnificent building with Adolf Hitler of Nazi Germany.

Rochdale Town Hall is a Victorian era town hall "widely recognised as being one of the finest municipal buildings in the country". The Grade I listed building is the ceremonial headquarters of Rochdale Metropolitan Borough Council and houses local government departments, including the borough's civil registration office and also holds the statue of its world famous citizen, the well loved, late Dame Gracie Fields (DBE) actor and singer. Built in the Gothic Revival style it was inaugurated on 27 September 1871. The architect, William Henry Crossland won a competition held in 1864. The town hall had a 240-foot (73m) clock tower topped by a wooden spire with a gilded statue of Saint George and the Dragon that were destroyed by fire on 10 April 1883. A new 191-foot (58m) stone clock tower and spire in the style of Manchester Town Hall was designed by Alfred Waterhouse, and erected in 1888. Art critic Nikolaus Pevsner described the building as possessing a "rare picturesque beauty". Its stained glass windows, some designed by William Morris, are credited as "the finest modern examples of their kind".

William Henry Crossland, from Huddersfied in Yorkshire, the architect of Rochdale Town Hall, was the great-uncle of my godfather Sam Crossland, who was the famous cross country and marathon runner. Sam was a member of Royton Harriers and he won many awards on their behalf in the north of England. Sam was also invited to attend trials in Manchester for the selection of athletes to represent Britain and run in the marathon race in the controversial Olympics of 1933, in Berlin, Nazi Germany. But he refused this invitation because of his repulsion of the anti-Semitic and anti-black overtone of this event. Sam Crossland was an avid member, supporter and past chairman of the Royton Harriers Club, of which I was also a member for a few years as a teenager, until I decided after coming last or second last in most of the races I ever entered that I was not an athlete? Royton Harriers & Athletic Club was founded in 1898 and still exists today as a private club. It is devoted to local athletics and the promotion of sporting excellence within the community.

Sam Crossland and his wife Anne never had any children so, being my godfather, he treated me like the son he never had. He later signed me up in the junior team of the Royton Cricket Club, of which he was also a member. I was selected to the fielding position of 'silly-mid-on'; this description is derived from the fact that the fielder is positioned so close to the batsman that he would be unable to take evasive action if the ball were to be hit very hard towards him. I was selected for this fielding position by the captain of the junior team; my friend Jack Greaves, for my first game at the 'Paddocks', the cricket field of the Royton Cricket Club, as I was told that I had a 'good eye' and was a 'good catcher', which was debatable. After I was hit on the head with the hard cricket ball I was carried off the cricket pitch on a stretcher with a lump on my head the size of a 'hen's egg'. I quickly decided that playing cricket was not for me, so my short career as a cricket player abruptly ended and I became an avid spectator of the game instead for the duration of my days in England.

The Berlin Olympic Games of 1933 are best remembered for Adolf Hitler's failed attempt to use them to prove his theories of Aryan racial superiority. As it turned out, the most popular hero of the Games was the African-American sprinter and long jumper Jesse Owens, who won four gold medals. Reich Chancellor Adolf Hitler saw the Games as an opportunity to promote his government and ideals of racial supremacy and anti-Semitism, and the official Nazi party paper, the *Völkischer Beobachter*, wrote in the strongest terms that Jews should not be allowed to participate in the Games. When threatened with a boycott by other nations, Hitler appeared to allow athletes of other ethnicities from other countries to participate. However, German Jewish athletes were barred or prevented from taking part by a variety of methods and Jewish athletes from other countries (notably the USA) seem to have been sidelined in order not to offend the Nazi regime.

A little known fact is that this magnificent building, the Town Hall in Rochdale in Lancashire, came to the attention of Adolf Hitler who was said to have admired it so much that he wished to ship the building; stone-by-stone back to Nazi Germany when the United Kingdom had been defeated in the Second World War. An unconfirmed rumor is that when the western allies eventually forced the Nazis into defeat in 1945, they found a dossier in the Nazi headquarters in Schloss Marburg (Marburger Castle), that contained numerous photographs and sketches with a fully developed plan, outlining how to dismantle and remove the British national treasure of the Rochdale Town Hall and ship it back to Nazi Germany. No doubt the photographs and other details were collected and secretly sent to the insane, megalomaniac Adolf Hitler by the many Nazi sympathizers who lived in England at that time, probably under the influence and control of the British fascist and traitor, Oswald Mosley. To quote from *The Guardian*:

> Sir Oswald Mosley's British Union of Fascists (later renamed the Union Movement) was active during the 1930s. To most of the electorate, Mosley's politics—of which anti-Semitism formed a key part, especially after 1934—were simply odious. So there was no outcry when he and his wife, Diana as well as some 800 of his followers, were interned in 1940 under *Defense Regulation* 18B.

An alternative account suggested that a personal visit to Rochdale was made in 1912-13 by Adolf Hitler himself, while staying with his half-brother Alois Hitler, Jnr. in Liverpool. If Adolf Hitler did stay in Merseyside, then it wouldn't have been difficult for him to visit Rochdale, and, as he was an aspiring landscape artist at the time, he would have been looking for interesting and beautiful subjects to paint. Whatever the reason and basis for Adolf Hitler knowing about Rochdale Town Hall, it is suggested and indeed noted that he admired the building so much that he issued orders that the Nazi air force, the Luftwaffe, was to avoid damaging it in their air-raids on Manchester, Oldham, Royton and the adjoining local areas, during his attempt to conquer the British Empire.

Appendices

One shudders to think of what the resolute and determined folk of Rochdale, back in the 1940s would have done to oppose this travesty of threatening the dismantling and blatantly stealing their treasured Town Hall by Nazi Germany, if Hitler had won the Second World War (1939-1945), and 'god-forbid' their reaction if he had indeed tried to steal their world famous, and much loved historic building. The people of Rochdale being true Lancastrians, and loyal to England, plus being the remnants of the Brigantes of Northern England, [Celtic tribe who in pre-Roman times controlled the largest section of what would become Northern England], they would have literally fought to the death to prevent this scurrilous theft of their precious Town Hall. Fortunately, as destiny unfolded, the men and women of Rochdale, and also the rest of the world, after 1945, breathed a sigh of relief when they were spared any further atrocities, theft or war crimes committed by the satanic Nazi empire of the Third Reich of Germany. As quoted in the BBC documentary *The History of the 2nd World War* (2011) on this individual: "Few names from history inspire such immediate and emphatic revulsion as that of Nazi leader Adolf Hitler. His hands are stained with the blood of millions killed in the devastation of the Second World War and the horror of the Holocaust."

In his book *Mein Kampf* (1925), Hitler is quoted:

> If you tell a big enough lie and tell it frequently enough, it will be believed. Make the lie big, make it simple, keep saying it, and eventually they will believe it. He alone, who owns the youth, gains the future.

Many readers will recognize this same tactic is used by many leading politicians and world leaders even today.

Amongst other records also discovered in Germany after 1945 were the "Windsor Files". Many historians have suggested that Hitler was prepared to reinstate the Duke of Windsor as King of England [Puppet King] and his American-born wife, Mrs Simpson as Queen in the hope of establishing a fascist Britain, if Edward agreed to do so after reaching Spain to hold special, secret meetings with the Third Reich. Documents recovered from the Germans in 1945 at Schloss Marburg [Marburger Castle], and later called the Windsor Files or the Marburg File, included relevant correspondence about the planned outcome of this plot, known as Operation Willi. This real event in history is so eloquently covered in the TV series *The Crown*. The Royal family of King George VI already had plans in place to relocate to Canada in the event of Nazi Germany invading England in 1940. With the evacuation of the approximately 400,000 British troops from Dunkirk [Dunkerque], France in 1940 and the now very real prospects of England falling to the German invading army. These events in history caused England to enter its "darkest hour".

Revealed earlier is the account that Edward the Prince of Wales (later to become King Edward VIII and then Duke of Windsor) arrived in Mombasa in 1928 aboard the ship *SS Malda*, accompanied by his brother Prince Henry, the Duke of Gloucester on an official visit to several East African countries. The 73-page report of this visit is contained in the *Colonial Annual Report to Parliament (Kenya)* (1928).

What does not appear in this report is an incident that our researchers have independently established—the visit that Edward made to Hugh Cholmondeley, 3rd Lord Delamere, and their secret meeting in 1928 at Soysambu, Hugh Cholmonderley's farm. This was to privately discuss the benefits of 'white supremacy', fascism and the promotion of anti-Semitic policies and how they could both mutually support and advance the extermination of the Jews in Europe and Africa, which of course eventually was attempted when Hitler and his Nazi party came to power in 1933, resulting in the Holocaust.

Photo of Rochdale Town Hall today, courtesy of Rochdale Town Council & Tim Green

Appendix 7: Royton Hall

During our research of the Great House and Estate of Vale Royal Abbey and also Baggrave Hall in Leicestershire, it became a stark reality that our national heritage sites in England must be preserved at all costs, as these ancient buildings are an integral part of our unique British history and so many have been lost through neglect and ignorance. We also became acutely aware how close the inhabitants of Cheshire, and for that matter the whole country of England, came to losing this magnificent building of Vale Royal Abbey, after it was recklessly abandoned by Hugh Cholmondeley, 3rd Lord Delamere, but we are now ever grateful that today it is registered as a scheduled ancient monument and recorded in the National Heritage List for England as a designated Grade II listed building.

However one glaring example of the ignorance and lack of foresight in the preserving of our National Heritage sites is that of the condition of the ancient building and estate of Royton Hall in Lancashire, England. This report from the archives of the *Oldham Evening Chronicle* puts it in a nutshell:

> Royton Hall is a typical example of how a historic and established ancient building; with intelligent foresight, could have been turned into a great opportunity as an international tourist centre, as it was directly related to the world famous, very well-known and highly respected Lord Byron, one of the greatest poets who ever lived. This carefully restored and preserved centre could have become a great tourist attraction and possibly include a top class restaurant and visitors centre, being of tremendous benefit to the local community of Royton and the surrounding area, as indeed the Vale Royal Abbey has now proved to be for the Cheshire community. But alas, the lack of foresight by the local officials of Royton back in 1939 has now permanently destroyed a great local asset and a heritage site that the local community could have preserved; benefitted from and enjoyed even today.

The Delamere Saga

For more information about Royton Hall, we recommend that you visit the web site of the Royton Local History Society at www.rlhs.co.uk

Royton Hall in 1795, courtesy of *Oldham Chronicle*

Another example, by contrast, is that of a local architectural treasure; Foxdenton Hall in Chadderton, a small town next door to Royton in Lancashire. Foxdenton Hall is now a country house which stands in Foxdenton Park and listed as a Grade II building by the National Trust in 1950. It is a two-storey Georgian house with an English garden wall bond exterior and its own private gardens. It was built between 1710 and 1730 for Alexander Radclyffe on the base of a previous hall built in 1620 for William Ratclyffe. The hall and the adjoining Park were leased by the Radclyffe family in 1922 to Chadderton Council, who opened the site to the public. In 1960 the council took over ownership of the hall, by which time it was in a state of disrepair. They fully restored it in 1965.

Appendix 8: Peterloo Massacre[36]

The Peterloo Massacre occurred at St Peter's Field, Manchester, England, on 16 August 1819 when cavalry charged into a crowd of 60,000-80,000 people who had gathered to demand the reform of parliamentary representation.

The end of the Napoleonic Wars in 1815 had resulted in periods of famine and chronic unemployment, exacerbated by the introduction of the first of the Corn Laws. By the beginning of 1819, the pressure generated by poor economic conditions, coupled with the relative lack of suffrage in Northern England, and had enhanced the appeal of political radicalism. In response, the Manchester Patriotic Union, a group agitating for parliamentary reform, organised a demonstration to be addressed by the well-known radical orator Henry Hunt. After the end of the Napoleonic Wars in 1815, a brief boom in textile manufacture was followed by periods of chronic economic depression, particularly among textile weavers and spinners (the textile trade was concentrated in Lancashire). Weavers who could have expected to earn 15 shillings for a six-day week in 1803, saw their wages cut to 5 shillings or even 4s 6d by 1818. The industrialists, who were cutting wages without offering relief, blamed market forces generated by the aftershocks of the Napoleonic Wars.

Exacerbating matters were the *Corn Laws*, the first of which was passed in 1815, imposing a tariff on foreign grain in an effort to protect English grain producers. The cost of food rose as people were forced to buy the more expensive and lower quality British grain, and periods of famine and chronic unemployment ensued, increasing the desire for political reform both in Lancashire and in the country at large.

Shortly after the meeting began, local magistrates called on the Manchester and Salford Yeomanry to arrest Hunt and several others on the hustings with him. The Yeomanry charged into the crowd, knocking down a woman and killing a child, and finally apprehending Hunt. However, in the midst of the throng they

---
[36] As sourced from *Wikipedia*.

became separated into small groups and halted in disorder. The 15th Hussars were then summoned by the magistrate, Mr Hulton, to disperse the crowd. They charged with sabres drawn, and, in the ensuing confusion, 15 people were killed and 400-700 were injured. The massacre was given the name Peterloo in an ironic comparison to the Battle of Waterloo, which had taken place four years earlier.

Historian Robert Poole has called the Peterloo Massacre one of the defining moments of its age. In its own time, the London and national papers shared the horror felt in the Manchester region, but Peterloo's immediate effect was to cause the government to crack down on reform, with the passing of what became known as the Six Acts. An estimated 18 people; including four women and a child died from sabre cuts and the trampling of the crowds in the confusion. Nearly 700 men, women and children received extremely serious injuries all in the name of liberty and freedom from poverty. The Massacre occurred during a period of immense political tension and mass protests. Fewer than 2% of the population had the vote, and hunger was rife with the disastrous Corn Laws making bread unaffordable. As 600 Hussars, several hundred infantrymen, an artillery unit with two six-pounder guns, 400 men of the Cheshire cavalry and 400 special constables waited in reserve, the local Yeomanry were given the task of arresting the speakers. The Yeomanry, led by Captain Hugh Birley and Major Thomas Trafford, were essentially a paramilitary force drawn from the ranks of the local mill and shop owners.

The crowd that gathered in St Peter's Field arrived in disciplined and organised contingents. Each village or chapelry was given a time and a place to meet, from where its members were to proceed to assembly points in the larger towns or townships, and from there on to Manchester. Contingents were sent from all around the region, the largest and "best dressed" of which was a group of 10,000 who had travelled from Oldham Green [thought to be where Tommyfield Market now stands], comprising people from Oldham, Royton, Crompton [which included a sizeable female section, including my great grandmother, Mary Todd from High Crompton], Lees, Saddleworth and Mossley.

On horseback, armed with sabres and clubs, many were familiar with, and had old scores to settle with the leading protesters. In one instance, spotting a reporter from the radical *Manchester Observer*, a Yeomanry officer called out "There's Saxton, damn him, run him through." Another recorded command from the Leader of the Soldiers said, "Down with 'em! Chop em down my brave boys: give them no quarter as they want to take our Beef & Pudding from us! & remember the more you kill the less poor rates you'll have to pay so go at it Lads, show your courage."

Heading for the hustings, they charged when the crowd linked arms to try and stop the arrests, and proceeded to strike down banners and people with their swords. Rumours from the period have persistently stated the Yeomanry was drunk.

One direct consequence of Peterloo was the foundation of the *Manchester Guardian* [now known as the respected and outspoken *The Guardian*] newspaper in 1821 by the Little Circle group of non-conformist Manchester businessmen headed by John Edward Taylor, a witness to the massacre. The prospectus announcing the new publication proclaimed that it would:

> zealously enforce the principles of civil and religious Liberty ... warmly advocate the cause of Reform ... endeavour to assist in the diffusion of just principles of Political Economy and ... support, without reference to the party from which they emanate, all serviceable measures.

The year 2019 marks the centenary of this tragic event.

The town of Oldham's involvement in the Peterloo meeting was sizeable and was the largest contingent that attended. The tragedy that was to follow could not have been predicted and it is only right to acknowledge it two centuries on.

The Delamere Saga

The Battle of Peterloo by Richard Carlile (1819), courtesy of Manchester Library

Veterans of Peterloo, assembled at Failsworth (1884); my paternal great-grandmother is the girl on the left of the three women, courtesy of *Creative Commons* and the *Oldham Chronicle* archives

Appendix 9: Cowlishaw Village or Hamlet in Crompton, Lancashire[37]

Extract from the book *History of Parochial Chapelry of Oldham* (1826) by James Butterworth:

> Cowlishaw is a small village and lies near the town of Crompton & Shaw and contains a considerable number of well-built houses and bears the mark of antiquity. There is a very neat-built house in the village owned by a Mr. Jones and occupied as a "public house". There also exists in the locality, School-croft Lane, Rushy-fields, Leonardien-cross, Narrow-gate Brow and Fir Lane, the last three which jointly form another unnamed small village and all lie on the eminence of the above Cowlishaw Village aforesaid.

Also Cowlishaw is described in the *British Parliamentary Records* of the 18th century as "The hamlet of Cowlishaw, within the township of Crompton, in the parish of Prestbury, Lancashire."

During the later Middle Ages, Crompton was a collection of scattered woods, farmsteads, moorland, swamp and a single corn mill, occupied by a small and close community of families. The area was thinly populated and consisted of several dispersed hamlets, including Whitfield, High Crompton, Cowlishaw, Birshaw and Bovebeale (above Beal). These hamlets were situated above the waterlogged valley bottoms and below the exposed high moors.

The dual name of both Shaw and Crompton has been said to make the town "distinctive, if not unique", while preference of Shaw over Crompton and vice versa has been (and to a limited extent remains) a minor local controversy and point of confusion.

The name Shaw is derived from the Old English word *sceaga*, meaning "wood". The name Crompton is also of Old English derivation, from the words crom or crumb, meaning "bent" or "crooked", and ton, for "hamlet or village". A local historian stated that "this name aptly describes the appearance of the place, with its uneven surface, its numerous mounds and hills, as though it

---

[37] From *Wikipedia*.

had been crumpled up to form these ridges". The University of Nottingham's Institute for Name-Studies has offered the suggestion that the name Crompton means "river-bend settlement", which may reflect Crompton's location on a meander of the River Beal.

The manufacture of textiles in Crompton can be traced back to 1474, when a lease dated from that year outlines that the occupant of Crompton Park had spinning wheels, cards and looms, all of which suggest that cloth was being produced in large quantities. The upland geography of the area constrained the output of crop growing and so prior to industrialisation the area was used for grazing sheep, which provided the raw material for a local woolen weaving trade. Wills and inventories from the 15th and 16th centuries suggest most families were involved with small scale pasture, but supplemented their incomes by weaving woolens in the domestic system, and selling cloth, linen and fustians to travelling chapmen for the markets in Manchester and Rochdale.

Although the industry endured, as imports of cheaper foreign yarns increased during the mid-20th century, Shaw and Crompton's textile sector, as did their neighbours in Royton, declined gradually to a halt; as with many other towns in Lancashire, and was said to have over-relied upon the textile sector, cotton spinning reduced in the 1960s and 1970s. By the early 1980s only four mills were operational. In spite of efforts to increase the efficiency and competitiveness of its production, the final cotton was spun in Shaw and Crompton in 1989, in the Lilac and Park mills. Of the 48 cotton mills that have occupied Shaw and Crompton, only six are still standing, all of which are now simply used as warehouses used as local distribution centres.

Appendices

Appendix 10: Carnegie Library in Royton, Lancashire

Royton Public Library, built in 1905, is a famous building in the North of England because of its history and connection with Andrew Carnegie the American millionaire. Royton was one of the few towns in Northern England to be privileged to receive one of these generous grants to build this very impressive structure, which was of tremendous value to the forward looking people of Royton, including my Grandfather Herbert Green.

Carnegie Library, Royton, courtesy of Stanley Walker

Andrew Carnegie believed in giving to the "industrious and ambitious; not those who need everything done for them, but those who, being most anxious and able to help themselves, deserve and will be benefited by help from others". Most of the library buildings were unique, constructed in a number of styles, including Beaux-Arts, Italian Renaissance, Baroque, Classical Revival, and Spanish Colonial. Scottish Baronial was one of the styles used in Carnegie's native Scotland. Each style was chosen by the local community. The architecture was typically simple and formal, welcoming patrons to enter through a prominent doorway, nearly always accessed via a staircase. The entry staircase symbolized a person's elevation by learning. Similarly, outside virtually every library was a lamppost or lantern, meant as a symbol of enlightenment. Carnegie's grants were very large for this time in history and his library philanthropy is one of the largest philanthropic activities, by value, in history. Small towns received grants of $10,000 that enabled them to build large libraries that immediately were among the most significant town amenities in hundreds of communities, including the historic town of Royton in Lancashire, where I was born in 1939.

Books and libraries were important to Carnegie, beginning with his early childhood in Scotland and his teen years in Allegheny, Pittsburgh in the USA. There he listened to readings and discussions of books from the Tradesman's Subscription Library, which his father helped to create. Later, while working for the local telegraph company in Pittsburgh, Pennsylvania, Carnegie borrowed books from the personal library of Colonel James Anderson, who opened his collection to his workers every Saturday. Anderson, like Carnegie, resided in Allegheny.

In his autobiography, Carnegie credited Anderson with providing an opportunity for "working boys" [that some said should not be "entitled to books"] to acquire the knowledge to improve themselves. Carnegie's personal experience as an immigrant, who with help from others worked his way into a position of wealth, reinforced his belief in a society based on merit, where anyone who worked hard could become successful. This conviction was a major element of his philosophy of giving in general, and of his libraries as its best-known expression.

Andrew Carnegie in his generosity donated this building and library to the people of Royton for perpetuity.[38] A news article in 2018 revealed that the local municipal officials are planning to close it down and move the contents of this world-famous library

---

[38] Perpetuity is an annuity that has no end or that continues forever, ad infinitum).

to nearby inferior premises and then sell this magnificent building to a local developer, who could possibly convert it into a seedy night club, which is the last thing the upright citizens of Royton need. Poor Andrew Carnegie would turn in his grave if he knew of this scandalous act that is a direct violation of the "title deeds" of this property and a blatant breach of international law and the ignorant misuse of his generous, dedicated gift of this spectacular Carnegie Library that he made to the genuine, forward-looking people of Royton.

Appendix 11: Mau Mau Uprising in Kenya (1952-1960)[39]

The Mau Mau groups of people, politically dominated by the Kikuyu people, fought against the white European settlers in Kenya and the British Army, e.g. the local Kenya Regiment (British, auxiliaries, and pro–British Kikuyu people).

The capture of rebel leader Dedan Kimathi on 21 October 1956 signaled the defeat of the Mau Mau, and ended the British military campaign. The Mau Mau failed to capture widespread public support, partly due to the British policy of divide and rule, and the movement remained internally divided, despite attempts to unify its various strands. The British, meanwhile, could draw upon the strategy and tactics they developed in putting down another rebellion that happened in Malaya in the Far East.

The Mau Mau was basically a secret insurgent organization in Kenya, comprised mainly of Kikuyu tribes. They were bound by oath to force the expulsion of white settlers from Kenya. In 1952 the Mau Mau began reprisals against the Europeans, especially in the 'white highlands', claimed as Kikuyu lands. The settlers of course retaliated and non-participant Kikuyu were killed by the Mau Mau. Jomo Kenyatta and other nationalist leaders were imprisoned. By 1956, however, British troops had hunted down the Mau Mau in the mountain forests. Most leaders were captured and executed. Later the entire Kikuyu tribe was resettled within a guarded area. The state of emergency decreed in 1952 in Kenya was ended in 1960 and Kenyatta was released; he subsequently became prime minister (1963) upon independence, and then later the president (1964) when the country became a republic.

The uprising created a rift between the European colonial community in Kenya and the metropole, but also resulted in violent divisions within the Kikuyu community. The origin of the term Mau Mau is uncertain. According to some Mau Mau, they never referred to themselves as such, instead preferring the military title, Kenya Land and Freedom Army (KLFA). Some publications, such

---
[39] From *Wikipedia*.

as Fred Majdalany's *State of Emergency: The Full Story of Mau Mau*, claim it was an anagram of Uma Uma [which means "get out get out"] and was a military codeword based on a secret language-game Kikuyu boys used to play at the time of their circumcision. Majdalany goes on to state that the British simply used the name as a label for the Kikuyu ethnic community without assigning any specific definition.

A feature of all settler societies during the colonial period was the ability of European settlers to obtain for themselves, a disproportionate share in land ownership. Kenya was no exception, with the first settlers arriving in 1902 as part of Governor Charles Eliot's plan to have a settler economy pay for the recently completed Uganda Railway. The success of this settler economy would depend heavily on the availability of land, labour and capital, and so, over the next three decades, the colonial government and settlers consolidated their control over Kenyan land, and 'encouraged' native Kenyans to become wage labourers.

Coupled with an increasing native Kenyan population, the land expropriation became an increasingly bitter point of contention. The Kikuyu, who lived in the Kiambu, Nyeri and Murang'a counties of Central Province, were one of the ethnic groups most affected by the colonial government's land expropriation and European settlement. By 1933, they had had over 109.5 square miles (284 km^2) of their potentially highly valuable land alienated. In terms of lost acreage, the Massai and Nandi people were the biggest losers of land. The Kikuyu did mount a legal challenge to the expropriation of their land, but a Kenya High Court decision of 1921 reaffirmed its legality.

The colonial government and white farmers also wanted cheap labour, which for a period, the government acquired from native Kenyans through force. Confiscating the land itself helped to create a pool of wage labourers, but the colony introduced measures that forced more native Kenyans to submit to wage labour: the introduction of the Hut and Poll Taxes (1901 and 1910, respectively); the establishment of reserves for each ethnic group, which isolated ethnic groups and often exacerbated overcrowding; the discouragement of native Kenyans' growing cash crops; the *Masters and Servants Ordinance* (1906) and an identification pass known as the *kipande* (1918) to control the movement of labour and to curb desertion; and the exemption of wage labourers from forced labour and other compulsory, detested tasks such as conscription.

Kenyan employees were often poorly treated by their European employers—sometimes even beaten to death by them, with some settlers arguing that native black Kenyans "were as children and should be treated as such". Some settlers flogged their servants for petty offences. To make matters even worse, native Kenyan workers were poorly served by colonial labour-legislation and a prejudiced legal-system. The vast majority of Kenyan employees' violations of labour legislation were settled with "rough justice" meted out by their employers. Most colonial magistrates appear to have been unconcerned by the illegal practice of settler-administered flogging. Indeed, during the 1920s, flogging was the magisterial punishment-of-choice for native Kenyan convicts. The principle of punitive sanctions against workers was not removed from the Kenyan labour statutes until the 1950s.

Many excellent books have been written about the Mau Mau Uprising and we recommend that readers who are interested in this devastating period of the history of Kenya research some of these journals and books reviewed in Amazon.com:

Squatters & the Roots of the Mau Mau: 1905-63 by Tabitha Kanogo:

> This is a study of the genesis, evolution, adaptation and subordination of the Kikuyu squatter labourers, who comprised the majority of resident labourers on settler plantations and estates in the Rift Valley Province of the White Highlands. The story of the squatter presence in the White Highlands is essentially the story of the conflicts and contradictions that existed between two agrarian systems, the settler plantation economy and the squatter peasant option.

Fighting the Mau Mau: The British Army and Counter-Insurgency in the Kenya Emergency by Dr. Huw Bennett:

> British Army counterinsurgency campaigns were supposedly waged within the bounds of international law, overcoming insurgents with the minimum force necessary. This revealing study questions what this meant for the civilian population during the Mau Mau rebellion in Kenya in the 1950s, one

of Britain's most violent decolonisation wars. For the first time Huw Bennett examines the conduct of soldiers in detail, uncovering the uneasy relationship between notions of minimum force and the colonial tradition of exemplary force where harsh repression was frequently employed as a valid means of quickly crushing rebellion. Although a range of restrained policies such as Special Forces methods, restrictive rules of engagement and surrender schemes prevented the campaign from degenerating into genocide, the army simultaneously coerced the population to drop their support for the rebels, imposing collective fines, mass detentions and frequent interrogations, often tolerating rape, indiscriminate killing and torture to terrorise the population into submission.)

Kenya, the Kikuyu and Mau Mau by David Lovatt Smith:

This is a history of the colonial period of Kenya 1885-1963. The book traces Britain's record from her original involvement in eastern Africa with the slave trade, to the agreement on 'Spheres of Influence' at the 1885 Berlin Conference; thence to the European settlement in Kenya and finally to the Mau Mau Emergency. The archival research includes interviews with former colonial officials and settlers. The author appends first-hand accounts together with his own interpretations after more than 50 years association with the country. This is a primary source book aimed particularly at students of African colonialism.

Ideology, Theory, and Revolution: Lessons from the Mau Mau of Kenya by Mazrui, Al-Amin:

The author has depicted peasant reaction against colonialism in Africa (including the militant Mau Mau reaction) as somewhat spontaneous, conceptually parochial, and lacking ideological foundation.1 This view is, in fact, not uncommon and can be found in a number of historical accounts of the Mau Mau movement in colonial Kenya. But how valid is this conception of the anti-colonial efforts of the peasantry in Africa? To what extent can we regard the specific instance of the militant Mau Mau insurrection against British colonial rule in Kenya as nonideological in its direction? This question obviously demands at least a

The Delamere Saga

> brief and broad consideration of the history of the Mau Mau movement, to which we will turn first. The massive land estates expropriated by the British community at the inception of colonial occupation of Kenya, which required an abundant supply of cheap labor, not only displaced thousands of (predominantly Kikuyu) Kenyans and rendered the African land reserves intensely overcrowded, but also transformed thousands of others into landless rural proletarian squatters within the British-occupied farms, generally the most productive agricultural territory. And during the state of emergency (declared in October, 1952) the squatters were forcibly evacuated en masse from the squatments to join the already congested, uprooted, and unemployed population. To aggravate this already volcanic situation, rigid 'Apartheid' restrictions were imposed on the Africans in the production and sale of certain cash crops as well as in the social and political spheres.

Mau Mau Rebellion: The Emergency in Kenya 1952–1956 by Nicholas van der Bijl:

> In the 'Mau Mau Rebellion', the author describes the background to and the course of a short but brutal late colonial campaign in Kenya. The Mau Mau, a violent and secretive Kikuyu society, aimed to restore the proud tribe's pre-colonial superiority and rule. The 1940s saw initial targeting of Africans working for the colonial government and by 1952 the situation had deteriorated so badly that a State of Emergency was declared. The plan for mass arrests leaked and many leaders and supporters escaped to the bush where the gangs formed a military structure. Brutal attacks on both whites and loyal natives caused morale problems and local police and military were overwhelmed. Reinforcements were called in, and harsh measures including mass deportation, protected camps, fines, confiscation of property and extreme intelligence gathering employed were employed. War crimes were committed by both sides.

Imperial Reckoning: The Untold Story of Britain's Gulag in Kenya by Caroline Elkins:

> A major work of history that for the first time reveals the violence and terror at the heart of Britain's civilizing

mission in Kenya. As part of the Allied forces, thousands of Kenyans fought alongside the British in World War II. But, just a few years after the defeat of Hitler, the British colonial government detained nearly the entire population of Kenya's largest ethnic minority, the Kikuyu, some one and a half million people.

The compelling story of the system of prisons and work camps where thousands met their deaths has remained largely untold, the victim of a determined effort by the British to destroy all official records of their attempts to stop the Mau Mau uprising, the Kikuyu people's ultimately successful bid for Kenyan independence. Caroline Elkins, an assistant professor of history at Harvard University, spent a decade in London, Nairobi, and the Kenyan countryside interviewing hundreds of Kikuyu men and women who survived the British camps, as well as the British and African loyalists who detained them.

European Imperialism: 1830-1930 by Alice L. Conklin:

This book deals with many of the major theories on the cause of European imperialism and why it is that it ultimately failed (there are even writings from Lenin and Gandhi in this book on the subject of imperialism). One of the most interesting things I learned about European imperialism is that the Europeans taught their colonial subjects about their own struggles for independence, rights and representative government, inadvertently planting and watering the seeds of colonial independence. They even have a section where a native of the Dutch colony of Indonesia (who was interested in Indonesian independence) wrote to and lectured the Dutch colonial authorities about this very thing.

Imperialism, Race and Resistance by Barbara Bush:

This book marks an important new development in the study of British and imperial interwar history. Focusing on Britain, West Africa and South Africa, Imperialism, Race and Resistance charts the growth of anti-colonial resistance and opposition to racism in the prelude to the 'post-colonial' era. The complex nature of imperial power is explored, as well as its impact on the lives and struggles of black men and women in Africa and the African Diaspora. Barbara

Bush argues that tensions between white dreams of power and black dreams of freedom were seminal in transforming Britain's relationship with Africa in an era bounded by global war and shaped by ideological conflict.

Selected Bibliography

Al-Amin, Mazrui. *Ideology, Theory, and Revolution: Lessons from the Mau Mau of Kenya*. New York: Sage Publications. 1987.

Andrews, Allen. *The Kings & Queens of England*. Singapore: Marshall Cavendish Publishers. 1976.

Barnes, Juliet. *The Ghosts of Happy Valley: Searching for the Lost World of Africa's Infamous Aristocrats*. London: Aurum Press, Ltd. 2013.

Beechey, Frederick William. *Narrative of a Voyage to the Pacific and Beering's Straits*. London: Henry Colburn & Richard Bentley Publishers. 1831.

Bevan, R. M. *The Donnes*. Chester: Cheshire Country Publishing. 1960.

Booth, Charles. *Inquiry into Life and Labour in London* (17 volumes). London & New York: Macmillan and Company, 1889.

Brownbill, John. *Vale Royal Ledger, Book of 1662*. Manchester: Manchester Record Society, Manchester University. 1914.

Bumsted, J. M. *Peoples of Canada*. Oxford: Oxford University Press. 1992.

Burke, Bernard. *Burke's Landed Gentry*. London: Shaw Publishing Company. 1898.

Bush, Barbara. *Imperialism, Race and Resistance*. London: Routledge Publishing. 1999.

Butterworth, James. *History of Parochial Chapelry of Oldham*. Oldham & Manchester: J. Dodge & Company Printers. 1826.

Cambridge University Staff. *The Journal of African History* (60 volumes). Cambridge: Cambridge University Press, 1960.

Carpenter, William. *Peerage for the People*. London: Palala Press. 1837.

Cholmondeley, Lionel. *The History of the Bonin Islands from the Year 1827-1876, and the Story of Nathaniel Savory, One of the Original Settlers*. London: Constable & Company Ltd. 1915.

Churchill, Winston. *History of the English Speaking Peoples* (four volumes). Oxford: Marlboro Books, 1956.

Cibber, Theophilus. *Lives of the Poets of Great Britain & Ireland*. London: Griffiths Press, 1753.

Collier, Ann. *Handbook of Textiles*. Manchester: Woodhead Publishing. 1974.

Conklin, Alice. *European Imperialism: 1830-1930*. Boston: Wadsworth Cengage Publishing. 1999.

Daniel, William Dukinfield. *History of Colonel Robert Dukinfield*. Cambridge: Cambridge University Press. 1758.

de Figueiredo, Peter & Julian Treuhertz. *Cheshire Country Houses*. Chichester: Phillimore Press, 1988.

Dickenson, H. P. *Walpole and the Whig Supremacy*. London: English Universities Press. 1973.

Editorial Staff. *Encyclopedia Britannica* (15th Edition). New York & London: Encyclopedia Britannica Inc, 1992.

Editorial Staff. *Oxford Bibliographies*. Oxford: Oxford University Press, 1856.

Egerton, Wilbraham. *Indian and Oriental Armour*. New Delhi, India: Asian Educational Services. 1906.

Elkins, Caroline. *Britain's Gulag in Kenya*. London: Jonathan Cape Publishing. 2005.

Farrell, Patricia. *Writer on the Edge*. (part of her Perspectives of Africa series, 1997-2015). Harare: Zimbabwe Publishing House. 2015.

Fischer, Louis. *Life of Mahatma Gandhi*. London: Harper-Collins. 1950.

Funigiello, Philip. *Florence Lathrop Page: A Biography*. Charlottesville: University of Virginia Press. 1994.

Gaunt, Peter. *The English Civil War*. London & New York: I B Tauris Publishers. 2014.

Godfrey, Barry. *The Digital Panopticon*. Liverpool & Sheffield: Liverpool University Press. 2017.

Grindon, Leo Hartley. *Summer Rambles in Cheshire, Derbyshire, Lancashire & Yorkshire*. London: Wentworth Press. 1866.

Hallett, Robert. *History of Kenya*. Cambridge.

Cambridge University Press. 1970.

Hanbury, Liz. *Regency Wagers*. London: Moonstone Solutions. 2009.

Herne, Brian. *White Hunters*. New York: Henry Holt & Company, LLC. 2001.

Hesler, John. *Henry II: Medieval Soldier of War*. London. Brill Publishing. 2007.

Hitler, Adolph. *Mein Kampf*. Berlin, Germany: Franz Eher Nachfolger. 1925.

Hopkirk, Mary. *Life at Vale Royal Great House 1907-1925, the Memoirs of Mary Hopkirk*. Chester, England: Heritage Society Publications. 1926.

Hoppit, Julian. *A Land of Liberty, England 1689-1727*. Oxford & London: Oxford University Press. 2000.

Hubbard, Edward. *The Works of John Douglas*. London: Victorian Society Publishing. 1991.

Huxley, Elspeth. *White Man's Country- Lord Delamere & The Making of Kenya* (two volumes). London: Chatto & Windus Publishing. 1935.

Ingham, Alfred. *History of Cheshire (Its Traditions & History)*. Manchester: Pillans & Wilson Publishers. 1920.

Jeffreys, Lord George. *The Tryal of Henry Baron Delamere for High Treason*. New York: Gale Publishing (Making of Modern Law). 1686.

Kanog, Tabitha. *Squatters & the Roots of the Mau Mau: 1905-63*. Athens, Ohio: Ohio University Press. 1987.

Kennedy, Dane. *Islands of White*. Durham, North Carolina: Duke University Publishing. 1987.

Langford, Paul. *Eighteenth-Century Britain - Walpole and the Rise of Robinocracy*. Oxford & London: Oxford University Press. 2000.

Lasky, Kathyrn. *The Royal Diaries of Elizabeth, the Red Rose of the House of Tudor*. New York: Scholastic Inc. Publishers. 1999.

Lee, Sydney, ed. *Dictionary of National Biography (1885-1900)*. Oxford: Oxford University Press. 2004.

Lester, W. R. *Unemployment and the Land, 1936*. Washington, D. C.: United Committee for Taxation of Land. 1994.

Lyttelton, George. *The History of the Life of Henry the Second* (five volumes). London: Sandby & Dodsley Printers. 1772.

Miller, Charles. *The Lunatic Express: An Entertainment in Imperialism*. London: MacMillan and Company. 1971.

Myers, Norman. *The Long African Day*. London & New York: MacMillan Publishing. 1972.

Nash Ford, David. *Royal Berkshire History*. Wokingham: Nash Ford Publishing. 1996.

National Geographic Staff. *History of Delamere Forest*. London & Oxford: National Geographic Society. 1930.

O'Gorman, Frank. *The Long Eighteenth Century: British Political And Social History, 1688-1832*. London & Oxford: Bloomsbury Publishing. 1997.

Ormerod, George. *The History of the County Palatine and City of Chester* (three volumes). London: Forgotten Books Publishing. 1819.

Parliamentary Staff. *Parliamentary Records (Ref. Vol.1715-1754*. London: Parliamentary Press Offices. 1754.

Parliamentary Staff. *The Cheshire Election of 1715*. London: History Records of Parliament. 1790.

Pevsner, Nikolaus Bernhard Leon. *The Buildings of England (1951–74)* (46 volumes). London: Faber & Faber Publishing. 1974.

Reader, John. *A Biography of the Continent of Africa*. New York: First Vintage Books. 1997.

Riley, Glenda. *Taking Land, Breaking Land: Women Colonizing the American West and Kenya*. Albuquerque: University of New Mexico Press. 2003.

Roosevelt, Theodore. *An Autobiography by Theodore Roosevelt*. New York: Charles Scribner & Sons. 1923.

Smith, Warren Thomas. *John Wesley & Slavery*. Cambridge: Cambridge University Press. 1986.

Steele, Philip. *British History*. London: Miles Kelly Publishing. 2003.

Taylor, James. *Great Historic Families of Scotland*. London: J S Virtue & Company, Ltd. 1880.

Terry, Samuel & Brown, Alexander. *Smith's Strangers Guide to Liverpool, Its*

Environs & Parts of Cheshire. Liverpool & Sydney: Sagwan Press. 1843.

Thornton, Tim. *Prophecy and the Revolution Settlement*. New York: Bowden & Brewer Publishers. 2006.

Thornton, Tim. *Prophecy & Politics of Early Modern England*. Woodbridge, England: Boydell Press. 2006.

Thurman, Judith. I*sak Dinesen: The Life of a Storyteller*. New York: Picador Press. 1995.

Unknown author. *Nixon's Original Cheshire Prophecy*. Derby, England: Thomas Richardson Publishers. 1938.

Unstead, R. J. *Looking at History*. London: A & C Black Publishers, 1953.

van der Bijl, Nicholas. *Mau Mau Rebellion: The Emergency in Kenya 1952–1956*. Barnsley, Yorkshire: Pen & Sword Books, Ltd. 2017.

Ward, Edward. *The London Spy*. London: J. How and Company, 1698.

White, Gilbert. *Natural History and Antiquities of Selborne*. London: Ben White Publisher. 1789.

Wilson, John. *Imperial Gazetteer of England & Wales*. London & Edinburgh: Fullerton and Company, 1870.

Wood, Amos. *Floyd County, Virginia. A History of Its People and Places*. Radford, Virginia, USA: Commonwealth Press. 1981.

About the Author

Geoffrey Hebdon was born and brought up in Lancashire, England, in the heart and region of the cotton industry. After leaving college, having studied textile engineering, he embarked on the vocation of education, including lecturing, teaching and evangelical work. He and his wife Pauline lived and served in various parts of the United Kingdom, including Scotland, Yorkshire, Cheshire, Warwickshire, Northamptonshire, Cambridgeshire, Bedfordshire and Buckinghamshire.

After starting a family in the 1970s Geoffrey and Pauline decided to relocate to South Africa and for almost 30 years were based in Cape Town. While working there, Geoffrey, a dedicated educationalist, along with a business partner, decided to open a private academy with campuses in Bellville, the northern suburbs of Cape Town, and also in Central Cape Town with plans to open a third campus in the African township of Khayelitsha in the Western Cape, to offer career training courses, including business management, computers, travel and tourism, journalism, plus health and beauty. This private academy later expanded its offerings to the more disadvantaged students of southern and eastern Africa, with the help of the Department of Education plus generous private subsidies and sponsorships.

After semi-retiring in 2000, Geoffrey and Pauline relocated their family to the United States and lived in Salt Lake City, Utah, for eight years before moving to Los Angeles, where they are currently based. Geoffrey is still involved with research, reporting and writing.

www.ingramcontent.com/pod-product-compliance
Lightning Source LLC
Chambersburg PA
CBHW050333230426
43663CB00010B/1847